Praise for

RUSSIAN POET/SOVIET JEW
The Legacy of Eduard Bagritskii

by Maxim D. Shrayer

"A welcome and challenging assessment of an original, unduly neglected voice in Soviet Russian poetry. Shrayer's translations of Bagritskii's verse are masterful; his approach to the material, with its emphasis on the complicated, often dangerous process of the writer's coming to grips with his Jewish identity, is highly suggestive and satisfying. . . . This book opens to a diverse readership some entirely new and previously obscured vistas on twentieth-century Russian, and Russian-Jewish, literary achievement."
—Stanley Rabinowitz, Amherst College

"In his definitive book, Shrayer makes the problematic world of Bagritskii and his poetry available to the English reader for the first time. . . . This will remain one of the standard studies of Russian-Jewish culture in the early twentieth century."
—Sander L. Gilman, University of Chicago

"Eduard Bagritskii has long been neglected in the West, both as a poet and as a personality. In this thoughtful, subtle, and carefully drawn study, Shrayer has installed Bagritskii where he belongs: among the leading Russian Jewish figures of the Soviet period. I highly recommend this book to anyone with an interest in Russian or Jewish literary culture."
—Joshua Rubenstein, author of *Tangled Loyalties: The Life and Times of Ilya Ehrenburg*

"In a virtuoso performance of solid scholarship and artful prose, Shrayer unmasks the dark demons haunting Soviet society and literature during the twentieth century through his enlightening study of Bagritskii. Shrayer's muscular critique of the pathos of Stalinism, of hyphenated Jewish life, of virulent anti-Semitism, along with his exquisitely moving translations of Bagritskii's poetry, combine to render *Russian Poet/Soviet Jew* a compelling achievement."
—Harvey J. Fields, Senior Rabbi, Wilshire Boulevard Temple

"An extremely well-informed introduction to a vibrant poet and a persuasive exploration of dual identity."
—Victor Erlich, Yale University

RUSSIAN POET/SOVIET JEW

The Legacy of Eduard Bagritskii

MAXIM D. SHRAYER

ROWMAN & LITTLEFIELD PUBLISHERS, INC.
Lanham • Boulder • New York • Oxford

ROWMAN & LITTLEFIELD PUBLISHERS, INC.

Published in the United States of America
by Rowman & Littlefield Publishers, Inc.
4720 Boston Way, Lanham, Maryland 20706
http://www.rowmanlittlefield.com

12 Hid's Copse Road
Cumnor Hill, Oxford OX2 9JJ, England

British Cataloging in Publication Information Available

Library of Congress Cataloging-in-Publication Data

Shrayer, Maxim, 1967–
    Russian poet/Soviet Jew : the legacy of Eduard Bagritskii / Maxim D. Shrayer.
        p. cm.
    Includes bibliographical references and index.
    ISBN 0-7425-0780-7 (alk. paper)
    1. Bagritskii, Eduard, 1895–1934—Criticism and interpretation. 2. Russian
poetry—Jewish authors—History and criticism.

PG3476.B23 Z84 2000
891.71'42—dc21   00-025454

Printed in the United States of America

♾™ The paper used in this publication meets the minimum requirements of American
National Standard for Information Sciences—Permanence of Paper for Printed Library
Materials, ANSI/NISO Z.39.48-1992.

For Karen

And thus: his tales of hunting have become a prophecy, and his childishness has become wisdom, because he was a wise man, conjoining a member of the Komsomol with Ben Akiva.

Isaak Babel

My Judaic pride sang,
Like a string stretched to its limits.

Eduard Bagritskii

I had long undervalued Tsvetaeva, just as in different ways I had also undervalued many others—Bagritskii, Khlebnikov, Mandelstam, Gumilev.

Boris Pasternak

Contents

Illustrations

Reprinted by permission of the Russian State Archive of Literature and the Arts (RGALI), Moscow, and the Manuscript Division of the Institute of World Literature (IMLI), Moscow.

Cover photo: Eduard Bagritskii. Moscow, 1928.

1. Bagritskii's father, Godel´ Moshkovich Dziubin (sitting), with sister of Bagritskii's mother, Polina, and her husband, David Roitman. Odessa, 1910.
2. Bazarnaia (Kirova), 40, in courtyard of the house where Bagritskii was born. Odessa.
3. Remeslennaia (Osipova), 4, the house where Bagritskii spent his childhood. Odessa.
4. Bagritskii. Odessa, 1899.
5. Bagritskii. Odessa, 1903.
6. Bagritskii. Zhukovskii School. Odessa, 1910.
7. Playbill of a reading by young Odessan writers, 10 October 1918. The participants include E. Bagritskii, V. Kataev, Iu. Olesha, and Z. Shishova, and others.
8. Bagritskii with son Vsevolod (Seva). Kuntsevo (presently a district of Moscow). Winter 1928–29.
9. Bagritskii. Kuntsevo, 1930.
10. Pionerskaia, 17 (Bagritskogo, 7), the house the Bagritskiis rented and lived in through 1930. Kuntsevo. Here Bagritskii wrote "Origin."
11. Bagritskii (third from left), with fellow members of the Literary Center of Constructivists. From left to right: V. Asmus, A. Kviatkovskii, E. Bagritskii, K. Zelinskii, N. Aduev, I. Sel´vinskii, B. Agapov (standing), V. Lugovskoi, G. Gauzner (standing), V. Inber, and E. Gabrilovich. Moscow, 1929.
12. Bagritskii (wearing what appears to be a yarmulke), with his wife, Lidiia Gustavovna Bagritskaia, née Suok, and his dog, Rait. Moscow, 1931.
13. Bagritskii (second from right), with a group of literary colleagues. From left to right: M. Ia. Ignatova, V. Kataev, N. Aseev, E. Bagritskii, and L. Nikulin. Barvikha, outside Moscow, summer 1933.

Acknowledgments

The research toward this book would have never been completed, and the book never written, without the generous financial support of the following institutions: Boston College, Kennan Institute for Advanced Russian Studies, Lucius N. Littauer Foundation, and Memorial Foundation for Jewish Culture.

This project has been in the making for almost as long as I have lived in the United States. It originated in Albert S. Cook's seminar on modern poetry and poetics at Brown in the spring of 1988. The late Albert S. Cook, poet and scholar, inspired me, then a twenty-year-old émigré fresh out of the Soviet Union, to undertake the English translation of Eduard Bagritskii's *February*; he read and commented on an early draft of my translation. After a hiatus of over six years, I returned to Bagritskii in the summer of 1995. At that time I was beginning to study the Jewish question in Russian culture, while on the whole my research interests were moving away from the crystal palace of pure poetics and toward the bathhouse of literary politics. In the spring of 1998, I conceived of a book with a double purpose: to introduce the major Russian-Jewish poet Eduard Bagritskii through translations of his principal works and to examine his art and life through the prism of Jewish history. This book thus brings together my earlier attempts at rendering in English Bagritskii's poetic idiom and my present concerns with the dynamics of Jewish culture and identity in Russia and the former Soviet Union.

A number of colleagues have commented on parts of this project, and I acknowledge their contributions with gratitude: Golfo Alexoupolus, Martin Cohen, Alexandra Kirilcuk, Gary Saul Morson, and Valerie Sperling. I am particularly grateful to Ruth Rischin and Thomas Seifrid, who read a late draft and offered their detailed, erudite, and immensely helpful suggestions. Albert S. Cook, Edwin Honig, Lawrence G. Jones, Karen E. Lasser, Askold Melnyczuk, Yasmina Mesiya, and Bernard Waldrop read drafts of my translations at different stages of their completion and offered precious advice. Patricia Herlihy generously answered my queries about Odessa's history and names of its streets and districts. Ruth Langer kindly helped me with questions of Judaic law. I thank my

colleagues at Boston College's Department of Slavic and Eastern Languages—
M. J. Connolly, Cynthia Simmons, and Margaret Thomas—for their support.
Last but not least, I thank my Moscow friend Maksim Mussel´ and his family for
their hospitality during my research trips to Russia in 1998–2000.

Stephen Vedder and Sarah Bastille of Boston College's audiovisual services
provided invaluable help with archival photographs. Daniel Benedetti, Mar-
guerite J. McDonough, Ellen E. Salah, and the staff of the interlibrary loan serv-
ices at Boston College's O'Neill Library have been unfailingly attentive to my
unending requests. Lisa Senay, Rachel Skiba, Julia Scorupsky, and Tim Tran-
chilla, my research assistants, have made the completion of this book less toil-
some for me. I also wish to thank my editors at Rowman & Littlefield—Serena
Leigh, Lynn Gemmell, and Shana Harrington. Mikhail Aivazian, head of the
Department of Manuscripts, Institute of World Literature (Moscow), and N. B.
Volkova, director of the Russian State Archive of Literature and the Arts, have
both assisted me in my research and have given me permissions to reproduce
archival materials. Isaac Babel's widow, A. N. Pirozhkova, has granted me per-
mission to translate and publish Babel's comments about Bagritskii.

If it were not for my parents, Emilia (Polyak) Shrayer and David Shrayer-Petrov,
who paved our way to emigration with nine hellish years as Jewish Refuseniks, I
would have never had the privilege of writing freely about Bagritskii and the Jewish
question. This book is but a small token of my love and gratitude.

M.D.S.
Boston
March 2000

Note on Transliteration, Dates, and References

Unless otherwise specified, a parenthetical date refers to the first publication of a literary work; in some cases, the date of completion precedes if it differs significantly from the date of publication. For information on the history of the creation and publication of Bagritskii's works, see the chronology following the main text of this book. Parenthetical dates for critical studies always refer to the date of publication. When two dates are provided for a historical event, the first refers to the Julian calendar, used in Russia prior to 1918, the second to the Gregorian calendar.

A simplified Library of Congress system for transliterating the Russian alphabet is used throughout. The only exceptions in the main text, but not in bibliographical references and works cited, are the Russian names that have gained a common spelling in English (for example, Joseph Brodsky instead of "Iosif Brodskii"; Mandelstam instead of "Mandel´shtam"; Babel instead of "Babel´").

Unless specified, all quotations from Bagritskii's works are from the Biblioteka poeta edition, Eduard Bagritskii, *Stikhotvoreniia i poemy* (Moscow: Sovetskii pisatel´, 1964). All translations into English are mine unless noted otherwise. The translations of "Origin" and *February* seek to render the originals' language and prosody, and I alone am responsible for the infelicities of these translations. The other translations in this book do not aspire to capture the originals' artistry but rather attempt to be literal insofar as that is possible. Russian originals of "Origin" and *February* are reprinted in the appendix, as is the Russian of all poetry lines quoted in the text in English translation.

INTRODUCTION

~

Bagritskii's Jewish, Russian, and Soviet Legacy

For a Russian Jew, becoming a Russian writer has often amounted to an ultimate act of identity remaking. In some cases, a Russian-Jewish writer's conversion to Christianity facilitated the process of becoming culturally Russian (Osip Mandelstam); in others, Zionist thinking was combined with an acute aesthetic sense of one's Russianness (Vladimir [Ze´ev] Jabotinsky). By writing in Russian, a Jew becomes a Russian. But does he also cease to be Jewish and, furthermore, what shape does this cultural assimilation take when riddled by Soviet rhetoric on Jewish identity? This was the central dilemma of Eduard Bagritskii's life and poetry, and is the one this book investigates.

Russian Poet/Soviet Jew: The Legacy of Eduard Bagritskii aims to fill a gap in Russian literary history as well as the history of Jewish writing in Diaspora. My main concern in this first English-language book about Eduard Bagritskii (1895–1934) is to highlight his career as a major Russian-Jewish poet. My goal is to situate Bagritskii's writings within the ideological and aesthetic contexts of the early Soviet period as well as within the postwar Soviet and Western debates on the meaning of Jewish identity. Post-Soviet voices in the currently rampant and alarming polemics on the place of Jews in Russian culture will also be given speaking parts in the book. Finally, and because Eduard Bagritskii is hardly a household name with the larger reading public in the West, my book is intended as an introduction to Bagritskii's art and life.

The problem of identity has been a central one throughout the millennia of Jewish Diaspora. This study of Bagritskii's poetry probes the very heart of Jewish culture and history by testing the limits of cultural assimilation. In our age, when people and even whole countries are increasingly concerned with defining their identities, *Russian Poet/Soviet Jew* tells the story of the writer's attempt at becoming Russian while also remaining Jewish. Like a raindrop reflecting the tall summer sky, Eduard Bagritskii's captivating life typifies the destinies of many Jewish artists struggling to enter the mainstream of gentile culture in the twentieth century. Of all modern Russian-Jewish artists, Bagritskii has received the greatest share of violently and markedly anti-Jewish detractions. His career has become a remarkable case study of the culture and politics of anti-Semitism.

*   *   *

"In his entire psychological mold, in his perception of life Bagritskii was a poet in the highest sense—with a splendid understanding of the poetic craft, with a passionate love for the sounding verse," the prominent critic Lidiia Ginzburg wrote in 1966.[1] Russian-Jewish poet Eduard Bagritskii had many admirers, and yet literary history has not been kind to him.[2] Although famous on the early Soviet literary scene for his vibrant, metaphorical, and masterfully crafted verse, following his untimely death Bagritskii's life and poetry were contrived into a Soviet literary legend. Born out of Bagritskii's funeral on the eve of the First Congress of Soviet Writers (August 1934), which codified socialist realism as the official method of Soviet literature and art, this legend was initially given its shape by the sobbing obituaries and reminiscences of Bagritskii's own literary comrades, themselves already sensing the advent of the Great Terror. Sounded in the horns and brass of the Young Pioneers and the hooves of the Red Army squadron that was ordered by the Soviet Minister of Defense Kliment Voroshilov to escort Bagritskii's coffin, this Soviet legend reduced Bagritskii's multifarious poetic heritage to a standard set of anthologized poems and ideologically correct themes.[3] Diligently dressing and redressing the poet's oeuvre in the official uniform of a Romantic tribune of the Revolution, Bagritskii's early Soviet critics circumnavigated the poet's questioning of both the oppressive bureaucracy of Soviet life and the dissolution of revolutionary equalitarian ideals. But above all, they feared like the plague a discussion of Jewish questions in Bagritskii's life and art.

One step below Vladimir Maiakovskii in the Soviet literary pantheon,[4] Bagritskii was given the most legitimacy as the author of the long poems *Death of a Young Pioneer Girl* (1932) and *The Lay of Opanas* (1926), the former about a Soviet girl's fatal break with both Orthodox Christianity and the philistinism of her familial past, the latter about class and ethnic struggle in the Ukraine during the Civil War of 1918–22.[5] The protagonist of *The Lay of Opanas*, a commissar, dies by the hands of a Ukrainian folk chieftain, the pogromist Opanas. And yet, while praising Bagritskii's remarkable epic poem, Soviet critics always tiptoed around the fact that the protagonist, Commissar Iosif Kogan, is Jewish.[6] In fact, Bagritskii's Jewish theme—which reached a peak in his last and finest work, *February*, and formed a central nerve of his entire oeuvre—remained a forbidden subject even at the height of Khrushchev's Thaw. For instance, when Andrei Siniavskii—who was to become a dissident writer—published a lengthy chapter about Bagritskii in

1958, he avoided any mention of the poet's Jewish theme. Western investigations of Bagritskii's writings are also far from complete, which provides an additional compelling motivation for the present discussion.

As an ideological simulacrum of a literary life, Bagritskii's Soviet legend both concealed and covered up. It obfuscated his real, unparalleled aesthetic achievement as one of the foremost voices of the first generation of Soviet Russian poets—the pleiad of poets, a number of them Jewish, who were born in the 1890s and 1900s; came of age at the time of World War I, the February and October 1917 Revolutions, and the Russian Civil War; and entered the literary mainstream during the period of the New Economic Policy (1921–28). This first generation of great Soviet Russian poets, which also included such splendidly talented masters as Nikolai Aseev, Vladimir Lugovskoi, Semen Kirsanov, Il´ia Sel´vinskii, Nikolai Tikhonov, and Nikolai Zabolotskii, followed in the footsteps of the Russian Silver Age and the prerevolutionary avant-garde. Especially important for this pleiad of poets were Innokentii Annenskii, Aleksandr Blok, Nikolai Gumilev, Velimir Khlebnikov, Mikhail Kuzmin,[7] Vladimir Maiakovskii, and Igor´ Severianin. Having composed and published much of their best verse before the total institutionalization of Soviet culture in the mid-1930s, the early Soviet Russian poets produced the literary equivalent of the great early Soviet Experiment in the visual arts and cinema by blending elements of futurist and constructivist design with inherited elements of the symbolist and acmeist grammars of poetry. Their contributions to modern Russian poetry can be easily compared to those of Sergei Eisenstein, Vsevolod Pudovkin, and Dziga Vertov to Soviet cinema, and of Kazimir Malevich, Aleksei Rodchenko, and Vladimir Tatlin to Soviet visual arts. The formal innovations of Bagritskii and his peers in early Soviet poetry were especially striking in the area of versification, as they pioneered or further experimented with modern, nonclassical, tonic Russian meters (dol´nik; pauznik) and rhymes, introduced prose techniques into verse, and expanded the conventional boundaries of poetic language. In retrospect, and especially from a post-Soviet vantage point, one might think of the work of Bagritskii and his fellow poets as the poetry of Soviet modernism, a branch of European high modernism.[8] Most of them fellow travelers for almost as long as it was safe to remain fellow travelers, the poets of Soviet modernism created their best works in the 1920s and early 1930s. They later made aesthetic and ideological compromises to survive Stalinism and did not fully regain (if at all) the strength of their voices until the Thaw of the mid- to late 1950s.

Bagritskii, unlike most other members of that glorious first generation of Soviet Russian poets, died at the very height of his career, during a time that bore witness to the rise of Stalinism. He passed away three years following Vladimir Maiakovskii's epochal suicide. As in the case of Maiakovskii, the early death of Bagritskii enabled the evolving Soviet literary machine to conceal not only the blazing modernism of his verse but also the problematic (and forbidden) issues that Bagritskii increasingly raised in his works. One such problem is a wide range of Jewish questions debated in Bagritskii's writing, which include such topics as the Jewish participation in the Revolution, the architectonics of Jewish identity, and varieties of anti-Semitism and forms of Jewish assimilation. Another problem is that of the lost generation of intellectuals and artists who, sympathetic as they had been to the Bolshevik Revolution and its initially egalitarian program, found themselves at odds with the emerging Soviet state and its dystopian reality. Perhaps creating a Soviet version of Hemingway's "lost generation," Bagritskii wrote in 1926:

> From black bread and faithful wife
> A pale pestilence keeps us.
>
> Our age has been tested with hoof and with stone,
> Water is heavy with deathless wormwood,
> And the bitterness of wormwood is on our lips . . .
> A knife does not fit our grip,
> A pen—our temper,
> A pickax—our pride,
> And fame does not suit us.
> We are rusty leaves
> On rusty oaks . . .
> Should a wind flutter,
> A northern wind,
> We would fall.
> Whose passage do we carpet with our bodies?
> Whose feet shall walk on our rust?
> Will young trumpeters stomp us?
> Will alien constellations rise over our heads?
> We are the shaken comfort of rusty oaks. . . .[9]

"The shaken comfort of rusty oaks . . ."! Could a Soviet critic in the years following the early 1930s speak openly about an intellectual—be he a revolutionary or a fellow traveler—who finds himself so out of place in the Soviet present and alienated from the Soviet future? To compensate for the obscured truth about Bagritskii's modernism, his Jewish theme, and his equivocal treatment of Soviet reality, the forgers of his Soviet literary legend generated a set of generic, formal, and thematic clichés that continued to define his reception in the Soviet Union until well into the 1980s. These clichés included a view of Bagritskii as a leading figure of Soviet "revolutionary Romanticism." Also characteristic of Bagritskii's Soviet legend are the constant references to his "ceaseless" Soviet optimism despite his ever-failing health, as well as to his use of the motifs of Russian and Ukrainian folk poetry. Bagritskii's indebtedness to "the best and most talented poet of our Soviet epoch" Maiakovskii (Osip Brik's formulation that Stalin made official[10]), the "folk" Scottish Romantic Robert Burns, and the Ukrainian national poet Taras Shevchenko was deemed central to his development. At the same time, the impact of Bagritskii's beloved French symbolists (Arthur Rimbaud, Stéphane Mallarmé, Paul Verlaine), Parnassians (Leconte de Lisle), German Romantics (Heinrich Heine; Novalis), and Rudyard Kipling was downplayed. In Bagritskii's Soviet legend, the rebel Til Eulenspiegel (of Charles de Coster's novel) ousted both the sentimental fowler Didel' (fashioned after German Romantics) and the beautiful Creole (possibly conjured up under the spell of Gumilev's ethnographic poems). Nothing helps to understand how Bagritskii's Soviet legend was forged so well as the funeral issue of the leading Soviet cultural review, Literaturnaia gazeta ("Literary Gazette"), two-thirds of which was filled with obituaries and eulogizing editorials (see illustration 17). Here are a few excerpts from that issue, published on February 18, 1934, as Bagritskii's coffin stood at the Central Writers' House on Vorovskii Street in the center of Moscow. From the front page editorial:

> He was among those poets—birthed and raised by the Revolution—who have been coming closer and closer to the Party, who have realized ever more fully and organically the rightness of its task. . . . High in its artistry, deeply and organically revolutionary in its content, free of formalistic tricks and simple in form, [Bagritskii's poetry] deserves to be entered into the main artistic treasury created by Soviet poetry.[11]

Valerii Kirpotin, chief of the Literary Division of the Party Central Committee and one of the fathers of the doctrine of socialist realism, said of Bagritskii that "he was a Romantic, who strove through song and word to express the pathos and dream of the Revolution. His poetic artillery bombarded the old world."[12] And here is an obituary, signed by several Soviet literary luminaries, including Aleksei Tolstoi and Leonid Sobolev: "The finest revolutionary Romantic is dead, the Revolution's lyrical voice."[13] Only Bagritskii's friend Viktor Shklovskii, the tremendously savvy master of subtlety and euphemistic wisdom, managed to allude to the complexity and fruitful ambiguity of the late poet's vision:

> A stroboscope is a rotating disk, equipped around the periphery with a number of holes. . . .
> A poet contemplates the world through the stroboscopic light of his heart. . . .
> Bagritskii died at age thirty-seven. His hair was completely gray.
> A hundred and fifty steps of the staircase separated his room from the world. . . .
> He loved the sun, the south, watermelons, birds, the sea, spring and was separated from the world by his malady and the staircase's steps.
> In his room he kept fish; the fish swam in blue water. . . .
> The fish in colored water was the last bit of life he could see from his couch.[14]

Shklovskii's words—a tired shadow of his own brilliant early prose—were drowned in the droning dithyrambs of writers and critics who were writing their own salutary Soviet tickets while seeing off their colleague Bagritskii across the Stalinist Black River. Have we the right to judge them when the Great Purges were already upon them? Here is one of the many corrective statements about Bagritskii that his friend from their Constructivist years, the skillful navigator Kornelii Zelinskii, would make from the 1930s to the 1960s: "Bagritskii was a truly humanist poet, and that is why he became a poet of Communism. He wished to and managed to make his song a weapon in this struggle."[15] In summary, Bagritskii's Soviet interpreters honed down the ardent modernism of his polyvalent and richly orchestrated verses to a safe and unambiguous series of ideas. They focused on the allegedly life-affirming and heroic message of Bagritskii's poetry (the "singer of youth," as Vsevolod Azarov put it in 1960)—the message, they claimed, that leaned toward the soundproof ideology of Soviet Communism.[16] Bagritskii's Jewish questions were all carefully circumnavigated.

The late 1940s and early 1950s saw a sharp decline in the study of Bagritskii in the Soviet Union. The chief reasons for this was Zhdanovshchina—a period of reaction that began in 1946 and was named after Stalin's chief of ideology Andrei Zhdanov. The cultural purges did not end with Zhdanov's death in 1948, and one of their main features was a wave of official anti-Semitism.[17] No editions of Bagritskii's works were issued between 1949 and 1956, the first year of Khrushchev's Thaw.[18] The rabidly anti-Semitic years 1949–53, culminating with the execution of Yiddish writers and the so-called Doctors' plot (delo vrachei), were also the darkest period in the history of Bagritskii's legacy. In July 1949, an editorial in the leading Ukrainian cultural weekly, Literaturna hazeta, was followed by a half-page unsigned article in Moscow's Literary Gazette entitled "For the Ideological Purity of Soviet Poetry."[19] The targets of the attack were Bagritskii and his admirers and followers. The Lay of Opanas, Bagritskii's famous epic poem, was branded a "politically erroneous work where historical truth is distorted."[20] Both articles did their utmost in trying to disassociate Bagritskii's poem from the poetry of Taras Shevchenko, especially his long narrative poem Haidamaky ("The Haidamaks," 1841), which had served as one of Bagritskii's main literary models (Bagritskii used as his epigraph a quatrain from The Haidamaks). Bagritskii was posthumously charged with expressing a "disdainful attitude to the people," as opposed to Shevchenko's "deep respect for the freedom-loving Ukrainian people."[21] The articles, both the Ukrainian and the Russian, claimed that other works by Bagritskii, written before and after The Lay of Opanas, also testified to the poet's "ideological unsteadiness," and expressed "bourgeois-nationalist tendencies, the spirit of decadence and motifs of hoboism."[22] Finally, a number of Bagritskii's works were deemed harmful because of the influence they had exerted on other poets. Most indicative of the articles' anti-Semitic undercurrents is the fact that the two "influenced" poets they discussed were the Ukrainian-Jewish poets Leonid Pervomais´kyi and Sava Holovanivs´kyi.[23]

The 1949 editorials set the tone for the treatment of Bagritskii during the next seven years. In those cases where critics did discuss Bagritskii, their comments were in the destructive vein, as is evident in Anatolii Tarasenkov's well-known article on "bourgeois nationalism" in Soviet Russian literature and also in Semen Tregub's writings.[24] In 1949, broadcasting the official cultural line, Tregub juxtaposed Bagritskii's poetry of "hoboism and immoralism" with that of Maiakovskii, who "[would always] remain an edifying example for Soviet poetry."[25] Tregub charged Bagritskii's friends and followers with having "falsified" the poet's life and poetry by presenting his "crudely biological, cosmopolitan, decadent verses" as "revolutionary Romanticism."[26] Tregub also likened Bagritskii's "philosophy" to that of the "bourgeois English poet, the decadent [T. S.] Eliot."[27] It is ironic that, in revealing a textual parallel between Bagritskii's "From black bread . . ." (1926) and Eliot's *Wasteland* (1922), the Stalinist critic unwittingly testified to Bagritskii's greatness.

Bagritskii was returned to press and was re-legitimized as a major Soviet Russian poet during the Thaw.[28] Following some critical discussion, adjustments were made in the way Bagritskii was presented to the Soviet reading public.[29] Best exemplified by Andrei Siniavskii's long chapter in the Academy *History of Russian Soviet Literature* (1958), a revised view of Bagritskii as a classic of early Soviet poetry firmly entered the curricula of schools and universities in the 1960s. Consider these remarks from a university textbook of Soviet Russian literature, published in 1974:

> Thus developed Bagritskii's Romanticism—from the individual to the collective, from hoboism to a conscious struggle for a new beauty of ideals . . . Bagritskii's long and short poems acquired a socio-philosophical meaning. The cohesion of the poet's aspirations and the new popular ideals made his characters truly rich, enduring, full of life—differing in many ways from [his] early Romantic characters.[30]

Bagritskii's books went through numerous editions in the 1960s, 1970s, and 1980s. Some of his "Jewish" poems—such as *The Lay of Opanas* and "Origin"— were regularly reprinted, although an open discussion of their principal subjects remained a taboo until the time of perestroika.

Could Soviet educators teach Bagritskii as a classic of Soviet poetry without stepping into ideological quicksand? I still remember the rather disastrous results of being taught Bagritskii in middle school in the late fall of 1979—on the eve of the Soviet invasion of Afghanistan. We were forced to memorize *Smert´ pionerki* (*"Death of a Young Pioneer Girl,"* 1932), arguably the text where Bagritskii comes closest to co-opting Party doctrine. During break time, mumbling the poem's catchy trochees, my classmates and I changed the lines to indicate that we did not find the poem believable. Parodying the opening description of the

teenage girl dying of scarlet fever in a hospital ward and refusing to wear her bap-
tismal cross, we changed the third verse of "Valia, Valentina, / Chto s toboi
teper´? / Belaia palata. / Krashenaia dver´" ("Valia, Valentina, / What is with you
now? / White hospital room. Painted door") into "Na tebia upala, / Krashenaia
dver´," which altered the meaning to "Valia, Valentina, / What is with you now?
/ A painted door / Has fallen upon you." Soviet teenagers sensed a measure of fal-
sity in Bagritskii's poem, especially in contrast to his glorious "Watermelon"
(1924) or "Smugglers" (1927) that some of us had read at home. In "Smugglers,"
the balladic voice sides neither with the brazen Greek contrabandists from
Odessa, whom Bagritskii sings with such memorable expressionism, nor with the
lithe and alert coast guard patrol. Rather, the poem ends with a hymn to the
Black Sea, a boundary between the Soviet Union and Turkey, but also the ele-
ment that reconciles the poem's series of binary oppositions, the foreign smug-
glers' "cognac, nylons, / and French letters" and the Soviet officers' "motor boat"
and "six [vigilant] eyes." Past the middle of the poem and into the closure, the
lyrical voice refuses to take sides (a fatal mistake for a Soviet poet!) and thus
offers a disclaimer against the ideological and cultural violence that the reduc-
tive Soviet literary legend would render Bagritskii's heritage:

> So pulse through the veins,
>   Pour over the edge,
> You, homeless youth,
>   My rage!
> So human blood
>   Would fall like the stars,
> And I would be fired
>   Across the universe.
> So the frenzied waves
>   Would sing out loud,
> A vile song
>   Contorting my mouth,
> Singing, out of breath,
>   In the terrifying expanse:
> "Hey, Black Sea,
>   You are a good sea! . . ."[31]

The paucity of Bagritskii studies in the West (only a handful of articles and
sections in two monographs have been published to date) reflects Western
scholars' lukewarm interest in the pleiad of early Soviet poets to which Bagri-
tskii belonged. Many Western Slavists seem to have taken to heart Roman
Jakobson's partisan dictum, issued in 1931 following Maiakovskii's death:
"The verse of Aseev and Sel´vinskii is bright indeed, but it is a reflected light.
They do not announce but reflect the spirit of the times. Their magnitude is

a derivative quantity."[32] A less than favorable view of the first generation of Soviet Russian poets thus persisted, while much attention in the West was focused mainly on the works of Vladimir Maiakovskii and Sergei Esenin, as the two poets whose suicides, in 1925 and 1930 respectively, became the dominant motifs of their fervent literary legends. Overall, Western students of Russian literature gave little credit to Bagritskii's poetic generation, largely turning their attention to the works of several of their older contemporaries, who had made major contributions to prerevolutionary Russian poetry and continued to work during the Soviet period. Vera (Sandomersky) Dunham, an early translator of Bagritskii, best summed up this attitude: "They belong to the generation that followed Blok, Mayakovskii, Esenin and Pasternak. Not one among them is a 'great' poet or even an initiator."[33] The resplendent tetrad—stoical Akhmatova, martyred Mandelstam, teetering Pasternak, cornered Tsvetaeva—dominated Western studies of Russian poetry in the Soviet period until well into the 1970s. By the time Western Slavists turned their eyes to the second and third generations of Soviet Russian poets—Bella Akhmadulina, Joseph Brodsky, Boris Slutskii, Andrei Voznesenskii, and others—their predecessors had moved even further into oblivion. The only place one could read about Bagritskii, Tikhonov, Sel´vinskii, and their illustrious colleagues was in anthologies and surveys. Bagritskii's poems were included in English-language anthologies of modern Russian poetry, and in overviews a page or two was routinely assigned to his contribution.

American surveyors and purveyors of early Soviet poetry inherited some of the Soviet assumptions about Bagritskii's career. Consider a few characteristic observations. Leonid Znakomy and Dan Levin, in the 1941 *New Directions Anthology*: "[Bagritskii] laid the foundation for what was to become the school of 'romantic realism.'"[34] Alexander Kaun, in *Soviet Poets and Poetry* (1943): "Whatever the subject, even during the long torment of his dying days, Bagritskii expressed a passionate affirmation of life, an exuberant love for the sensuous, and an indestructible trust in man and mankind."[35] Above, the difference lies with the line "an exuberant love for the sensuous," for the sensuous was outside the scope of Soviet criticism.

Not all of the surveyors of Soviet literature accepted Bagritskii's Soviet literary legend to an equal degree. Take Gleb Struve, who thus characterized Bagritskii's poetry in his survey of early Soviet literature: "A decided Romantic who looked at the Revolution from outside, Bagritskii saw it as something strange and alien but recognized its elemental, sweeping force."[36] Take another émigré, Marc Slonim, who was a student and an enthusiast of Soviet poetry during his prewar years in Prague and Paris and who later became a professor of Russian literature in the United States. While reiterating the Soviet cliché regarding Bagritskii's "positive attitude toward reality," Slonim nevertheless warned his students of the challenges of studying the poet's heritage: "And since it could not be classified as anything even approaching socialist realism, Soviet critics have great trouble in finding a place for Bagritskii in their officially approved chart of post-revolutionary literature."[37]

Perhaps the shortsighted assessment by Renato Poggioli is most indicative of the amount of undoing that a student of early Russian Soviet poetry faces today. In *The Poets of Russia* (1960), Poggioli characterized Bagritskii's first collection as "the work of [a] jejune Pasternak."[38] Even a perfunctory glance at Bagritskii's *South-West* (1928) and Pasternak's output of the 1920s shows that one is dealing not only with starkly different (and entirely independent) aesthetic orientations but also with two dissimilar authorial worldviews. Poggioli—who published his book following the Pasternak Affair of 1958—objected less to the texture of Bagritskii's verse than to Bagritskii's Soviet legend of the revolutionary Romantic:

> It was by following the line of least resistance that these and other would-be pioneers of Soviet poetry were led into bypaths without issue. Starting as *neoteroi*, they ended as *epigones*, precisely because they failed to realize that the great achievements of art are attained only by those who stay on the royal road, which is often the hardest to travel on. No living Russian author seems to have known this as well as a poet slightly older than they, who became the master he was born to be by never deviating from the path marked for him by his star. . . . This poet was Boris Pasternak.[39]

What does "the royal road" mean in this skewed comparison of Bagritskii and Pasternak? Pasternak himself, writing in 1956–57 about his earlier misgivings regarding Marina Tsvetaeva's verse, confessed that he "had long undervalued Tsvetaeva, as in different ways [he] had also undervalued many others—Bagritskii, Khlebnikov, Mandelstam, Gumilev."[40] In Pasternak's postwar (and post-Stalinist) reckoning, Bagritskii strolls in the select company of great Russian poets. If, on the other hand, "the royal road" stands for a poet's politics (in this case, a poet's avoidance of Soviet politics), can one forget Pasternak's weaker, histrionic long poems *The Year 1905* (1926) and *Lieutenant Shmidt* (1927), both of which are near Marxist/Leninist in the dialectic of their plots? In these works, as well as in some of Pasternak's shorter poems of the late 1930s and 1940s, a survivalist imperative often lowered the aesthetic merits of the verse. Likewise, can one discount Bagritskii's ideological compromises? I raise these questions as I envision the objections of those who would readily point to Bagritskii's political curtsies, quoting, for example, from his "Verses about a Poet and Lady Romanticism" (1929): "A dispatch from Petrograd: terrifying news / Of Gumilev's black treason."[41] Should one explore the reasons behind Bagritskii's ignoble endorsement of Nikolai Gumilev's execution by the Bolshevik regime in 1921? Yes, and one is likely to discover that Bagritskii's irresponsible verdict was motivated less by his fidelity to the Revolution than by his resentment of Gumilev for his post-revolutionary plottings against Bagritskii's beloved poet Aleksandr Blok. One is also reminded of another of Bagritskii's low points, his poem "TBC" (1929), where the ailing asthmatic poet receives a visit by a specter of Feliks Dzerzhinskii, the founder of the Cheka, the Soviet secret police.[42] Revealing is a comparison of Bagritskii's "TBC" with Maiakovskii's often-quoted "Conversation with Comrade Lenin," published the same year as Bagritskii's poem. Maiakovskii pledges revolutionary allegiance to the dead Soviet leader: "Comrade Lenin, I am reporting to you / not as a service, but as my heart's duty" (*"ne po sluzhbe, a po dushe"*).[43] In Bagritskii's poem, however, the leader, and not the poet, does most of the talking and politicking.[44] Dzherzhinskii, and not Bagritskii's lyrical voice, pronounces what amounts to a historical justification of political terror:

And the century awaits on the pavement,
Alert, like a sentinel.
Go, and do not be afraid of standing beside him.
Your loneliness befits the century.
Should you turn back—enemies are all around you;
You reach out your hands—and your friends are no more;
But if it [the century] should say "Lie," then tell a lie.
But if it should say "Kill," then kill. . . .[45]

Written in mighty four-stress accentual verse and replete with Bagritskii's signature tropes, such as anthropomorphisms and likening of natural objects with human anatomical parts, this poem exemplifies his original voice, his own unique poetic intonation. And here Victor Terras's thoughtful comment is especially appropriate: "Somehow even [Bagritskii's] propaganda poetry has a ring of sincerity."[46]

Should Bagritskii's political pitfalls affect one's judgment of his verses? To what extent, if any, should a Soviet poet's politics be considered in a study of his or her poetry? This issue seems to be most fascinating today when students of Soviet culture have achieved a post-Soviet critical vantage point. Ideology is bound to vanish into oblivion—do most of us think of Catullus's or Propertius's politics when reading their lyrics? What about the passionate monarchism of André-Marie Chénier, guillotined in 1794? Would it occur to many to judge and dismiss Fedor Tiutchev's poems on the basis of his loyalist lines written for the czar? Clearly, a poet's politics are important as the footlights that illumine the stage of his verses, but not as a sole source of judgment about the poet's work. As soon as one political era is swept over by the next one—and I would argue that this is especially true in post-totalitarian times—a poet's ideology starts fading into the background, while the verses, the form, the language remain. Only a poet with an original talent, organic to his time and milieu but also translatable into other ages and cultures, could have created such powerful shorter lyrics as Bagritskii's "The Watermelon" (1924; 1928), "Verses about a Nightingale and a Poet" (1925), "Spring" (1927), "The Swamp" (1927), "Origin" (1930), and others.

And I have no doubt that Bagritskii's long narrative poems, *The Lay of Opanas* (1926), *The Last Night* (1932), *Man from the Suburb* (1932), and his last—and greatest in my judgment—work, *February* (1933–34; 1936), will be read and studied among the crowning achievements in the tradition of the Russian *poema* ("long poem"). They will also be reevaluated as visionary interpretations of this century's catastrophic events: World War I and the Russian revolutions.

The recent, post-Soviet comments by the critics Natal´ia Bank, Mikhail Sinel´nikov, and Monika Spivak point in the direction of a radical rethinking of Bagritskii's heritage, a process that Spivak has termed "the posthumous diagnostics of genius."[47] Sinel´nikov's remarks, published in 1995 in Moscow on the occasion of Bagritskii's centennial, reassess Bagritskii's unsettled place in modern Russian letters:

> Contemporaries have spoken of Bagritskii's human compromises and deformities, of his fears and daring moves. . . . Today's members of the Black Hundreds portray him as a monster who proclaimed lies, murder, and blasphemy. In actuality he was anguished and tormented by the catastrophe of Russian culture.[48]

But there is more to why we should revisit Bagritskii than undoing decades of silence, cover-up, and injustice. Consider this exchange, published in 1988, between a Lithuanian émigré poet, Tomas Venclova (b. 1937), and the late Joseph Brodsky (1940–1996), on the subject of early Soviet poetry:

[TV] And how do you feel about Lugovskoi? Or, let's say, about Tikhonov?
[JB] I'll answer that. My attitude to both is rather positive. . . . As a young man, I was terribly fond of [*mne uzhasno nravilsia*] Bagritskii.[49]

The study of Bagritskii's art and life is indispensable for a holographic understanding of the dynamics of Soviet Russian poetry not only during the Stalin era but also in the 1950s and 1960s. Along with Sel´vinskii and Lugovskoi, Bagritskii belonged to the Literary Center of Constructivists in the late 1920s, and the poetry of his latter years exhibits a Soviet literary version of high modernism. In much of his mature verse, Bagritskii created a deliberate constructivist poetics, where the meaning ("semantic dominant," as the constructivists termed it) of a poem defines the formal devices that the poet employs.[50] Bagritskii's shorter lyrics and longer narrative poems, often written in nonclassical meters, rhetorically supported by techniques of monologue and confession, usually focusing on a concrete natural object or a specific sociohistorical dilemma, and abounding in prosaic and anatomical details, suggested an effective literary method to subsequent generations of Soviet poets. This explains why many Soviet poets who entered literature in the 1930s and 1940s were so influenced by Bagritskii. An apprenticeship to Bagritskii is visible in the verses of Dzhek Altauzen, Semen Gudzenko, Boris Kornilov, Semen Lipkin, Aleksandr Mezhirov, Mariia Petro-

vykh, Aleksandr Prokof´ev, Boris Ruch´ev, Arkadii Shteinberg, Iaroslav Smel-
iakov, Arsenii Tarkovskii, and other poets of the second Soviet generation.
Referring to his generation of Russian Soviet poets, Iaroslav Smeliakov
(1913–1972) reminisced in his programmatic post-Gulag poem "Tri vitiazia"
("Three Noble Warriors," 1967): "Bagritskii's shadow hovered over us / And
Esenin rustled behind our back."[51] In a 1960 introduction to a posthumous vol-
ume of Boris Kornilov's verse, the poet Ol´ga Bergol´ts described vividly how
much the poets of her generation admired Aseev, Bagritskii, and Sel´vinskii. She
also pointed out that Bagritskii's intonations and Esenin's influence were visible
in Kornilov's poetry.[52]

Bagritskii even managed to give an impetus to the development of his junior
contemporaries representing a broad spectrum of Russia's poetic schools and tra-
ditions, from the Odessan Jew Mark Tarlovskii (1902–1952) to the Cossack poet
Pavel Vasil´ev (1910–1937), who was executed during the Great Purges. A wit-
ness of and coparticipant in Bagritskii's Odessan adventures in life and poetry,
Tarlovskii immortalized his older friend in several pyrotechnically perfect poems
as well as a memoir in verse, *Veselyi strannik* ("Merry Stranger," 1935).[53] Vasil´ev's
remarkable long poems of the late 1920s and 1930s, including *The Salt Mutiny* and
Prince Foma, recall the rhythms and intonations of Bagritskii's narrative poems.
Aleksandr Mezhirov (b. 1923), known for choosing his words carefully, has stated
that Bagritskii's talent was greater and more original than that of Osip Mandel-
stam.[54] In his memoirs, the gifted poet and translator Arkadii Shteinberg wrote of
Bagritskii's place in his own life and in Russian culture:

> Bagritskii's influence on me was very strong. Later, not without difficulty, I tried to
> free myself of this influence. . . . When he died suddenly, I was really orphaned
> because he was a remarkable person. I think that Bagritskii's destiny is a tragedy of
> Russian poetry, as he was, I believe, a person of late development, and everything
> that he managed to write during his short life were merely approaches to the verses
> he would have created at fifty. And he died at thirty-nine.[55]

In 1998, a prominent Soviet poet of the second generation, Viktor Bokov (b.
1914), told me of his admiration for Bagritskii and quoted these lines from
"Spring" as an example of the poet's metaphoric genius[56]:

And the train, slithering
  In wet grass—
A monstrous creature
  With a light in its head.[57]

Among the so-called generation of the 1960s (*shestidesiatniki*), a number of poets
shared in Bagritskii's poetics—Iunna Morits (b. 1937) and Evgenii Rein (b.
1935) immediately come to mind. Bagritskii was an especially captivating influ-
ence upon poets in their youth, as in the case of the Petersburgian Viktor

Krivulin (b. 1944).[58] While by the age of twenty Krivulin had turned to other models, Rein, a major voice in postwar Russian poetry, to this day remains Bagritskii's most faithful and conscious disciple.[59] Finally, of the younger Russian poets, the metametaphorists/metarealists—chiefly, Aleksandr Eremenko, Il'ia Kutik, Aleksei Parshchikov, and Ivan Zhdanov—utilized Bagritskii's experience in their verses.[60]

A number of Russian poets of the Soviet period, whom Bagritskii helped as a mentor and editor, later recalled him with fondness and gratitude. There were those, however, who dismissed the works in which Bagritskii treated ideological subjects, while they still admired his verses about nature. Some were also terrified of endorsing Bagritskii's writings about the Jews. Exhibiting ingratitude, Bagritskii's disciple and protégé in the 1920s, the poet and translator Semen Lipkin (b. 1911) spoke thus of his mentor's later works: "Bagritskii's poems like 'TBC,' *Death of a Young Pioneer Girl*, or *February* are not a struggle with God, but a shameful— and even more shameful because sincere—capitulation to the Devil."[61] In January 2000, visiting Lipkin and his wife, Inna Lisnianskaia, also a poet, in their country home outside Moscow, I asked the eighty-nine-year-old Lipkin whether in his youth he really loved Bagritskii and his poetry. Lipkin replied: "Yes. I understood his weaknesses, such as the poem about Dzerzhinskii ['TBC'] with its lines 'But if it should say "Lie," then tell a lie. / But if it should say "Kill," then kill.' I fought with him over this. [Bagritskii] replied rudely. [He said] that I was too removed from real life, and that is why I had a hard time publishing my poetry, that one should go abreast with life, that I did not understand life. . . . I met him when I was fifteen going on sixteen. He died in 1934, when I was twenty-three." Bewildered, I asked Lipkin to explain the meaning of his scathing remarks about *February* and several other poems by Bagritskii. He said this: "Well, I did not like in them this desire to justify everything Soviet, to justify everything the Bolsheviks did. This I did not like. . . . I told him this—the way a younger person tells an older one, the way a student tells a teacher—politely, but quite seriously. . . . The whole intonation of *February* is alien to me."[62]

While in the pages to come I will speak at length about the achievements of *February,* and especially the profoundly biblical message of its ending, one thing should be said here in reply to Lipkin and Bagritskii's other self-righteous critics. Regrettably, Lipkin—an Odessan Jew and one of the last survivors of early Soviet culture—seems incapable of dealing with the complexity and ambiguity of Bagritskii's message, hiding instead behind the reductive safety of binary oppositions.

While a critical examination of Eduard Bagritskii's Soviet literary legend could alone amount to a book-length study, one glaring omission serves as my principal motivation for this book: the Jewish question in Bagritskii's life and art. His short life, encompassing the first three decades of the twentieth century, typifies the destinies of Russia's Jewish artists born in the late 1890s and early 1900s—the artistic generation whose lives were forever changed by the February and October 1917 Revolutions. Born in 1895 in Odessa, Bagritskii was raised in a family where Judaic traditions and rituals were respected, while the lifestyle was that of a modern and largely secularized urban petite bourgeoisie. As a teenager, he experienced firsthand the pogroms of 1905 and the anti-Semitic quotas of the czarist educational system (for details, see the chronology following the main text of this book). He received a mediocre education and debuted as a poet on the eve of World War I in Odessa's literary publications. Bagritskii welcomed the February Revolution and during the spring and summer of 1917 served in the law enforcement organs created by the Provisional Government. In 1918–20, he was a political officer in the Red Army, writing agitational poetry and propaganda leaflets.[63] Following the end of the civil war in European Russia, Bagritskii rejoined Odessa's cultural life, which had grown considerably more provincial after the departure of many of Bagritskii's stellar colleagues, the representatives of the South-Western School (Viktor Shklovskii's term). Bagritskii married a non-Jewish woman, Lidia Suok, in 1920, and their son Vsevolod was born in 1922. In 1925, upon the insistence of his friends, Bagritskii moved to Moscow, following Isaac Babel, Il´ia Il´f and Evgenii Petrov (who coauthored their main works), Valentin Kataev, Iurii Olesha, Lev Slavin, Konstantin Paustovskii, and other Odessan writers, many of them Jewish. In a relatively short time, he gained wide acceptance and admiration in Moscow as one of the most talented new authors. His literary affiliations bespeak the fluctuations of a fellow traveler: briefly a member of the Pass (Pereval)—a politically moderate group that stressed an intuitively organic approach to a realistic depiction of life—and later a member of the Literary Center of Constructivists (LTsK). In 1930, Bagritskii joined the Russian Association of Proletarian Writers (RAPP). Between 1925 and 1934, he published eight books of verse. By the time of his premature death in 1934, he had firmly installed himself in the new Soviet literary establishment, regularly contributing to the foremost literary periodicals and serving as an editor at Federatsiia ("Federation") Publishing House and as a member of the editorial board of the Literary Gazette. The asthmatic Bagritskii spent his latter years confined to his apartment in the center of Moscow, writing, editing, mentoring younger writers, and taking care of his beloved fish (Bagritskii liked to say that his profession was ichthyology).

However schematic, this outline of Bagritskii's career betokens several emblematic facts for the history of Jews in the late imperial and early Soviet period: his upbringing in a mercantile Jewish family and some exposure to Judaism; his cultural Russianization through education, voracious reading, and group literary activities; his enthusiastic endorsement of the Revolution and engagement in the events of the civil war; his assimilation through marriage to a non-Jew; his move from the former Pale of Settlement to Moscow; his major literary success following the move to the Soviet capital; and his service in the developing apparatus of Soviet culture.

In Bagritskii's Soviet literary legend, the fact of the poet's Jewishness is marginalized to the point of oblivion. The following comments by Elena Liubareva come from her introduction to the 1964 volume of Bagritskii's collected works: "The poet's parents were typical representatives of Jewish petite bourgeoisie (as Bagritskii would subsequently characterize his father). Their interests did not extend beyond those of narrow practical concerns. . . . Religious traditions exacerbated the poverty of their spiritual life."[64] Thus, Bagritskii's Jewish ethnic origin is stated in conjunction with a set of (negative) Soviet-Marxist class-based associations, while his Judaic religious upbringing is condemned outright. In most cases, discussions of Bagritskii's Jewishness—much like that of other Russian-Jewish authors—followed the prescribed formula of the passage I have just quoted. Ironically, the fact of Bagritskii's Jewishness was given full billing only in those instances when he became the object of violent anti-Semitic attacks, first at the height of Stalin's anti-Jewish campaign of 1948–53 and later in the diatribes of the founders of the Russian ultranationalist movement in the 1970s and 1980s (Igor' Shafarevich, Stanislav Kuniaev). To Judeophobes, Bagritskii's career as a Russian-Jewish writer symbolizes everything that supposedly went wrong with Russian culture after the Bolshevik Revolution.

Bagritskii's Jewishness was a central predicament of his identity. Jewishness gave his poetry a major theme that reached an explosive crescendo in his last work, *February*. Needless to say, Bagritskii was not the only Russian-Jewish poet to achieve fame during the first Soviet decade: both the virtuosic and ambitious Il'ia Sel'vinskii and the skillful and politically correct Iosif Utkin enjoyed great success (in emigration, Dovid Knut stands as a major Russian-Jewish poet of that generation). However, owing to his natural artistic predilections and the epoch and place in which he was born and formed as a poet, but also to the legend-proof brevity of his career and the pathologically high number of his anti-Semitic detractors, Bagritskii cuts a most controversial and colorful figure among the Russian-Jewish poets of the early Soviet period. His career mirrors that of his coeval, the great Russian-Jewish prose writer Isaac Babel (1894–1940), and in many respects Bagritskii was the Babel of Russian poetry.

Of all Russian-Jewish poets, Bagritskii most summons comparison with Osip Mandelstam (1891–1938), one of this century's greatest poets and Bagritskii's senior by four years.[65] Bagritskii's derogators make this comparison to prove that although Mandelstam and Bagritskii were both born Jewish, Mandelstam has become an integral part of Russian poetry, whereas Bagritskii has allegedly remained an anomalous and "un-Russian" tree in its groves. At the same time, Bagritskii's admirers have juxtaposed Bagritskii with Mandelstam to highlight an alternative path for a Jew assimilating into Russian culture, a path that does not lie through conversion to Christianity.

Indeed, the dynamic of Bagritskii's life shares some important features with that of Mandelstam's but also differs from it in crucial ways.[66] Mandelstam converted to Lutheranism in 1911, not only to sidestep the czarist anti-Jewish quotas but also in an effort to embrace the Christian heritage of Western civilization and enter the mainstream of Russian culture. As I see it, the early part of Mandelstam's career was one of an abnegation of his Jewish self, while Hellenism ousted Judaism as a spiritual and ethical foundation of Mandelstam's version of Christian culture. Due in part to Mandelstam's professional misfortunes and his subsequent persecution by the Stalinist regime, his latter years were marked by a growing acknowledgment of his Judaic roots. For the Mandelstam of the late 1920s and 1930s, the Jew equaled the ultimate "outsider for life" (Clare Cavanagh's expression[67])—more in keeping with Marina Tsvetaeva's famous dictum of 1924: "In this most Christian world / poets are the Yids," than owing to Mandelstam's identification with the millennia of Jewish history.[68] Furthermore, and despite his discursive and poetical lapses into Jewish topics, his reactions to his un(der)assimilated Russian-Jewish contemporaries were predominantly ones of shame and embarrassment, as was his attitude to Yiddish and its cultural heritage. Put simply, the Petersburgian Osip Mandelstam found it bewildering to be a Jew in Russian culture—not a refined and tormented poet-Yid but a provincial Jew reading his Russian poems with a Yiddish accent, whereas the Odessan Eduard Bagritskii saw no problem with it.

As did Mandelstam, in the early part of his career Bagritskii engaged in active identity remaking. In the initial steps of Bagritskii's cultural assimilation, the riches of Russian poetry served a role not dissimilar from that of the heritage of European Christian culture in Mandelstam's, although conversion to Christianity was never an option that Bagritskii entertained. Following the October Revolution, enthralled by the idea of a Soviet state in which there would be "neither Hellene, nor Jew," Bagritskii made assimilationist—and occasionally anti-Judaic—statements in tune with many other Jewish artists and intellectuals embracing Bolshevism as a modicum of political—and secular—Jewish liberation. "What do Bagritskii and Mandelstam both hate?" asked Shimon Markish, son of the great Yiddish poet Peretz Markish and himself a scholar of Jewish literature. And Markish thus replied to the question he posited in a discussion of the varieties of Russian-Jewish self-hatred:

Not a Jewish way of life (which they simply do not know), but a Jewish everyday living [ne evreiskoe bytie . . . , a evreiskii byt]. And furthermore: when and how do they hate it? In childhood, in young adolescence, as a brief paroxysm of disgust or a fierce rebellion taking the shape of a scandal. Then the child and the young adolescent grow up, and their reactions to Jewishness diverge both in terms of the everyday living and of the Jewish way of life: Mandelstam turns away and exits, Bagritskii stays.[69]

During the 1920s and early 1930s, Bagritskii agonized over the status of his Jewishness at the time of the growing antireligious campaign in the Soviet

Union. This was also the time when the artificial, ahistorical, supraethnic concept of the Soviet man was being brought forward. How can one become a Soviet man without shedding one's Jewishness? What is the goal of Jewish assimilation? Will Jewishness survive in Russia? These were the "overwhelming questions" Bagritskii struggled with at the time of his untimely death in 1934. As did Isaac Babel—his close friend since their shared Odessan youth—Bagritskii always maintained a personal live connection with the Judaic past and Jewish present, both in moments of antireligious blind rage and in those of messianic awakening.

Brief comments on the scope of this book are in order. Written from a post-Soviet critical vantage point, it attempts to reconstruct Bagritskii's career as a major Russian-Jewish poet by turning from his last work back to his literary and historical origins. While I examine Bagritskii's works written at various junctures of his life, I focus principally on his greatest contribution, the long narrative poem *February* (*Fevral'*, 1933–34; 1936). Its significance for a reconstruction of the poet's literary dynamic may be compared to that of the heartrending lyrics of Nikolai Nekrasov's *Last Songs,* written in 1876–77, or to Heinrich Heine's poems and aphorisms, composed in 1855–56 in the mattress crypt. As a story of the tragic formation of a Russian-Jewish identity in a time of historical and political cataclysms, *February* has plenty to tell a student of Jewish history and Soviet history. A document of immense literary and historical significance, *February* in its afterlife has emerged as a single work by a Russian-Jewish author most maligned by anti-Semitic critics. Dying of a poet's malady, Bagritskii wrote *February* at the time when his idealism crashed against the ferroconcrete dams of the emerging Stalinist state, when he witnessed the death of an idyll, the impossibility of a poet's harmonious existence in a world of cultural and political violence. He also realized that his hopes for the disappearance of anti-Semitism were but a beautiful dream, light years away from the reality of interethnic relations in the Soviet Union.[70]

This book is intended for anyone with a penchant for modern poetry, Jewish writing, and Russian culture and history. While it began as a work for students of Russian literature and history, it gradually changed its thrust as I grew more and more interested in the parameters of Jewish identity and cultural assimilation in Diaspora. A desire to make Bagritskii available to the reader in my adopted language and country impelled me to undertake the English translations of two of his major works about Jewish identity, "Origin" and *February.* This desire also explains my decision to provide a detailed chronology of Bagritskii's life and works.

As a cultural space where the Romantic myth of the poet as both prophet and martyr has survived much longer than in the West, Russia challenges her students to understand the ways her writers negotiate, formulate, and submit to the members of the general public the most pressing issues of their past and future. At the beginning of the twenty-first century, Bagritskii the person and the poet stands as a brave transgressor of boundaries—Jewish, Russian, and Soviet.

CHAPTER ONE

~

The Major Jewish Texts

1. "Origin": English Translation

Origin

I can't recall the exact night
When I felt the ache of life to come.
The world rocked and swayed.
4   A star stumbled on its way,
Splashing into a sky-blue basin.
I tried to grab the star. . . . Slipping through my fingers
It darted off, a carp with blazing fins.
8   Over my cradle rusty Jews
Crossed rusty blades of crooked beards.
And everything was upside down.
And nothing was ever right.
12   A carp pounded on the window;
A horse chirped; a hawk dropped into my hands;
A tree danced.
And my childhood went forth.
16   They tried desiccating it with matzos.
They tried deceiving it with candles.
They pushed its nose into the tablets—
Those gates that couldn't be opened.
20   Jewish peacocks on upholstery.
Jewish cream that always turned sour,
Father's crutch and mother's headscarf—
All muttered at me:
24   "Scoundrel! Scoundrel!"
And only at night, only on my pillow
Did a beard not split my world in two;
And slowly the water fell,

28   Like copper pennies from the kitchen faucet.
      The water dripped. Descending like a storm cloud
      It sharpened the crooked blade of its jet. . . .
      "Tell me, how could my Jewish disbelief
32   Believe in this ever-flowing world?"
      They taught me: a roof's a roof.
      The chair's hard. The floor dies under your feet,
      You must see, comprehend, and hear,
36   Leaning on this world, like on a counter.
      But the watchmaker's precision of a woodworm
      Already hollows the beams of my existence.
      "Tell me, how could my Jewish disbelief
40   Believe in this solid world?"
      Love?
      But what about lice-eaten braids;
      A jutting collar bone;
44   Pimples; a mouth, greased with herring;
      And a horsey curve of the neck?
      Parents?
      But aging in the twilight,
48   Hunchbacked, knotty, and wild,
      Rusty Jews fling at me
      Their stubbly fists.
      The door! Fling the door open!
52   Outside the stars have chewed all the leaves
      From their branches,
      The moon's crescent smokes in the middle of a puddle.
      A rook screams not knowing his kin.
56   And all that love,
      Rushing at me,
      And all the self-deprecation
      Of my fathers
60   And all the nebulae
      Creating the night,
      And all the trees
      Tearing through my face—
64   All this stood in my way
      Wheezing in my chest, whistling through my ailing bronchi:
      "Pariah! Take your poor belongings,
      Your cursedness and rejection!
68   Run away!"
      I'm abandoning my old bed:
      "Should I leave?
      I'm going!

72   Good riddance!
        I don't care!"

1930

Translated, from the Russian, by Maxim D. Shrayer

Note on the Text of "Origin"

"Origin" (Russian title "Proiskhozhdenie") was first published in the monthly review *Novyi mir* (*"New World"*) 11 (1930) and was later included in Bagritskii's second collection, *Pobediteli* (Victors, 1932), as well as in a number of his subsequent collections.

2. February: English Translation with Notes on the Text

February

Here I am again on this land.
                                Again
I walk under the young plane trees,
Again children run around park benches,
4   Again the sea lies in the steamers' haze. . . .

Volunteer, my shoulder straps
Decorated with multicolored cord;
That's me—the warrior, the hero of Stokhod,
8   The Knight of the Mazurran swamps,
Hobbling in blistered jack boots,
With a service cap cocked on the back of my head. . . .

On furlough I came home to take in with every muscle,
12   To feel with every tiny cell the tremor
Of wind, enmeshed in leaves,
The pigeon warmth of breath
Of suntanned boys, the play of spots
16   On the sand, the salty tenderness of the sea. . . .

Now I'm used to everything: from where
I escaped these things seemed trivial to me—
The world charred by a mortar shell,
20 Pierced by a bayonet, tightly wound
With barbed wire, the pungent stench
Of sweat and rancid bread. . . .

In this world I must find a place, a corner
24 Where a fresh towel on a hook has the scent of mother,
Where a shard of soap is aside the tap,
And the sun, passing through the window,
Doesn't burn your face like coal. . . .

28 Here I am again on the boulevard.
                                    Again
Cowwheats blossom on flower beds,
A man in a Navy cap is reading
A book in a raspberry binding;
32 A girl in a short dress
Is playing yo-yo; on a balcony
A parrot screams from his silver cage.

Now I am almost equal to them, if I want
36 I sit, if not—I walk around, or even smoke
(Unless I see an officer nearby)
Watching the smooth flight of a leaf
Above the benches and the sparrows passing
40 By the town hall clock. . . .

What's most important will happen
At four sharp.
                    From behind the kiosk
A girl in a pelerine will come
44 Swinging her striped satchel,
All of her as if flung open
To the cool sea breath, to birds and sun rays,
In her green dress of weightless wool
48 She flows as if into a dance,
Into the whirling of leaves and the trembling
Of flowers and butterflies over the lawn.

Home from high school . . .
                              Together with her
52 From a forgotten world—
Trills of school bells, announcing breaks,

Whisper of girlfriends, angel from a notebook,
Teacher's footfall in the corridor.
56   Stately plane trees sing her name,
And the sea wheezes a goodbye. . . .

I never loved properly . . .
A little Judaic boy,
60   I was the only one around
To shiver in the steppe wind at night.

Like a sleepwalker, I walked along tram tracks
To silent summer cottages, where in the underbrush
64   Of gooseberry or wild blackberry bushes
Grass snakes rustle and vipers hiss,
And in the thickets, where you can't sneak in,
A bird with a scarlet head darts about,
68   Her song is thin as a pin;
They've nicknamed her "Bull's eye." . . .

How did it happen, that born to a Hebrew,
And circumcised on the seventh day,
72   I became a fowler—I really don't know!

I loved Brehm better than Mayne Reid!
My hands trembled with passion
When I opened the book at random—
76   Birds would leap out at me from chance pages
Looking like letters of foreign alphabets,
Sabers and trumpets, globes and rhombuses.

I imagine the Archer once paused
80   Above the blackness of our dwelling,
Above the notorious Jewish smoke
Of goosefat cracklings, above the cramming
Of tedious prayers, bearded faces
84   In family pictures. . . .

I didn't peep, like others
Into chinks of bathing huts.
                              I never tried
To pinch a girl as if by chance. . . .
88   Shyness and vertigo
Tormented me.
                        I tried to run
Sideways, unnoticed, through the garden

With girls in high school dresses singing.

92   But lost in reverie, not noticing
It myself, I could thoughtlessly
And stupidly stare at the bare legs
Of a young woman;
                standing on a stool
96   She wiped store windows with a rag. . . .

Suddenly glass whistled like a bird
And scattered around in front of me
Golden buntings and dry leaves,
100   Swamps strewn with forget-me-nots,
Women's shoulders and birds' wings,
The whistle of wings and babble of skirts,
The nightingale's chattering and the song
104   Of the girl on the other side of the street;
And, at last, clearer and purer,
In the world of customs and rituals,
Under the oil lamp of my home
108   The eyes of a nightingale on the face of a girl. . . .

This time, again, peering in under her hat,
In a slight shadow I saw her eyes;
Full of nightingale tremble,
112   Swaying, they flowed in tune with her heels,
A lock of her hair trailed down,
Shooting gold on her skin. . . .

Down the alley, along the lawn,
116   A high school dress was walking;
Fifty yards behind, like a killer,
Stumbling on benches, bumping
Into people and trees, whispering curses,
120   I walked in big jack boots,
In a green greasy blouse; cut short
In accordance with the field manual,
Still not cured of stooping my shoulders—
124   The company's dodger, a Jewish boy. . . .

She looked into store windows, and amidst
Transparent silks and perfume bottles
Her water-face was reflected,
128   Mysterious and unearthly. . . .

She stopped at flower stands,
Her fingers would pick a rose,
Swimming in an enameled bowl
132   Like a small double fish.

A smell of coffee and cinnamon
Wafted from the colonial shop,
And muffled by that smell, wet rose in hand,
136   Above baskets with heaps of leaves
She looked like an exotic bird
Having flown out of Brehm's book. . . .

.   .   .   .

I evaded the front: I tried everything. . . .
140   How many crumpled rubles
Escaped from my hands to the clerks'!
I bought my sergeants vodka,
I bribed them with cigarettes and salt pork. . . .
144   I roamed from ward to ward
Coughing in a paroxysm of pleurisy,
Puffing and gasping,
Spitting into bottles, drinking medicine,
148   Standing naked and unshaved
Under stethoscopes of all the doctors. . . .

When I was lucky enough by truth
Or lie—who can remember?—
152   To get a leave pass,
I would shine my boots,
Straighten my blouse, and sharply
Walk to the boulevard, where an oriole sang
156   In the treetops, its voice like baked clay,
Where above the sand of the path
A green dress swayed
Like a slender strand of smoke. . . .

160   Again I dragged on behind her,
Dying of love, swearing, stumbling into benches. . . .
She would go into a movie theater,
Into the rattling darkness, the tremble
164   Of green light in a square frame,
Where a woman beside a fireplace
Wrung her alabaster hands,

And a man in a granite vest
168   Was shooting from a silent revolver. . . .

I knew the faces of all her admirers,
I knew their habits, smiles, gestures,
How their steps slowed down, when on purpose
172   With chest, hips or palms
They would feel through a dainty cover
The anxious tenderness of a girl's skin. . . .

I knew it all . . .
              Birds flew away . . .
176   Grass withered . . .
                   Stars collapsed . . .
The girl walked around the world,
Picking flowers, lowering her eyes. . . .
Autumn . . .
           The air is soaked with rain,
180   Autumn . . .
            Rage, hurt and anguish!
I'll go up to her today.
              I'll stand
Before her.
          I won't let her turn away.
Enough of this hustle.
           Be strong!
184   Take yourself in hand.
           Stop dawdling!
The kiosk is boarded up . . .
           Pigeons fuss
Around the town hall clock.
           Soon it'll be four.
She appeared an hour earlier;
188   A hat in her hands . . .
           Her coppery hair—
Translucent in the chilly sun—
Streaming down her cheeks . . .
           Silence.
            And the voice
Of a tomtit, lost in this world . . .
192   I must go up to her.
           I must
Certainly go up to her.
           I must
Really go up to her.

Don't think,
Just go after her.
Enough gibbering! . . .
196 But my legs didn't move,
As if made of stone.
My body
As if chained to the bench . . .
Couldn't get up. . . .
Idler! Loser!

200 The girl had already approached the square,
And in the dark gray circle of museums
Her dress, flying in the wind,
Looked thinner and greener. . . .

204 I tore myself from the bench
With such effort, as if I had been
Bolted to it.
And not turning back
Rushed after her toward the square.
208 All the things I used to read at night—
Sick, hungry, half-dressed—
Birds with non-Russian names,
People from an unknown planet,
212 World where they play tennis,
Drink orangeade and kiss women—
All that was now moving before me,
Dressed in a woolen dress,
216 Flaming with copper locks,
Swinging a striped satchel,
Heels running over cobblestones. . . .

I'll put my hand on her shoulder,
220 "Look at me!
I am your misfortune!
I'm dooming you to the torment
Of incredible nightingale passion!
Wait!"
But there, around the corner.
224 Twenty steps away her dress shows green . . .
I am catching up with her.
A little farther on
And we shall stride abreast. . . .

I salute her as my superior,

228   What shall I tell her? My tongue
    Mumbles some nonsense,
                "Will you . . .
    Don't run away . . .
            May I
    Walk you home? I was in the trenches! . . ."

232   She is wordless.
              Not even a look
    In my direction.
             Her steps get faster.
    I run beside her, like a beggar,
    Bowing respectfully.
             How on earth
236   Can I be her equal!
            Like a madman
    I mumble some ridiculous phrases. . . .

    And suddenly a halt.
             Silently
    She turns her head—I see
240   Her copper hair, her blue-green eyes
    And a purplish vein on her temple,
    Pulsating with anger.
    "Go away. Now." And her hand
244   Points to the intersection. . . .
            There he is—
    Placed to guard the order—
    He stands in my way like a kingdom
    Of cords, shiny badges, medals,
248   Squeezed into high boots,
    And covered on top by his hat,
    Around which whirl in a yellow
    And unbearably torturous halo
252   Doves from the Holy Scriptures,
    And clouds, twisted like snails;
    Paunchy, beaming with greasy sweat,
    A policeman,
            from the early morning pumped
256   With vodka and stuffed with pork fat. . . .

    . . . .

    Students' blue peaked caps;
    Soldiers' astrakhans; fur hats; derbies;
    Steam, erupting from chilled throats;

260   Clouds of shag smoke floating around. . . .

A dance of sheepskin coats and jackets,
Trench coats stinking of rancid bread,
And at the podium, near a big carafe—
264   So unexpected in this disarray—
An agitated man in a leather jacket,
Worn over a ripped shirt,
Shouts in a strained voice
268   While spreading his arms
In a gesture of victory.
                        Large doors
Open wide.
                From a February night
People flow in; blinded by bright light,
272   They stamp in place, shake the snow
Off their sheepskins, and here they're
With us: talking, shouting, raising hands,
Damning, weeping,
                        puffing, coughing.

276   Railings crack in the galleries
Under the push of shoulders.
Smeared with dirt and caked blood
Fists rise like soiled luminaries. . . .

280   That night we went to take over
A police station:
                Myself, my friend—a student,
And a Socialist professor with red hair.

Body fills with the blood of courage,
284   Wind of courage rounds out the shirt.
Youth is over . . .
                Maturity is next. . . .
Crush the butt against cobblestones! Tear off your hat!

The shape of the world is changing.
                        Just this morning
288   Plane trees rustled their blessings.
                        The sea
Made its home in the gulf.
                        In summer cottages
Girls sang in circles.
                        In the book
Dr. Brehm was resting, his double-barrel

292 Pressed against a boulder.
My parents' house
Was lit by tongues of candles and the Biblical kitchen. . . .

The shape of the world is changing . . .
Tonight
Hoar frost is covering trees,
296 Branches get in the eyes, like hands.
The sea
Has lapped over the empty boulevard.
Steamers wheeze, sinking.
Summer cottages
Have all been boarded up.
Rats march
300 On deserted porches.
Dr. Brehm puts down a book
And lifts his rifle at me with a threat. . . .
My parents' house has been robbed.
A cat
On the cold stove raises his claws. . . .

304 Youth is over today . . . Peace is but a dream. . . .
Feet splash through the mud.
Damn it!
Lift your collar and wrap up your shoulders!
Okay, gotta go!
Don't fret, my friend!
308 Rain!
Squabble of fussy crows
On the acacias.
Rain.
Out of nowhere
Motorcyclists roll out, enshrouded
In acetylene light.
And again the black
312 Tunnel with no beginning or end.
Blind wind, blowing in all directions.
Patrols,
Splashing through puddles.
And again—
Rain.
We're alone in this world of wet.

316 Stumbling on curbstones near back alleys,
Knocking into each other, falling

Like cobbles on the roadway, by midnight
We reached the station. . . .
　　　　　　　　　　　Here it is:
320　The stone box, protected by hundreds
Of rusty chains and thirty-pound hooks,
The box, filled with fever
And typhoid chill, with drunken
324　Delirium, mumbled prayers, forbidden songs. . . .

Two gendarmes, wearing wide trousers,
At the entrance stood guard,
Both of them were mighty and stout
328　Like mustached samovars. . . .

From somewhere in the bowels of autumn,
Fizzing with raindrops, came the round
Neighing of a horse and the wondrous
332　Crying of a rooster.
　　　　　　　　　　The porter
Opened some sort of chink.
　　　　　　　　　　　　We entered and the locks
Clanked again, blocking our exit. . . .

We walked through corridors, looking
336　Like nightmares.
　　　　　　　　　Crooked lanterns
Swayed over our heads.
　　　　　　　　　　　Slanted shadows,
Bunching into lumps, rolling into spirals
Ran up the walls
340　Toward protruding ceilings. . . .
Policemen snored on long benches
Resting their heads on sword hilts;
The labyrinth led
344　To oak gates with a square
Brass plate: "Sheriff."

Pinkish, with sky-blue whiskers,
Heaving from the lightest blow of air,
348　Like an angel from a high school notebook
He soared over his inkstand,
Made from shrapnel shells,
He faintly smiled, melting, dying
352　Of cordiality, tenderness, and pleasure
To see the Committee delegates. . . .

And we . . . we just stood there, stepping
In indecision, staining with our heels
356   The unbelievable horses and parrots
Embroidered on the carpet. . . .
                               Naturally
We weren't up to smiling.
                      That's enough . . .
Just give us the keys and get the hell out!
360   There's nothing to talk about.
                         Goodbye!

We took over the station.
                   We roamed
Around the corridors.
                     In one of the rooms
We found a tower of Brownings
364   And revolvers, piled like potatoes;
We counted all the weapons.
                     By morning,
Drowsy, tired of the night jobs,
Covered with the station's dust,
368   We found a prisoner's tin kettle—
Dirty and dented—and we drank,
Burning and pouting our lips,
The winners' first tea, the tea of freedom. . . .

372   Blue rains washed the soil;
At night—when no one could see it—
Proud chestnut trees started to blossom.
The soil dried up.
                  The brine of salt air
376   Wafted from the shore.
                     In the orchestra's shell,
Lost in the thick of plane trees,
The Marseillaise, raised up on the bows,
Disappeared amid lanterns and leaves.

380   Our street, washed to brilliance
By summer downpours, was drifting away
Toward the bay girded by a green fence
Of tall plane trees;
384   In the tree crowns, in curls of foam
The cardboard Battleship Sinope
Rocked on the waves.
                  And a pennant wriggled

Like a fiery worm on a purple cloud. . . .
388   Shedding acacias.
                                    Invisible odor
Of rotting flowers reached the shore,
Where sailors danced hugging
Buxom girls from blue-collar districts.

392   Behind fishermen's homes, on the slopes
Of mountain passes, overgrown with tufted mint,
Under smashed boats, near demolished
Bathing huts the fearless lads—
396   Deserters with dangling shoulder straps—
Played blackjack, go fish, and crazy eights
While the coiled pipe of the still
Snuffled in the cave like a suckling calf.

400   I stayed in the area. . . .
                                    I worked
As deputy commissar.
                                    At first
I spent many nights in damp sentry boxes;
I watched the world, passing by me,
404   Alien and dimly lit by crooked streetlamps,
Full of strange and unknown monsters
Oozing from thick fumes. . . .

I tried to be ubiquitous. . . .
                                    In a gig
408   I churned rural roads, searching
For horse thieves.
                                    In the middle of night
I rushed out in a motorboat
Into the gulf, curved like a black horn
412   Around rocks and sand dunes.
I broke into thieves' lodgings
Reeking of overfried fish.
I appeared, like the angel of death,
416   With a torchlight and a revolver, surrounded
By four sailors from the battleship
(Still young and happy. Still rosy-cheeked.
Sleepy after a night of reckless fun.
420   Cocked caps. Unbuttoned pea jackets.
Carbines under their arms. Wind in their eyes.).

My Judaic pride sang,

Like a string stretched to its limit. . . .
424 I would've given much for my forefather
In a long caftan and fox fedora,
From under which fell gray spirals
Of earlocks and clouds of dandruff
428 Flushing over his square beard,
For that ancestor to recognize his descendant
In this huge fellow, rising, like a tower,
Over flying lights and bayonets,
432 From a truck, shaking off midnight. . . .

.   .   .   .

I was startled.
The telephone rang,
Grinding right by the ear.
"The Commissar? Speaking. What do you want?"
436 And the voice, hidden in the receiver,
Told me that on Richelieu Street,
In the teahouse of Mrs. General Klements
All three were getting together:
440 Sam Rabinovitch, Pete Flounder and Moe Diamond,
The train robbers,
The movie heroes,
Gangsters with cases, containing a set of
444 Drills and saws, sweet-smelling cigarettes
To put to sleep a fellow traveler. . . .
These gangsters flew over train tops
In black capes flapping in the wind,
448 With revolvers up the sleeves of their tuxes;
They embraced hundred-ruble houris,
And now at Mrs. General Klements'
We'll get them.
Basta!

452 My lads from the battleship were drinking tea
And playing checkers in the mess hall.
Their striped T-shirts
Bulged around their muscles. . . .
456 Rosy with the rosiness of childhood,
Big-armed and blue-eyed,
They moved the checkers
From square to square, delighted,
460 Blinking and stirring their lips;
Singing with zeal and passion,

Keeping time with their heels. . . .

We climbed onto the carriage,
464   Holding on to each other's waists,
And an angular ancient jade
Drove us into warm darkness. . . .

All it took was to stick a revolver
468   In the chink of the gate, and the porter,
Yawning and pulling up his pants,
Opened the squeaky gate.
                  Silently
We ascended the long red
472   Carpeted staircase.
              Alone
I approached the door.
              My lads,
With carbines between their knees,
Leaned against the wall.

476   Everything like in a decent home:
A pendant lamp with a dark blue shade
Above the dinner table.
              Velvet curtains,
Chairs with soft backs.
              Piano,
480   Bookcase, Tolstoy's bust on top.
Kindness and coziness
In the warm air.
              Streams of steam
Around the samovar. A cloth
484   Of knitted wool.
              Everything in place. . . .

We walked in like a storm, like a breath
Of black streets, not wiping our boots,
Not taking off our pea jackets.
              Bowing
488   And nervously rubbing her hands
With many rings, a bewigged lady
Smelling of powder minced out to greet us;
Fat, with flabby cheeks.
492   "Mrs. Antonina Klements?
We need to talk to you,"
I said, opening the door ajar.

A conversation at the table.

Three

496   Young men in the National Guard uniform,
Young ladies modestly laughing,
Candy and cake on the table.

I came in and stood still, dumbfounded. . . .
500   Hell! What a stupid mistake!
This—a teahouse?
Friends over for tea.
Why am I intruding? . . .
504   Maybe I also should sit
In a cozy room, talking about Gumilev's verses,
Instead of sneaking around at night, like some detective,
Or break into quiet homes
508   Looking for nonexistent gangsters. . . .

But one of my sailors came up to the table
And barked out:
"I know those three.
512   Hands up!
Take 'em, guys! . . .
Where's the fourth one? . . . Ladies step aside! . . ."
And then it all started.
Then it really started!
We unfastened holsters from the bellies
516   Of those fancy fellows, of course
They were the gangsters we were looking for.
We locked them up in a storage room
And stationed a sailor to guard them.

520   We pushed doors open.
We entered rooms,
Where air was soaked with sultry powder,
With semen and the sweet stupor
Of coffee liqueur.
Through the languish
524   Of blue fog a streetlamp's light
Was piercing, barely visible (as through water).
In beds, under blankets,
Narrow bodies swam
528   Like fish. A man's head
Rose from pillows
As if from heavy foam. . . .
We checked documents,

532   Closed the doors, apologizing,
         And continued the search.
                    Again
         We were overcome
         With sweet hot air.
               Again
536   Heads rose from pillows
         And dived back into silky foam. . . .

         In the third room we found
         A fellow in sky-blue long johns.
540   He stood with his legs apart.
         Slowly rocking his torso.
         He waved a Browning,
         Like a glove. . . . He winked at us:
544   "Wow! A whole fleet's here! With my gun
         I can't whack you all! All right, I surrender. . . ."

         Behind him, bare-legged,
         In a nightgown sliding down
548   Her shoulders; biting a cigarette,
         Half asleep, silently sat on the bed
         She, the girl whose nightingale glances
         And flight of shoes across slippery asphalt
552   Had so tormented me. . . .

    .   .   .   .

         "Dismissed!" I told the mates.
         "The search is over! Take the fellow!
         I'll stay with the girl!"
                 Awkwardly
556   Rumbling their carbines, my sailors
         Made for the door.
              I remained
         In the stuffy semidarkness, in hot drowsiness,
         With the girl sitting on the bed. . . .
560   "Remember me?" but she didn't speak,
         Weightless hands covering
         Her pale face.
              "Now you remember?"
         Still more silence.
             Angry, I blurted out,
564   "How much do you want for the hour?"
         Quietly, not parting her lips, she said,

"Have pity . . . I don't want the money. . . ."

I tossed her the money.
                              I threw myself down—
568   Not pulling off my boots, not taking off the holster
Or unbuttoning my shirt—
Right into the mess of feathers, into the blanket
Under which all my predecessors
572   Had throbbed and sighed, into the somber
Muddled flow of visions,
Screams and unencumbered movements,
Into darkness and awesome light. . . .

576   I am taking you because my age
Was shy, because I am so bashful,
Because of the shame of my homeless ancestors,
Because a chance bird twitters!

580   I take you to avenge the world
From which I couldn't break away!

Let me into your empty womb,
Where grass cannot take hold,
584   Maybe my night seed
Will fertilize your desert.

There'll be rainfalls, southern winds will blow,
Swans will make again their calls of passion.

1933–1934
Translated, from the Russian, by Maxim D. Shrayer

Note on the Text of *February*

The Russian Original and Its English Translation

Eduard Bagritskii worked on *February* from the end of 1933 until his death in February 1934. The title was assigned in the first publication in 1936 on the basis of a contract that Bagritskii had signed with Federatsiia for a trilogy of long poems to include *February* and two more works that he never wrote. The published Russian text was put together posthumously by its editors, V. Trenin and N. Khardzhiev, who transcribed, compared, and merged two manuscript versions: the first, a complete rough draft, and the second, a reworked and semipolished draft of the first two-thirds of the text. The last third of the poem was published on the basis of the rough draft alone. Manuscripts of both drafts can be found in a single-lined notebook that is kept among Bagritskii's papers at the Institute of World Literature (IMLI) in Moscow.[1]

The text of the English translation is exactly the same length as the Russian original (see the appendix); the number of lines within each of Bagritskii's stanzas has also been preserved in translation. The rows of dots indicate the places where Bagritskii planned but did not have a chance to make additions. Those additions were to include a song between lines 138 and 139, a lyrical digression between lines 552 and 553, and a transitional passage between lines 256 and 257. Finally, the place between lines 432 and 433—where the first two-thirds of the second draft and the last third of the rough drafts converge—is also marked with a row of dots.

The meter of the original, the flavor of which I have tried to preserve here in translation, is *dol´nik*. *Dol´nik* (plural, *dol´niki*) is a Russian nonclassical tonic meter here based on a pattern of a fixed number of recurrent strong syllables (ictae) in combination with a varying (0–2) number of syllable intervals and anacruses. In the case of *February*, one observes a mix of unrhymed and occasionally rhymed three- and four-ictus *dol´niki*, whose general schemes would be, respectively, 2/0—2/1—2/1—2/0 and 2/0—2/1—2/1—2/1—2/0, with the obligatory stress on the final ictae.[2] In three instances in *February*, Bagritskii employs rhymed *dol´niki*. Lines 219 to 222 of the Russian text are rhymed with feminine clausulae to signal the intensity of the protagonist's emotions in the moment of confessing love. Likewise, lines 325 to 328 of the original are rhymed with feminine clausulae to enhance the satirical description of the policemen. Additionally, Bagritskii rhymes lines 403 to 411, 419 and 421, and 447 and 449, also employing feminine clausulae. Only shadows of the episodic rhyming have been preserved in translation. In the poem's conclusion, where the narrative and emotional tension reach a climax, lines 479 to 498 and 505 to 587 are in blank trochaic pentameter (Tr 5) with all feminine clausulae; the switch from a nonclassical *dol´nik* to a classical trochee has been rendered only in the last two lines of the translation. The (Maiakovskiian) stepladder layout of some 10 percent of the original verses has been preserved in translation, as have been Bagritskii's various stanzaic units of four to twenty-four lines.

The Historical Background

The events of *February* unfold in Bagritskii's native city of Odessa between the autumns of 1916 and 1917. The opening scene (lines 1–256) takes place in September or October of 1916, as is evident from the reference to the Stokhod operation of July–August 1916, in which the protagonist has participated (line 7). The next episode (lines 257–371) depicts the February 1917 Revolution: a political rally, and a transfer of power to the organs of the Provisional Government.

Czar Nicholas II abdicated on March 15 (2), 1917. In Odessa, the power of the Provisional Government was established on March 25 (12), 1917. The takeover of a local police station by the protagonist and his cohorts could have taken place at the earliest after the March 22 Circular by the Provisional Government regarding the organization of a temporary militia in place of the czarist police force. On April 17, 1917, a permanent militia was established by a ukase of the Provisional Government.[3]

The next, transitional episode (lines 372–432), in which the protagonist describes his activities as a deputy commissar of the militia, takes place in the spring and summer of 1917. The final scene (lines 433–587) at the house of prostitution ("teahouse") most likely occurs in September–October 1917, and definitely prior to the Bolshevik coup d'état of November 7 (October 25), 1917; in Odessa, the local soviet assumed the power in December 1917.

The following notes on the text, identified by the line numbers of the English text, might be helpful to the English-language reader:

8   Mazurran swamps: this refers to the area of Masurian (Mazurran) Lakes in the northeast of Poland (formerly East Prussia), famous for the defensive operations of the Russian army in February 1915.

33   yo-yo: the Russian original has "d´iabolo"; I have chosen a similar game, popular in the United States.

51   high school: the Russian original has "gimnaziia" (*gymnasium*), a secondary school, based on the classical model, that prepares students for the university.

64   wild blackberry: "ozhina," a Russian dialectal term for "ezhevika," is used in the original.

70   ". . . born to a Hebrew, / And circumcised on the seventh day." This is a curious mistake on Bagritskii's part: in Judaism, the ritual of circumcision (*brit milah*) occurs on the eighth, not the seventh, day of a boy's life. Note that from the point of view of the meter, "vos´moi" ("eighth") would have worked just as well as does "sed´moi" ("seventh") because both Russian words have two syllables and the stress on the first syllable.

73   Brehm: Alfred Edmund Brehm (1829–1884), world-renowned naturalist. Brehm's books include *The Animals of the World* and *Bird-Life, Being a History of the Birds*. Brehm's books, written in German and translated into Russian, were extremely popular among Russian teenagers.

73   Mayne Reid: Mayne Reid, also known as Main Rid (1818–1883), American author. His novels of adventure include *Adventures among the Indians; or the War Trail and the Hunt of the Wild Horse* (1853); *Afloat in the Forest* (1866), *The Headless Horseman* (1866); and *Chris Rock, A Lover in Chains* (1889). Reid's

books were translated into Russian, and they enjoyed much popularity both in Czarist and Soviet times.

79   Archer: "sozvezd´e Strel´tsa" in the original; Archer, or Sagittarius, is the ninth zodiacal constellation.

282   Socialist professor; the original has "privat-dotsent iz eserov"; the protagonist's colleague, an adjunct university professor, is a member of the Socialist-Revolutionary (SR) party.

438   teahouse: the original has "chainyi domik," here a euphemistic term for a bordello.

440   Sam Rabinovich, Pete Flounder, Moe Diamond: I have translated and anglicized the names of the Jewish gangsters; in the Russian text, they are *Semka Rabinovich, Pet´ka Kambala,* and *Monia Brilliantshik.*

454   striped T-shirts: "tel´niashka" in the original, a traditional sailor's undershirt with blue stripes.

496   National Guard uniform: the original has "v zemgusarskoi forme"; "zemgusary" was a mocking nickname for the members of the Vserossiiskii zemskii soiuz ("All-Russia Zemstvo Union"), an organization operating in Russia during World War I; a rough equivalent of the National Guard.

505   Gumilev: Nikolai Gumilev (1886–1921), prominent Russian poet; executed for allegedly taking part in an anti-Bolshevik conspiracy.

Top: Bagritskii's father, Godel´ Moshkovich Dziubin (sitting), with sister of Bagritskii's mother, Polina, and her husband, David Roitman. Odessa, 1910.

Bottom: Bazarnaia (Kirova), 40, in courtyard of the house where Bagritskii was born. Odessa.

3

4

Top: Remeslennaia (Osipova), 4, the house where Bagritskii spent his childhood. Odessa.

Bottom: Bagritskii. Odessa, 1899.

5

6

Left: Bagritskii. Odessa, 1903.

Right: Bagritskii. Zhukovskii School. Odessa, 1910.

Студенческій Литературно-Художествен. Кружокъ
I-й Четвергъ 1918-19 г.

10 н. с. Октября 1918 г.
Зданіе Юридическаго Факультета
Преображенская, 24.
АУДИТОРІЯ № 8. ——— АУДИТОРІЯ № 8.

ПРОГРАММА.

ОТДѢЛЕНІЕ I-е.

Петръ Ершовъ	. . . докладъ „Тургеневъ и мы“.
Валентинъ Катаевъ	. „Октавы“.
Георгій Долиновъ	. . Мелодекламація „На пляжѣ“ исп. Вадимъ Долиновъ, у рояля авторъ.

Антрактъ 5 минутъ.

ОТДѢЛЕНІЕ II-е.

Ефимъ Бриль	. . . . „Сѣдая дѣвушка“, стихи.
Валентинъ Катаевъ	. . „Нервы“, разсказъ.
Вадимъ Долиновъ	. . „Передъ дорогой“, стихи.
Зинаида Шишова	. . Циклъ стиховъ.
Анатолій Фіолетовъ	. Стихи.
Эдуардъ Багрицкій	. 4 пѣсни поэмы „Послѣдній перевалъ“.
Корчмаревъ	. . . . Собственныя призведенія для фортепіано.

Антрактъ 5 минутъ.

ОТДѢЛЕНІЕ III-е.

Юрій Олеша	. . . . „Пракситель“, „Нарциссъ“, стихи.
Аддалисъ	. . . . . . Изъ цикла „Афродитѣ— Аддалисъ“.
Сергѣй Гольденфельдъ	„Мелькартъ“, „Милетъ“, стихи.
Георгій Долиновъ	. . „Третій“, стихи.
Э. Соминскій	. . . . Ритмическая мелодекламація къ стихамъ В. Катаева исп. В. Долиновъ, у рояля авторъ.

Conferencier Лидія Скрынникова.

Начало ровно въ 7 часовъ.

Правленіе.

Playbill of a reading by young Odessan writers, 10 October 1918. The participants include E. Bagritskii, V. Kataev, Iu. Olesha, and Z. Shishova, and others.

8

9

10

Top Left: Bagritskii with son Vsevolod (Seva). Kuntsevo (presently a district of Moscow). Winter 1928–29.

Top Right: Bagritskii. Kuntsevo, 1930.

Bottom: Pionerskaia, 17 (Bagritskogo, 7), the house the Bagritskiis rented and lived in through 1930. Kuntsevo. Here Bagritskii wrote "Origin."

11

12

Top: Bagritskii (third from left), with fellow members of the Literary Center of Constructivists. From left to right: V. Asmus, A. Kviatkovskii, E. Bagritskii, K. Zelinskii, N. Aduev, I. Sel´vinskii, B. Agapov (standing), V. Lugovskoi, G. Gauzner (standing), V. Inber, and E. Gabrilovich. Moscow, 1929.

Bottom: Bagritskii (wearing what appears to be a yarmulke), with his wife, Lidiia Gustavovna Bagritskaia, née Suok, and his dog, Rait. Moscow, 1931.

13

14

Top: Bagritskii (second from right), with a group of literary colleagues.
From left to right: M. Ia. Ignatova, V. Kataev, N. Aseev, E. Bagritskii, and
L. Nikulin. Barvikha, outside Moscow, summer 1933.

Bottom: Bagritskii hunting in the north of Russia. Left to right: E. Tverdov, V. Kokushkin,
A. Tarasov, and Bagritskii with his dog Rait. Niandoma, Arkhangel´sk Province, 13 August 1928.

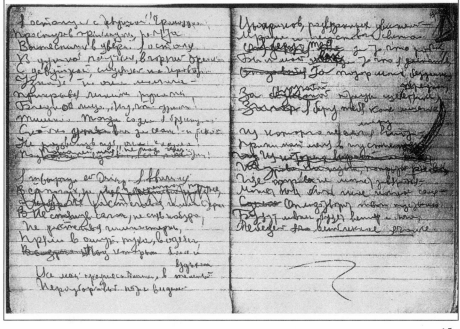

15

Facsimile of the last page of the manuscript of the
long poem *Fevral'* (*February*, 1933–34; 1936).

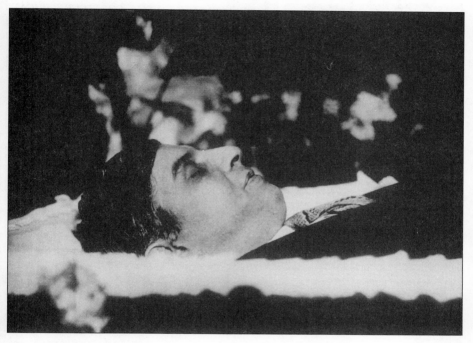

16

Bagritskii lying in state. Moscow, 18 February 1934.

МАЯ 7 1934

ЦЕНА № 90 КОП.

Пролетарии всех стран, соединяйтесь!

Литературная газета

ОРГАН ОРГКОМИТЕТА СОЮЗА
СОВЕТСКИХ ПИСАТЕЛЕЙ СССР и РСФСР.

ПОД РЕДАКЦИЕЙ: В. БАГРИЦКОГО, А. БОЛОТНИКОВА, В. ВИ... ПОВА, В. ЛИДИНА, А. СЕЛИВАНОВСКОГО, М. СЕЛЬВИНСКОГО, В. СУ... РИНОВ..., М. СКРЫПНИК..., А. ЧАРНОГ..., Б. УСИЕВИ...

| № 19 (334) | 18 ФЕВРАЛЯ 1934 года | ВЫХОДИТ ЧЕРЕЗ ДЕНЬ |

Литературной газеты

боевую активность бойцов культурного фронта.

Редакция «Истории заводов» утвердила заявку бригады писателей, работающей над книгой о великой сибирской магистрали. Это будет, вероятно, даже не одна книга. «История великой сибирской магистрали», так она будет называться, включит в себя историю КВЖД и целый ряд проблем истории русского и японского империализма на Дальнем Востоке (боксерское восстание, русско-французский альянс, русско-японская война, авантюра в Корее, поездка Николая в Японию и т. д.), проблему роста Сибири и ее народности и историю рабочего революционного движения («Амурская колесуха», забастовки 1905 г. и др.).

Богатейший материал для этой истории заключают значительные документальные воспоминания участников строительства дороги, воспом...

ния политкаторжан, архивы царских министерств, архивы НККС, архивы революции и архивы ДВР и журналы того времени.

«История великой сибирской магистрали» будет распадаться на три периода (вероятно, сообразно с этим на три тома): с 50-х годов XIX века до 1905 г., с 1905 г. до 1917 г. и последний период—с 1917 г. до наших дней. Последний период включает в себя историю интервенции-интервенции Сибири и интервенции на КВЖД.

Уже утверждена ориентировочный объем работы—60 печ. листов. Бригада писателей еще окончательно не сформирована. Пока над разработкой плана работают инициативная группа (С. Виноградская, Б. Лапин, И. Рахтанов, Л. Рубинштейн, Е. Соболевский, С. Третьяков, М. Шкапская, В. Шкловский, О. Эрдберг, Л. Авербах).

Замысел «Истории великой сибирской магистрали» был одобрен А. М. Горьким.

ПЛЕНУМ ОРГКОМИТЕТА ССП СССР

5 марта созывается пленум Оргкомитета союза советских писателей СССР.

В повестке дня пленума два больших вопроса: «Итоги XVII партийного съезда и задачи литературы», «О подготовке оргкомитета к всесоюзному съезду писателей» (доклады оргкомитетов ССП Украины, Белоруссии, Грузии, Азербайджана, Армении, Узбекистана, Туркмении, Таджикистана, Татарии). Пленум республиканских оргкомитетов.

Всесоюзный Оргкомитет предложил оргкомитетам предварительно проработать и обсудить стоящие на повестке для всесоюзного пленума вопросы. Для этого оргкомитеты на местах предлагают широкие собрания писателей с участием руководящих работников республик, краев, областей, г. биное, литераторов фабрик, заводов, колхозов и частей Красной армии. Республиканские, краевые и областные оргкомитеты должны будут представить к всесоюзному пленуму письменные доклады с полной характеристикой работы местного оргкомитета и подготовки его к съезду писателей СССР. Эти доклады также будут предварительно обсуждены на широких заседаниях.

я французская литература

Д ПОЛИ НИЗАНА В ГИХЛ

Показатель фашизации правого в буржуазного крыла очень широк. Основным из них сквозящим сейчас в краю буржуазной цивилизации, в его нынешнем виде. Южный рынок буквально затоплен литературными рецептами «всякаря капитализма». Одну «рецептуру» предлагает Поль Моран, другую—Жюль Ромен, третью— Андре Морьяк. Некоторые из этих писателей стремятся придать себе фашистским положением демократическим прикрытием. Жюль Ромен, например, это такого, который марксизма, но такого, который «согласит ... гений французской нации.

Другая характеристика-черта фашизации ... все усиливающееся роли науки и техники и возможности самого прогресса. Если страх где-то недавно, еще в период Золя, господствовала натурализм, связанный с материалистической фило-

доктриной. Возникло даже целое течение; возглавляемое Франсуа Морьяком, которое пытается противопоставить марксизму историтуалистическую католицизму. Самое замечательное в том, что у этих писателей Морьяка опираются в своих теориях, не в малой степени на помощь идей из лагеря Троцкого и Суварина.

У всех этих фашистов имеется наложный шеф и покровитель—Жан на д'Арк, которая сейчас является знаменем фашистского движения во Франции. Это новые и историко-интеллектуальные установки фашистской клики и основные еи фило-философии.

Но имеются и другая разновидность фашистов; они оперируют на не жизни «шеф» и «покровитель»—Жан на 2 Арк, которая называет нео-социал-жей—группа тех назад «нео-социалистов во главе с Марселем Деа, писателей, сплотившихся вокруг журнала «Памфлет»—Жэ Превэ, Дэ миньян, Альфред Люс, пытаясь

ЭДУАРД БАГРИЦКИЙ

Гриппозное воспаление легких, соединение с зимней вьюгой, оставило жизнь крупнейшего советского поэта—Эдуарда Багрицкого.

Тов. Багрицкому было 37 лет. Он принадлежал к тому иному поколению интеллигенции, которое кровью связало свою судьбу с судьбой за социализм, начиная с первых лет Октябрьской революции. Он прошел свои молодость на фронтах гражданской войны, в Красной армии. Он был в числе тех рожденных к восприятию нашей революционной поэтов, которые не редко подходили к партии, все полнее и органичнее осознавали правоту ее дела и без остатка отдавали свои творческие силы пролетариату, создаваемому в ожесточенной борьбе с врагами бесклассового социалистическое общество.

Болезнь—астма—та последние годы приковала его к постели. Его редко можно было встретить на больших писательских собраниях и дискуссиях. Но тем не менее его внимание, высокая по своему мастерству, глубокая и органически революционная по своему содержанию, чуждая всем формалистическим выкрутам в простая по форме ...по праву занять было заметно в основной творческий фонт, созданный советской поэзии. Стихи Багрицкого читали, читают и будут читать сотни тысяч и миллионы строителей социализма и наши строители и друзья СССР за рубежом,— по этим стихам учатся многие молодые талантливые советские поэты. Три небольшие книги стихов («Юго-Запад»—1928 г., «Победители»—1932 г. и «Последняя ночь» 1932 г.) в поэтический текст поэмы «Дума» про Опанаса»—таково творческое наследство Багрицкого. Он был невзыскательным борцом за качество в искусстве, непримиримым врагом недобросовестного отношения к труду художника. Нередкого советского образа.

Творчество его становилось все более совершенным по мере того, как он продвигался в себе ряд пред

Очень большая сила была в этом человеке. Очень много восторга, много ненависти, много жадности и жизни. Хорошая книга могла сделать его счастливым. Плохая—заставить страдать. Литература была для него насущным, кровным, занимавшим все мысли делом. Он много читал, много учил и мало писал. Он хорошо знал разницу к тому, чтобы настоящий была у него в каждой строчке. Поэтому строк у него было мало. И большинство из них были настоящей поэзией.

Он был поэтом в полном смысле этого слова. Поэтом, каким мечтают быть поэты.

Его будут помнить, о нем будут долго рассказывать. И его будут очень долго читать.

Все мы, работавшие с ним, очень хорошо это знаем,

КОЛЛЕКТИВ РАБОТНИКОВ «ЛИТЕРАТУРНОЙ ГАЗЕТЫ»

ОРГКОМИТЕТ СОЮЗА СОВЕТСКИХ ПИСАТ...
со скорбью извещает о смерти крупнейшего сов...
ЭДУАРДА БАГРИЦКО...
СКОНЧАВШЕГОСЯ 16 ФЕВРАЛЯ 1934 г. ОТ ВОСПАЛЕНИЯ

СТИХИ БАГРИЦКОГО ПОЛНЫ РИТМОМ БОЛЬШЕВИЗМА

Этот человек ходил по Одессе и из его солнцем. Это было в его глазах стихи—свои и чужие,—читал истоки, что так сущность. В где придется, по случаю, страстно, громко, нем был яростная любовь к жизни сверкал серыми глазами. нераздельности большевизма. Поэ

Он зарядил нас любовью к то и в нем молодость—комсоэтом, иные разящих в советской мольцы, молодые вскармливают поэзии, дойдя ему свои поэти ...

Сегодня умер не только замечательный поэт, но перестал также существовать замечательный поэтический ...

17

Vsevolod Bagritskii's Soviet passport; his nationality (line 3) is listed as "Russian"; the blank triangular spot is the hole made by the Nazi bullet that killed him.

19

Facsimile of Isaac Babel's postcard to Lidiia Bagritskaia, dated 21 August 1935
and mailed from Odessa to Moscow.

CHAPTER TWO

~

The Poetics and Politics
of Russian-Jewish Identity

1. The Trials of Bagritskii's
Last Testament

The long poem *February* (*Fevral´*) was Eduard Bagritskii's last testament. Bagritskii died on February 16, 1934, of pneumonia that was exacerbated by the severe asthma that had plagued him since adolescence.[1] He did not expire in his native Odessa, where both he and Isaac Babel had always longed to return. In September of 1935, Babel wrote this in a postcard to Bagritskii's widow (see illustration 19):

> Dear Lidiia Gustavovna. Once again, my heart filled with emotions, I walk the streets of Odessa and sit in the sun by the sea. The summer is here in all its glory. Twice a day I eat mackerel cooked in all different ways. The first few days I stayed in Londonskaia Hotel, spending many hours with [Iurii] Olesha on a bench on the boulevard. . . . Are you thinking of visiting the home city? It is a bit shabby, but still beautiful as ever. . . . Yours, I. Babel.[2]

A year later, Babel reminisced in print about his last conversation with Bagritskii: "It was time, we both agreed, to leave the alien cities [*chuzhie goroda*] behind, . . . rent a little house in Near Mills [Blizhnie Mel´nitsy, in Odessa], write stories and grow old." Bagritskii and Babel both dreamed of sitting in the sun on an Odessan boulevard as "obese, shrewd old men . . . following women with long-drawn looks."[3] It was, however, in Moscow, where Bagritskii had immigrated in 1925, that he lay dying, wheezing and gasping for air in a room cluttered with fish tanks and manuscripts of verse. Bagritskii left a rough draft of the entire text of *February* as well as a second draft of the first two-thirds of this long narrative poem (*poema*).[4] He had still intended to insert a song and a lyrical digression, but otherwise the poem's text was complete. First published in 1936 in a memorial collection of writings by and about Bagritskii, *February* was due to appear in the second volume of Bagritskii's collected writings scheduled for 1939.[5] The entire second volume, prepared by Bagritskii's widow and the poet Vladimir Narbut, and edited by the Russian-Jewish poet Iosif Utkin, was derailed.[6] In fact both Narbut and the critic Dmitrii (Sviatopolk) Mirskii, who wrote an introduction to the 1936 memorial volume, were arrested in the Great Purges and disappeared in the Gulag. Bagritskii's wife, Lidiia Bagritskaia, was also arrested in 1937. Charged with having been a member of a "terrorist fascist organization" of writers, she spent seven years in a labor camp and almost ten in subsequent exile.[7] One can only wonder what would have been Bagritskii's own lot had he lived to see this first wave of Stalin's terror!

Following the poem's original publication in 1936, February—with its central Jewish theme—has forever remained a thorn in the sinewy side of the Soviet literary establishment.[8] A fairly consistent pattern emerges when one considers the publication history of this long poem against the backdrop of Soviet history. Despite the numerous editions of Bagritskii's other works, between 1936 and 1983 February appears to have been reprinted only three times, first in 1940, then in 1948, and finally in 1964.[9] In 1949–50, the poem was condemned as "erroneous" and "bourgeois-nationalist"[10] and subsequently was not reprinted for fifteen years.

Let me summarize the principal points of the plot as they relate to the poem's structure. February is set in Odessa in the 1900s and 1910s. The protagonist, a timid Jewish youth, a quixotic dreamer alienated from his petit bourgeois surroundings, is desperately in love with a girl who comes from an upper-class non-Jewish family, possibly from the nobility. The protagonist follows his beloved around, unable to approach her. The distance between the two is prohibitive: she—a glamorous student at a prestigious gymnasium; he—a painfully self-conscious son of Jewish shopkeepers from Bazarnaia (Market) Street.[11]

From the outset, and in anticipation of the reader's questions, I wish to make one point clear: I believe it is central to the meaning of the poem and to Bagritskii's design that the beloved of the male Jewish protagonist is not Jewish. Although this is never stated in the poem as a fact, much in the poem supports my conjecture. In the pages to follow, I will explore the significance of the girl's haughty rejection of her Jewish admirer, set against the monologue of the "little Judaic boy" about being unable to "love properly." I will also probe the poem's central opposition between the small and suffocating world of the Jews, from which the protagonist is trying to break away, and the large and luring world of the Gentiles, to which the protagonist's beloved belongs by right of birth. While this beauty with copper hair and green eyes could theoretically be an ethnic Russian, Ukrainian, or Pole in Odessa's multiethnic society, the logic of the poem's tragic ending further suggests that she is a Slav and a Christian, and not a Jew. In the eyes of the Jewish protagonist, the young lady symbolizes a mainstream Russia, both Slavic and Christian, that is off-limits to him in the early parts of the poem. Furthermore, to Bagritskii's anti-Semitic readers, the ending represents a ritualistic rape of Russia by the Jews.

To continue with my summary, participation in the battles of World War I, including the bloody Stokhod operation of 1916, gives the protagonist courage to confront the Russian girl while he is in Odessa on furlough. She refuses even to speak with him and threatens to enlist the help of a nearby police officer. Then the February 1917 Revolution turns the protagonist's life around. An equal citizen of a temporarily democratic Russia, he now works as deputy commissar of the militia, created by a decree of the Provisional Government in place of the czarist police force. His job is that of a criminal investigator. In the middle of the night, the protagonist receives a call informing him that three legendary gangsters are having a spree in a "chainyi domik" ("tea house"), an illicit house of prostitution. Accompanied by a unit of sailors, the protagonist raids the tea house and indeed finds and arrests the gangsters. He also discovers—in one of the bedrooms, in bed with a gangster—"the one whose nightingale looks" used to torment him. Shocked and enraged by the metamorphosis of his former beloved, an unearthly Slavic beauty turned prostitute, the young man offers to pay her for sex. "Have pity . . . I don't want the money," is the prostitute's plea. Both cruel and passionate in his revenge, the protagonist throws her the money and has sexual intercourse with her. With the exception of the final scene (and three rhymed quatrains in the middle), the poem is composed consistently in Bagritskii's celebrated *dol'niki*. However, in the scene of the night search, a classical meter, trochaic pentameter, grows out of the nonclassical *dol'nik* (the last two lines of the translation illustrate the original's trochaic pentameter). Otherwise devoid of a deliberate stanzaic structure, the poem ends with twelve verses of pure trochaic pentameter with feminine clausulae and a deliberate stanzaic configuration: a quatrain, a couplet, a quatrain, and another couplet. Blank trochaic pentameter perfectly suits the feeling of the protagonist's avenging "the world / From which [he] couldn't break away."

February occupies a prominent and still contested position in early Soviet poetry. It is also a literary document of unparalleled significance for historians of Russian-Jewish relations during the early Soviet period. To illustrate the place of *February* in the minds of postwar Russian readers and writers, I will quote from a memoir by Anatolii Naiman (b. 1936), a poet and Anna Akhmatova's secretary in the 1960s. Naiman, who was born Jewish, thus describes the beginning, in 1954, of his friendship with a fellow young poet, the ethnic Russian Dmitrii Bobyshev (b. 1936):

> On a sunny spring day, when Bobyshev and I talked to each other for the first time, we walked down Zagorodnyi, Vladimirskii and Liteinyi Prospects, across the Neva, then down Lesnoi Prospect, to my house near Lanskaia Station, reciting poetry without letting up, and then stamped in place before the gate for another hour, finishing Bagritskii's *February* and selections from [Nikolai] Tikhonov's *Orda* ["The Horde," 1922] and *Braga* ["The Mead," 1923].[12]

Responding to my query in the fall of 1999, Bobyshev confirmed Naiman's recollections: "*February* could not but produce an overwhelming impression

owing to its dazzling imagery, emotional vigor, verbal richness. And also—
because of the openness of its love descriptions." When asked to comment on
February's Jewish theme, Bobyshev said this: "[The Jewish theme] mars what is
almost a work of genius. It mars it because it explains the universally human
(humiliation, love, lust, power) in terms of the national, and this causes the read-
ers' reactions on the same level—that is, both negative and positive [reactions].
In essense, this long poem is 'an anti-Semite's find,' and I do not think this was
part of the author's intentions. . . ."[13] Made by a Russian Orthodox poet whose
verses document a universalist quest and place much emphasis on the continu-
ity of the Judeo-Christian tradition, these retrospective remarks illustrate that
February touches raw nerves even in Bagritskii's fans, let alone his derogators.
Why is it that the poet Bobyshev would seemingly have admired the poem more
had it simply been a story of love and desire at the time of the Russian Revolu-
tion? Why does Bagritskii's coupling of that which is universal and that which is
expressly Jewish—and Judaic—trouble some of his readers? In contesting the tra-
ditional boundaries of interethnic and interreligious relations, *February* chal-
lenges its readers to unearth and confront the question many of us keep buried
deep in our souls.

Despite its prominence and its impact upon postwar Russian poetry, *February*
has received little attention in studies of Soviet literature.[14] Not surprisingly, and
in no small measure due to a censorial plug on Jewish topics following the 1940s,
Soviet critics have had a perilous time with *February*.[15] They have disregarded
the poem completely or have mentioned it only in passing.[16] Pre–World War II
Soviet critics must have been fearful of the example of Dmitrii Mirskii, who paid
with his life for mixing intellectual honesty, ideological blindness, and residual
aristocraticism in his criticism. Consider Mirskii's remarks on *February*:
"Nowhere had Bagritskii portrayed with equal force the plebeian pathos of the
revolution."[17] Andrei Siniavskii devoted the poem but a few scant and noncom-
mittal lines in his 1958 long chapter on Bagritskii.[18] Later critics, including
Bagritskii's conformist biographer, Iosif Grinberg, and the minor classic of Soviet
poetry, Pavel Antokol´skii, avoided any discussion of the poem's Jewish theme.[19]
A run-of-the-mill response to the poem occurs in Elena Liubareva's monograph
of 1964, which fails to treat either the Jewish theme or the problematic final
scene: "And *February* ends on a lofty, joyous note."[20] An exception is found in
Irina Rozhdestvenskaia's 1967 book, where the Jewish question receives a limited
treatment.[21]

At the same time, *February* has been the target of some of the most vicious
attacks on Russian-Jewish creative artists. In 1950, Anatolii Tarasenkov, a
mouthpiece of official Soviet anti-Semitism, accused Bagritskii of Jewish nation-
alism—a charge that at the time amounted to a posthumous death sentence. In
1977, Tarasenkov's words were reiterated by Stanislav Kuniaev (b. 1932), a poet
and an inspired ideologue of the then-nascent ultranationalist Russian move-

ment (Kuniaev now edits the openly anti-Semitic monthly review *Nash sovre-mennik* [*"Our Contemporary"*]).[22] Finally, in the 1980s, the mathematician turned dissident turned ultranationalist Igor´ Shafarevich resorted to *February* to illustrate the anti-Semitic thesis of his treatise *Rusophobia:* "The poems of E. Bagritskii often communicate a cold estrangement from the surrounding people [that is, ethnic Russians], and in the poem *February* an extreme hatred breaks out."[23] As Kuniaev's recently published memoirs demonstrate, *February* continues to top the list of works that most enrage the Russian extremists.[24]

What were the reasons for the reluctance of even dedicated students of Bagritskii's life and oeuvre to engage in a discussion of *February*? Why did *February* become the object of pathological hatred by Russian nationalists?

In his swan song, Bagritskii was able to formulate with utmost clarity, narrate with maximum power, and render in an innovative poetic form one of the most fundamental and debated issues in twentieth-century Russian history. Written from the vantage point of the first decade and a half of Soviet history, *February* is about the making of the identity of a Russian-Jewish youth in the time of World War I and the February Revolution. The poem's Jewish protagonist grows up in the 1900s and 1910s, acutely aware of his otherness and the distance it creates between him and the non-Jews around him. The protagonist's identity is formed through rejection of the narrow Jewish world of his parents and identification with the larger Russian world. He is alienated from his native realm of "notorious Jewish smoke / Of goosefat cracklings, above the cramming / Of tedious prayers, bearded faces / In family pictures" (81–84). He is drawn to what he perceives as the splendid life of the mainstream Russian society. The February 1917 Revolution, the central historical event of the poem, also becomes the key event in the shaping of the protagonist's identity. As a Jew, he embraces the February Revolution, which has awarded him equal rights and opportunities.

One cannot overestimate the significance of Bagritskii's artistic decision to link the problem of Jewish participation in the Russian Revolution to the poem's love story. Bagritskii makes the controversial issue of Jewish identity in twentieth-century Russia not only one of history, ideology, and religion but also one of desire. The quest of the Russian-Jewish protagonist in *February* is the quest to be able to express himself freely as a Jew, as a Russian, and as a sexual subject. The protagonist's idealized beloved, equally graceful and unattainable before the February Revolution, is also, allegorically, the Russia of his destiny. Given its disturbing and prophesying conclusion—with its mixture of desire and violence and a blend of Judaic and Soviet discourses on Jewish identity—*February* is ultimately about the unsettled relationship between Jews and Russians and about the mission of the Jews in modern history.

A number of factors contributed to the making of the protagonist's Russian-Jewish identity in Bagritskii's *February*.[25] I am especially interested in the connections between Bagritskii's poem and Babel's oeuvre (Babel and Bagritskii are among the Russian-Jewish writers of the early Soviet period who were most pre-occupied with the formation of modern Jewish identity). After outlining the similarities and dissimilarities in Babel's and Bagritskii's constructions of a Russian-Jewish self, I will turn to the language of Bagritskii's protagonist. Unlike Babel, who created his own unmistakable artistic language for his Jewish characters, Bagritskii leaned upon the experience of Russian Silver Age poetry. He partook of the language of symbolist (and also acmeist and ego-futurist) poets, chiefly that of Blok, but also that of Briusov, Viacheslav Ivanov, Kuzmin, Gumilev, and Severianin, to build the internal monologue of the Jewish protagonist. My next goal will be to discuss Bagritskii's view of the historical role of the February Revolution in the life of Russian Jews. After considering Bagritskii's career in light of the contemporary Western and Russian debates about Jewish self-hatred, I examine the development of Bagritskii's Jewish theme. I will pay special attention to Bagritskii's reception by leading figures and spokesmen of Soviet and post-Soviet Russian anti-Semitism. In the conclusion I discuss Bagritskii's vision of the future of Russia's Jews.

2. Babel, Bagritskii, and the Jewish Trauma of Rejection

Isaac Babel's famous "childhood stories" were a major point of departure for Bagritskii's exploration of the making of a Russian-Jewish identity.[26] In fact, both writers intended for their works to become parts of larger autobiographical wholes, a novel-length cycle in the case of Babel's stories, a trilogy of long narrative poems in the case of Bagritskii's *February*.[27] Bagritskii (1895–1934) and Babel (1894–1940) were the same age and shared many experiences growing up in Odessa in Jewish petit bourgeois families.[28] Representatives of what Viktor Shklovskii termed the "South-Western School" (*iugo-zapadnaia shkola*) in Russian letters, both Bagritskii and Babel left Odessa to become major Soviet authors and recollect their childhood and youth from the vantage point of Moscow in the late 1920s and 1930s.[29] Bagritskii's narrating protagonist in *February* is the literary cousin of Babel's autobiographical narrator in such stories as "Detstvo. U babushki" ("Childhood. With Grandmother," 1915), "Istoriia moei golubiatni" ("The Story of My Dovecote," 1925), "Pervaia liubov'" ("First Love," 1925), and "Probuzhdenie" ("The Awakening," 1930). The Jewish boys see themselves as captives trapped in the narrow world of their fathers and forefathers. They are tormented by their own physical incapacity, a condition they tend to associate with being Jewish. "Like all Jews," proclaims the narrator of "The Story of My

Dovecote," "I was small of stature, puny and suffered headaches from too much study."[30] Bagritskii's protagonist refers to himself as a "malen´kii iudeiskii mal´chik" ("little Judaic boy," 58–59). Against the wishes of their kinsmen, Babel's and Bagritskii's Jewish boys idealize and aestheticize the world of the Gentiles while perceiving it as being devoid of strictures and prohibitions. It is hardly coincidental that both Babel and Bagritskii employ bird imagery to convey the Jewish boys' vision of the larger, non-Jewish world. (A bird catcher, a fowler, *ptitselov*, is a recurrent image in Bagritskii's poetry.) Birds symbolize freedom and lightness, and they embody immaterial things, particularly the soul.[31] In "The Story of My Dovecote," the protagonist confesses: "In my childhood I very much wanted to have a dovecote. Never in my life have I desired anything more intensely."[32] Like his literary predecessor, Bagritskii's Jewish boy, too, is passionate about birds:

I loved Brehm better than Mayne Reid!
My hands trembled with passion
When I opened the book at random—
Birds would leap out at me from chance pages
Looking like letters of foreign alphabets,
Sabers and trumpets, globes and rhombuses.
(73–78)

As a Russian-Jewish adult, the protagonist wonders "how [it happened], that born to a Hebrew, / And circumcised on the seventh [*sic*] day, / [he] became a fowler" (70–72). He is inclined to attribute his infatuation with birds to a fatidic intrusion: "I imagine the Archer once paused / Above the blackness of our dwelling, / Above the notorious Jewish smoke" (79–81). (The invocation of the zodiacal sign of the Archer [Sagittarius], a figure armed with a bow and arrow, may suggest a movement beyond traditional boundaries.)

Birds, pigeons and doves specifically, play a major role in staging the trauma of anti-Semitism that Jewish boys experience as they discover their otherness and their place within the desirable world of the Gentiles. In Babel's stories, the trauma is inflicted by a pogrom in the city of Nikolaev in the fall of 1905. The pogrom breaks out on the day the main character purchases the doves he had "desired" more than anything.[33] This event is preceded by another landmark in the life of Babel's Jewish teenager: he passes a challenging examination and is admitted to a privileged Russian high school, a *gymnasium*. Speaking in Hebrew during a celebration, the boy's teacher of the Torah

said that at the exam [the boy] had vanquished all [his] enemies, had vanquished the Russian boys with fat cheeks and the sons of our coarse men of wealth. Thus in ancient times had David, King of Judah, vanquished Goliath, and just as [he] had triumphed over Goliath, so would our stalwart people vanquish by the power of their intellect the enemies who had surrounded us and were waiting for our blood.[34]

Despite the warnings of their relatives and teachers, the innocent Jewish boys—both in Babel's stories and in Bagritskii's *February*—refuse to perceive the world of Gentiles as hateful and threatening. Babel's adolescent falls asleep while listening to his grandmother's advice:

> Study . . . you will attain wealth and fame. You must know everything. Everyone will fall down and abase themselves before you. Everyone must envy you. Don't have faith in human beings. Don't have friends. Don't lend them money. Don't lend them your heart.[35]

The horrible knowledge that Babel's protagonist acquires on the day of the pogrom destroys his idealized image of the non-Jewish world. His symbolic (and forbidden) pass to the future—the two pairs of doves that he desires to possess—acquires ominous associations. Among the symbolic connotations of the dove, one finds purity, peace (Noah's doves), and love (a pair of doves). Still, one must keep in mind the specifically Christian symbolism of the dove, that of the Holy Spirit. In Babel's story, a Russian cripple, who has the same name as the famous Soviet educator Anton Makarenko (1888–1939) and whom "children love," strikes the Jewish boy with one of the treasured doves:

> "Doves," he repeated, like an inevitable echo, and struck me on the cheek. He struck me a swinging blow, his hand now clenched; the dove cracked on my temple, Katyusha's [the cripple's wife] wadded posterior swayed before my eyes and I fell to the earth. . . . "Their seed ought to be destroyed," Katyusha said then, . . . "I cannot abide their seed and their stinking men. . . . "[36]

Supine, with the entrails of the dove "trickling" from his temple and "blinding" him, the Jewish boy shuts his eyes in order not to see the devastating metamorphosis of the world of the Gentiles: "Soft dove gut crept over my forehead, and I closed a last unstuck eye so as not to see the world that was spreading about me. That world was small and horrible. . . . My world was small and horrible."[37]

Thus, the boy's self-realization as a Jew in the alien world of native Russians and Christians occurs through the sacrificial killing of a dove on a Sunday, the Christian Sabbath. However traumatic, the experience of otherness is also liberating as it frees the Jewish boy from his illusions: "I walked along an alien street crammed with white boxes, I walked in an attire of bloodstained feathers, alone in the middle of pavements . . . and wept more bitterly, completely and happily than I have ever wept again in all my life."[38]

In *February*, Bagritskii focuses on a different, albeit no less traumatic, experience of anti-Semitism—the rejection of the Jewish protagonist by his prejudiced and haughty non-Jewish beloved. While this episode (and the centrality of bird imagery) will be considered below, it should be noted here that Bagritskii's protagonist links doves implicitly with the Czarist system of state-sponsored anti-Semitism. After the Jewish youth approaches the Russian girl, she threatens him with a nearby policeman, described in this way:

                    There he is—
Placed to guard the order—
He stands in my way like a kingdom
Of cords, shiny badges, medals,
Squeezed into high boots,
And covered on top by his hat,
Around which whirl in a yellow
And unbearably torturous halo
Doves from the Holy Scriptures,
And clouds, twisted like snails. . . .
(244–253)

Might the reference to the "doves from the Holy Scriptures" (252) signal yet another genetic tie between Babel's "The Story of My Dovecote" and Bagritskii's *February*? A careful reader will also notice that, in *February*, *golubi* (the same word—*golub´*, pl. *golubi*—is used for both "pigeon" and "dove" in the Russian) "fuss / Around the town hall clock" as the protagonist walks toward his non-Jewish beloved, intent on confessing his love.[39]

Another parallel between the shaping of a Russian-Jewish identity in Babel's stories and Bagritskii's long poem concerns the way in which the Jewish adolescents sexualize the world of the Gentiles. In Babel's "First Love," the ten-year-old protagonist falls in love with his neighbor's wife. The Jewish boy reads sex in the eyes of this Rubenesque Slavic woman, who "had not seen her husband for one and a half years."[40] Sexual visions of the unknown Russian world both horrify and beguile him: "In her exultant eyes I saw the wonderful, shameful life of all people upon earth, I wanted to fall asleep in an extraordinary slumber, in order to forget about that life that exceeded all my dreams."[41]

In *February*, Bagritskii connects sexual awakening with the protagonist's self-realization as a Jew in a strange Russian world. Having grown conscious of the opposite sex, the protagonist develops a pathological shyness:

I didn't peep, like others
Into chinks of bathing huts.
                    I never tried
To pinch a girl as if by chance. . . .
Shyness and vertigo
Tormented me.
              I tried to run
Sideways, unnoticed, through the garden
With girls in high school dresses singing.
(85–91)

Bagritskii emphasizes the sense of a boundary between his teenage protagonist and girls. The Jewish boy is drawn to Slavic girls from the *gymnasium*, not to Jewish girls from his native milieu. The reference to "girls in high school dresses" is hardly gratuitous, and later in the poem the protagonist links his beloved metonymically to a *gymnasium* uniform: "Vdol´ allei, mimo gazona, / Shlo gimnazicheskoe plat´ie" ("Down the alley, along the lawn, / A high school dress was walking").

While simultaneously discovering his sexuality and his place in the world of nightingales and women, Bagritskii's Jewish protagonist realizes that as a "little Judaic boy," he is neither capable nor destined to "love properly," without taboo or restriction. This confession, made in retrospect by a Russian-Jewish adult in the early 1930s, resonates with the heartrending if ironic self-awareness of the characters of the classic of Yiddish literature Sholom Aleikhem (1859–1916). Among works by Bagritskii's predecessors in late-nineteenth- and early-twentieth-century Jewish poetry, two works immediately come to mind. One is the narrative poem *Monish* (1888) by one of the greats of modern Yiddish poetry, I. L. Peretz. The other is "Ekhod, ekhod, veayn roeh . . ." ("One by One, without anyone seeing it . . . ," 1915), a lyrical meditation on the loss of childhood innocence by the classic of modern Hebrew letters Hayyim Nahman Bialik. In the case of Bialik's poem, Bagritskii definitely knew it—if not in the original, then in Viacheslav Ivanov's masterful Russian translation.[42]

The confession of Bagritskii's protagonist lends itself to several complementary interpretations. What does "kak nado" ("properly"; "as one should") mean in terms of a developing Russian-Jewish identity? Does it mean that he cannot follow in the footsteps of his forefathers and love only Jewish girls? Or does it mean that the Jewish adolescent cannot love like his Russian peers and will never be an equal to them in the eyes of non-Jewish girls? Caught in this dilemma of his emerging dual identity, Bagritskii's Jewish protagonist learns his traumatic lesson of rejection.

3. The Language of the Jews and the Russian Silver Age

In addition to the psychological (and sexual) trauma of discovering "that world," the Jewish adolescents in Babel's autobiographical stories and Bagritskii's *February* also face a linguistic challenge. Coming from an imperfectly bilingual, Yiddish- and Russian-speaking milieu, and learning much of their normative Russian from "Smirnovskii's grammar" and "Petsykovich's primer of elementary Russian history,"[43] they lack the necessary vocabulary to cognize—and, what is more, to describe artistically—the Russian-speaking world. A linguistic discovery of the larger world facilitates their "escape." Both Babel and Bagritskii deemed linguistic "awakening" a critical point in the making of their characters' Russian-Jewish identities. Babel's protagonist in "The Awakening" encounters a tutor, Judophile Smolich, who sees preparing Jewish boys to live in the larger world as his mission. Bagritskii's Jewish adolescent takes an alternative, autodidactic path, and reading becomes his main source of knowing the world of Gentiles. Before the awakening, the Russian world of Babel's and Bagritskii's Jewish boys is that of ideas of things, the idea of "bird" or the idea of "bush." Generally ignorant of the particulars, they are especially unaware of the world of nature. This strikes the benevolent tutor of Babel's teenager as outrageous, since his ward tries his hand at composing fiction in Russian: "And you presume to write? . . . A man who does not live in nature as a bird or an animal in it will never write two worthwhile lines in all his life. . . ."[44] This lesson amounts to a culture shock:

> "A feeling for nature," I thought. "My God, why did I never think of that before? Where am I going to find someone who can explain the calls of the birds and the names of the trees to me? What do I know about them? I might be able to recognize lilacs, when they're in bloom, anyway, lilacs and acacias."[45]

Babel's teenager has heard that Deribasovskaia and Grecheskaia Streets in Odessa are lined with lilacs and acacias. He has seen the trees in blossom. His linguistic awakening consists in establishing links between the Russian words *siren'* and *akatsiia,* and the physical objects to which they refer. Falling together like pieces of a strange mosaic, these small discoveries will eventually construct the Jewish boy's Russian world.

Early in the poem, Bagritskii's protagonist confesses that he "was [the only Jewish boy] around / To shiver in the steppe wind at night" (60–61). Infatuated with the world of nature, and especially with birds, whose names and habits he learns from the Russian translation of Alfred Brehm's popular books, he spends his spare time translating the book knowledge into firsthand experience. Nature is his passage into the larger world of the Gentiles:

> Like a sleepwalker, I walked along tram tracks
> To silent summer cottages, where in the underbrush
> Of gooseberry or wild blackberry bushes
> Grass snakes rustle and vipers hiss,
> And in the thickets, where you can't sneak in,
> A bird with a scarlet head darts about,
> Her song is thin as a pin;
> They've nicknamed her "Bull's eye." . . .
> (62–69)

Falling in love with the Russian girl, the Jewish protagonist of *February* extends the linguistic boundaries of a self-cognized non-Jewish world to encompass his beloved. He initially perceives and describes her as a perfect creation of nature, as a girl with the qualities of a beautiful bird. In the poem's prerevolutionary episodes, as the Jewish boy shapes his nascent larger world while also aestheticizing it, he parallels feminine beauty and the grace of birds:

Suddenly glass whistled like a bird
And scattered around in front of me [. . .]
Women's shoulders and birds' wings,
The whistle of wings and babble of skirts,
The nightingale's chattering and the song
Of the girl on the other side of the street.
(97–98, 101–104)

When his Russian beloved rejects him, he inevitably perceives this action as a rejection by the entire world of Gentiles that he had so desperately tried to become a part of. In the poem's narrative logic, the boy's trauma generates resentment that in turn gives way to his participation in the February Revolution.

Let us now turn to the specifics of the linguistic and cultural making of the Russian-Jewish identity. Against the background of a pogrom—of chaos, rubble, and the destruction of his father's store by a triumphant mob—Babel's Jewish adolescent in "First Love" imagines the Russian woman Galina (with whom he is infatuated) as dwelling "high up," in an almost otherworldly "blueness of the world" (*v vysote, v sineve mira*).[46] This is a typically Babel construction, employing pure colors and large-scale spatial tropes. In *February*, Bagritskii's protagonist envisions the arrival of his Russian beloved as follows:

And, at last, clearer and purer,
In the world of customs and rituals,
Under the oil lamp of my home
The eyes of a nightingale on the face of a girl. . . .
(105–108)

Similarly to Babel's youth, Bagritskii's young man contrasts the world of his beloved Russian woman with the Jewish "world of customs and rituals" that he is so ashamed of. And yet, the language of Bagritskii's protagonist and the structure and texture of his images tell the story of a different kind of a literary upbringing.

Bagritskii's *February* and Babel's "childhood" narratives are first-person autobiographical accounts. The first language of the protagonists' parents was presumably Yiddish, and at home the young protagonists were probably exposed to a Russian not unlike the one in Osip Mandelstam's description in "The Judaic Chaos," a section of *The Noise of Time*: "My father absolutely had no language; his speech was tongue-tie and languagelessness [*U ottsa sovsem ne bylo iazyka, eto bylo kosnoiazychie i bez´´iazychie*]."[47] Babel's and Bagritskii's heroes both narrate their stories as adults, and the language of their accounts is naturally Russian. Native as their command of Russian may be, it nevertheless constitutes a borderline case of an acquired language, a quasi-second language for expressing the protagonists' reconfigured, acculturated, and Russianized identities. (Incidentally, in Bagritskii's adulthood, his command of spoken Yiddish was quite limited, although he did retain a reading knowledge of both Yiddish and Hebrew.)

In Babel's case, his autobiographical stories deal with a synchronic cut, concentrating on a few days ("The Story of My Dovecote") or months ("Awakening") in the life of the narrator as a young adolescent. In several works, most notably in "The Awakening," Babel masterfully investigates the problem of a Jewish boy's linguistic awakening to the riches of the Russian language. At the same time, Babel does not seek to capture in the Russian language of his Jewish narrators the trajectory of their linguistic development. Babel tells his autobiographical stories in the kind of uniquely expressive Russian that became one of his achievements. Put simply, Babel's stories, from beginning to end, sound and read as Babel's stories. What I wish to emphasize here is that in his stories, and particularly in the confessional ones like "The Story of My Dovecote," Babel's narrator speaks a sui generis artistic form of Russian, a language that combines inventions of Babel's own linguistic genius with the borrowed flavor of native speakers of Yiddish or the peculiarities of the Odessan dialect.

In Bagritskii's *February*, one observes a qualitatively different linguistic scenario. Here the Russian-Jewish protagonist speaks of his youth in a pure literary Russian free of Yiddishisms and nearly free of Odessan dialectal flavor (the latter are found in his other poems; both Odessan flavor and Yiddishisms were abundant in Bagritskii's own everyday speech). In Bagritskii's *February*—a Russian Jew's poetical bildungsroman—the language of the transformed (and partly translated) identity of the Russian-Jewish protagonist reflects the literary history of *how* this identity was shaped. In the prerevolutionary episodes, the poetics of the protagonist's emerging Russian-Jewish identity point to Bagritskii's apprenticeship under the poets of the Russian Silver Age.

As a young Jewish man in love with a Russian girl, Bagritskii's protagonist is unable to produce his own unparalleled language of love in the early parts of the poem. The quasi-native and dull Russian spoken in his parents' Jewish environment could not yield the lyrical and sensuous power of the confessional monologue in *February*. Bagritskii has his Jewish protagonist draw on ready-made Russian literary models. Throughout the prerevolutionary episodes of *February*, the protagonist perceives reality as split into two worlds. In his mind, the mundane world—first the Jewish shopkeepers' milieu, then the trenches of World War I—is juxtaposed with an idealized world. The Jewish boy initially discovers his idealized world through reading and populates it with exotic birds. Later, as a sexually budding adolescent, he conflates birds and women within an idealized world of fancy. After he falls in love with the girl from privileged Russian society, the Jewish youth makes her the center-piece of this idealized world:

> She looked like an exotic bird
> Having flown out of Brehm's book. . . .
> (137–138)

The imagery and two-world structure of *February's* prerevolutionary sequence (lines 1–256) may be generally attributed to the influence of the symbolist aesthetics that were organic to Bagritskii's own development in the 1910s. One finds in *February* a number of references to the writings of Aleksandr Blok, one of Bagritskii's most beloved poets.[48] Blok's works that make appearances in Bagritskii's text include "Neznakomka" ("An Unknown Lady," 1906), *Vozmezdie* (*"Retribution,"* 1910–19; 1917–21), and *Solov'inyi sad* (*"Nightingale Garden,"* 1915).[49] Compare, for instance, a description of the Jewish protagonist's beloved with the one in Blok's celebrated poem "An Unknown Lady." In *February:*

> She looked into store windows, and amidst
> Transparent silks and perfume bottles
> Her water-face was reflected,
> Mysterious and unearthly. . . .
> (125–128)

And in Blok's "An Unknown Lady": "Devichii stan, shelkami skhvachennyi" ("The maiden's waist, wrapped in silk"; compare with Bagritskii's "sredi . . . shelkov"); "V tumannom dvizhetsia okne" ("Moves in the misted-over window"; compare with Bagritskii's image of the girl's reflection in the shop window); "Dysha dukhami i tumanami" ("Permeated with perfume and fog"; compare with Bagritskii's "sklianki" = "perfume bottles"); and "Glukhie tainy mne porucheny" ("Grave mysteries have been entrusted to me"; compare with Bagritskii's "tain-stvenno" = "mysteriously").[50]

Among the Blokian subtexts in *February*, of special significance is the long poem *Nightingale Garden*. In constructing the language of love that his protagonist uses first to describe his beloved and later to address her, Bagritskii draws on Blok's imagery and the language of Blok's main character. The specific architecture of the narrative space in the early episodes of *February* also resembles that of *Nightingale Garden*. Both underprivileged protagonists, Bagritskii's Jewish youth and Blok's poor toiler, associate the garden with singing and nightingale grace. In Blok's poem, the protagonist worships the mysterious "nightingale garden" by the sea where "an unknown melody / rings":

I, a poor toiler, wait,
Repeating the unknown tune
Ringing in the nightingale garden.[51]

Bagritskii's narrator speaks with angst of trying to "run / Sideways, unnoticed,
through the garden / With girls in high school dresses singing." Leaning on Blok's
experience of reworking a medieval literary topos, Bagritskii's Jewish youth links
his love for the Russian girl with nightingales. In the following revelatory pas-
sage (the protagonist stares at a young woman's legs in a shop window), his love
for the Russian girl emerges out of a stream of ornithological and feminine
images and acquires concrete nightingale associations:

Suddenly glass whistled like a bird
And scattered around in front of me
Golden buntings and dry leaves,
Swamps strewn with forget-me-nots,
Women's shoulders and birds' wings,
The whistle of wings and babble of skirts,
The nightingale's chattering and the song
Of the girl on the other side of the street;
And, at last, clearer and purer,
In the world of customs and rituals,
Under the oil lamp of my home
The eyes of a nightingale on the face of a girl. . . .
(97–108)

And only a few lines later, Bagritskii's protagonist speaks of the eyes of his
beloved:

In a slight shadow I saw her eyes;
Full of nightingale tremble [. . .]
(110–111)

Both poems, Blok's and Bagritskii's, describe protagonists who cannot resist their
passions despite their awareness of the immense social boundaries separating
them from the objects of their love. It is no accident that the nightingale—a
symbol of love but also of yearning, pain, and sleeplessness—is chosen as the
semantic dominant in both poems (forms of *solovei*, "nightingale," occur six
times in Blok's poem; five times in Bagritskii's).[52] Blok's protagonist realizes that
"the nightingale song"—now synonymous with love—is incapable of "deafening
the thunder of the sea." As a poor toiler outside the boundaries of the nightin-
gale garden, he longs to unite with his beloved. Having joined her and surren-

dered his soul to the nightingales ("Vziali dushu moiu solov´i" ["The nightingales have taken my soul"]), he yearns for his habitual domain, the seacoast, as well as for his hoe and donkey.[53] When Bagritskii's protagonist—the "little Judaic boy"—finally confesses his love to the Russian girl, he, like Blok's character, also links nightingale passion with torment and doom:

> I'll put my hand on her shoulder,
> "Look at me!
>   I am your misfortune!
> I'm dooming you to the torment
> Of incredible nightingale passion!
> Wait!"
> (219–223)

The prerevolutionary episodes of *February* are Bagritskii's tribute to his Russian literary origins.[54] Subsequently, in the episodes depicting the February Revolution, Bagritskii's protagonist leaves behind the grammar of Silver Age Russian poetry. He enters a vastly different cultural space, where the revolutionary aesthetics push him toward a discovery of his own literary voice.

4. Jewish Identity and Russian Revolution

Bagritskii had originally considered inserting a lyrical transition from the prerevolutionary sequences in the second half of the poem to the part dealing with the February 1917 Revolution (between lines 256 and 257). He apparently gave up the idea of the transitional episode and crossed it out in the manuscript.[55] In the published text (from which the present English translation was made, although the manuscript was also consulted), the prerevolutionary episode on an Odessan boulevard—where the Russian girl haughtily rejects the Jewish protagonist and threatens him with the police—is followed directly by a political rally in March 1917.

The February Revolution transforms the life of the young Jewish man. It is noteworthy that in the eyes of the protagonist, the February Revolution debunks the previous division of life into two worlds, the smaller, Jewish world and the larger world that the protagonist had in turn identified with exotic birds, mainstream Russian society and, finally, his idealized beloved, who is not Jewish. One of the great accomplishments of the February Revolution was the March 20, 1917 ukase "Abolition of Restrictions Based on Religion and Nationality."[56] To quote from the ukase, "All the laws and statutes are abolished, whether in effect throughout all Russia or in its various parts, which establish—on the basis of the adherence of citizens of Russia to a particular religious denomination or sect or by reasons of nationality—any restrictions. . . ."[57] For the Jews of the former Russian Empire, this meant a historical breakthrough: abolition of the Pale of Settlement, of official discrimination at all levels of society, including quotas at institutions of learning.

In the episodes describing the February Revolution, the Jewish protagonist no longer renders reality as split into the narrow world of the Jews and the spacious world of the Russians. As one might have expected, the new opposition is between the old world of czarist Russia and the world of new Russia—an opposition that is political and historical, not ethnic, religious, and cultural:

> The shape of the world is changing.
> Just this morning
> Plane trees rustled their blessings.
> The sea
> Made its home in the gulf.
> In summer cottages
> Girls sang in circles.
> In the book
> Dr. Brehm was resting, his double-barrel
> Pressed against a boulder.
> My parents' house
> Was lit by tongues of candles and the Biblical kitchen. . . .
> (287–293)

The old world now encompasses attributes of the protagonist's own past that had previously been in opposition to each other: the girls from the *gymnasium* represents the "old" Russian world, while the "Biblical kitchen" refers to the "old" Jewish world. "The shape of the world is changing" becomes the poem's new leitmotif:

> The shape of the world is changing . . .
> Tonight [. . .]
> Steamers wheeze, sinking.
> Summer cottages
> Have all been boarded up.
> Rats march
> On deserted porches.
> Dr. Brehm puts down a book
> And lifts his rifle at me with a threat. . . .
> My parents' house has been robbed . . .
> (294, 298–302)

In this passage, the coming of the new world demands the uprooting of the old world. Bagritskii removes the image of "singing girls"—previously linked with his

62 ⁓   Chapter Two

Russian beloved—from the "summer houses" that have been abandoned. The protagonist speaks of revolutionary violence and the destruction of his parents' home.[58] For the protagonist, the Revolution marks the end of youth, and he affords a passing note of regret if not nostalgia, addressed either to himself or to an implied revolutionary comrade: "Chto zhe! Nado idti! Ne goriui, priiatel´!" ("Well! Got to go! Don't fret, my friend!").

Bagritskii avoids references to the protagonist's Jewishness in his meditation on the world's changing image. This should hardly be a surprise. As the protagonist participates in the February Revolution and rejoices at its ending the oppression of the Jews in Imperial Russia, his own identity is in flux. He is no longer the "little Judaic boy" lost in the world of Russians, but he is as yet uncertain about his new status in Russia's changing society. He himself resembles a "black tunnel with no beginning or end," described in the following chain of images:

Rain!
    Squabble of fussy crows
On the acacias.
        Rain.
            Out of nowhere
Motorcyclists roll out, enshrouded
In acetylene light.
            And again the black
Tunnel with no beginning or end.
Blind wind, blowing in all directions.
            Patrols,
Splashing through puddles.
        And again—
Rain.
    We're alone in this world of wet.
(308–315)

This description evokes a sense of transition if not transformation, while "we" stands for the protagonist and his two comrades heading out to take over the police station. In fact, for several pages of the poem (lines 333–371), the protagonist surrenders his individual identity and speaks in a collective revolutionary voice [added italics]:

Opened some sort of chink.
    We entered [. . .]
(333–334)

We walked through corridors [. . .]
(335)

And *we* . . . *we* just stood there, stepping
In indecision [. . .]
(354–355)

We took over the station.
(361)

We found a prisoner's tin kettle [. . .]
(368)

And it is not until the protagonist is appointed deputy district commissar of
the militia, a new law-enforcement agency established by a ukase of the Provi-
sional Government, that he regains his individual voice.[59] In the passage describ-
ing the protagonist's responsibilities, the word "I" occurs nine times and punctu-
ates the verse as a kind of semantic anacrusis:

I stayed in the area. . . .
                          I worked
As deputy commissar.
                  At first
I spent many nights in damp sentry boxes;
I watched the world, passing by me,
Alien and dimly lit by crooked streetlamps,
Full of strange and unknown monsters
Oozing from thick fumes. . . .

I tried to be ubiquitous. . . .
                          In a gig
I churned rural roads, searching
For horse thieves.
                  In the middle of night
I rushed out in a motorboat
Into the gulf, curved like a black horn
Around rocks and sand dunes.
I broke into thieves' lodgings
Reeking of overfried fish.
I appeared, like the angel of death.
(400–415)

The new status that the protagonist wins as a result of the February Revolution
allows him to speak without shame or bewilderment about his Jewish origins. His
unabashed words belong to the most explicit statements by Russian-Jewish authors
about the role of the February Revolution in the destiny of Russia's Jews and the
shaping of their identity. These words have infuriated many a Russian nationalist:

My Judaic pride sang,
Like a string stretched to its limit. . . .
I would've given much for my forefather
In a long caftan and fox fedora,
From under which fell gray spirals
Of earlocks and clouds of dandruff
Flushing over his square beard,
For that ancestor to recognize his descendant
In this huge fellow, rising, like a tower,
Over flying lights and bayonets,
From a truck, shaking off midnight. . . .
(422–432)

In January 1950, at the height of the ominous campaign against the so-called "bourgeois nationalist" and "cosmopolitan" trends in Soviet culture—which also involved the liquidation of Yiddish culture in the Soviet Union with genocidal plans under consideration—the critic Anatolii Tarasenkov published an essay, "On National Traditions and Bourgeois Cosmopolitanism," in *Znamia* (*"The Banner"*), a leading Moscow journal.[60] (This was the same Tarasenkov who, in 1934, had signed Bagritskii's obituary along with a group of young editors and critics who had worked with him.[61]) The main targets of Tarasenkov's attack were two major poets, Eduard Bagritskii and Il'ia Sel'vinskii (1899–1968), both of whom were Russian Jews, and the brilliant prosaist Aleksandr Grin (1880–1932), who was not. Quoting in full Bagritskii's passage about "Judaic pride," Tarasenkov said this: "In the long poem *February*, written in 1933–34 and published posthumously, Bagritskii develops nationalistic ideas. The main character of this poem participates in the revolution only in order to affirm his racial 'full worth' [*rasovuiu polnotsennost*]."[62] Tarasenkov skillfully avoided any mention of the fact that *February* was about the February 1917 Revolution, not the October 1917 Bolshevik Revolution. In fact, Bagritskii did not ever mention the Bolshevik Revolution in the poem. He had considered a digression about the political climate of the spring and summer of 1917 but then crossed out the following lines in the manuscript: "Pervye bol'sheviki—na zavodakh— / Bratan'e. Vybory. Lenin" ("First Bolsheviks—at factories— / Fraternization. Elections. Lenin").[63] He did, however, speak of non-Bolshevik political parties and forces that were active in the February Revolution. For example, the protagonist takes over the police precinct together with a member of the Socialist-Revolutionary Party. Such an avoidance of references to the Bolsheviks strikes me as deliberate on Bagritskii's part.

In his menacing critique, Tarasenkov contrasted Bagritskii and the "classic" of Soviet poetry, Vladimir Maiakovskii (1893–1930), claiming that "neither Bagritskii, nor Sel'vinskii could, or had any political right to, take Maiakovskii's place, to say nothing of the fact that they bear no comparison to the great poet of the Revolution."[64] Although Tarasenkov made no mention of it, he most likely had in mind a juxtaposition between *February* and Maiakovskii's earlier poem of the same title. The rally scene in Bagritskii's long poem resembles the first part of Maiakovskii's "February" (1927):

The crowd flows
                    and again
                                  runs aground.
and flows again,
                    digging
                              a riverbed in the rock.
             [. . .]
They carry banners,
                    carry
                         and carry.
The color scarlet in their hands,
                                  their hearts,
                                            their button holes.[65]

In Bagritskii's *February:*

[. . .] and here they're
With us: talking, shouting, raising hands,
Damning, weeping,
                        puffing, coughing.
[. . .]
Smeared with dirt and caked blood
Fists rise like soiled luminaries. . . .
(273–275, 278–279)

Unlike Bagritskii in his long poem *February*, Maiakovskii builds up an opposition between the February and October Revolutions. He calls the Prime Minister Alexander Kerensky a "compromiser and a liar" (*soglashatel´ i vrun*), and ends his poem with a staunchly Bolshevik statement:

But we
          replied
                    seething with anger:
"The Earth
          will not
                    turn backward.
Let's
          convert words into action!"

And we
   reached the goal
      and completed in October
That which February had not finished.

(In Maiakovskii's original, "Oktiabr'" ["October"] is deliberately capitalized because it refers not only to the month but also to the Bolshevik revolution, whereas "fevral'" ["February"] is not capitalized.)

Might Bagritskii's refusal to speak of either Bolshevism or the October Revolution in *February* have been a polemical gesture aimed at Maiakovskii's earlier poem, which sends a stringently Bolshevik message? Such a meaningful silence on Bagritskii's part—a silence that is a commentary in and of itself—would be further evidence that he wished for his deathbed poem to be a tribute *exclusively* to the February Revolution. In fact, one the most rewarding discoveries I made while studying the drafts of *February* was that Bagritskii crossed out an unfinished and unpolished digression following the description of the "the first tea of winners, the tea of freedom" (line 371; after the taking over of the police station in March 1917). In this crossed-out passage, the February Revolution is candidly given a key role in the formation of the protagonist's identity:

All my love, all my voice and vision,
Blood, that had not yet been spoiled,
Bones, yet untouched by rheumatism,
Sweet youthful inspiration,
[. . .]
The unspoiled word: freedom!
All have been given without reservation,
To March of 1917.[66]

The absence of references to the October Revolution in *February*, written in 1933–34, seems even more striking, given the fact that Bagritskii was not disinclined to discuss the Bolshevik Revolution in his previous works. For the sixth anniversary of the February Revolution in 1923, Bagritskii whipped up a short poem that was also entitled "February" and that began: "Temnoiu volei sud'biny . . ." ("By destiny's dark will . . ."); it portrayed the events of February 1917 as having laid a foundation for the October 1917 Revolution:

New horizons have opened,
New horizons—to sunrise.
Thus we labored in February,
In order to win in October![67]

Bagritskii's "February" of 1923, as well as a poem of the same name he composed in 1926 ("Gudela zemlia ot moroza i v'iug . . . ," = "Earth hummed with frost and storms"), struck a note that was ideologically similar to the one expressed in Maiakovskii's 1927 poem.

It also should not escape one's attention that Bagritskii did not introduce any Jewish questions into both of his earlier poems with the title "February." In contrast to these earlier poems of the same title, the problem of Jewish identity was the focus of the long poem *February*. In it, Bagritskii showed that the February Revolution, and not the October Revolution, was the principal event in the liberation of the Jews of the Russian Empire. Such a Judeocentric perspective was, of course, threatening to the official Soviet historiography, in which the February Revolution was treated as a "bourgeois" revolution, at best a prelude to the October Revolution and in no way a defining historical event. Consider a typical example of an official Soviet treatment of the role of the Bolshevik Revolution in Jewish history, in a book entitled *Jews in the USSR* (1932): "The Jewish question was solved completely and finally by the Socialist Revolution of the working class."[68] In fact, Bagritskii has been faulted by Soviet scholars for having "misrepresented the events of the February Revolution"[69] and misunderstood the role of the October Revolution.

I believe that Soviet ideological leadership (critic Tarasenkov was executing a political order during the anti-Semitic campaign of 1949–53) decided to exorcise Bagritskii posthumously in 1950 for two principal reasons. One was Bagritskii's praise of the February "bourgeois" and not the October "socialist" Revolution in his last work. The other was his declaration of "Judaic pride" and his open identification with the faith and history of his forefathers. Bagritskii's parameters of a Jewish identity in *February* go against the very grain of the Soviet conception of the Jews as an ethnic group with a spoken Germanic language (Yiddish). It is significant that in three pivotal moments in the poem, Bagritskii opted for the adjective *iudeiskii* ("Judaic," derived from the noun *iudei*—used in Russian primarily in reference to the religious tradition of Judaism) instead of *evreiskii* ("Jewish," derived from the noun *evrei*, which is used primarily in reference to the historical and ethnic origins of the Jews). Two of the three instances occur in the monologue describing the teenage protagonist's sense of his place in the world: "Malen'kii iudeiskii mal'chik" ("A little Judaic boy," line 59); "rozhdennyi ot iudeia" ("born to a Hebrew," line 70). The third instance occurs in the poem's Judeocentric monologue invoking the protagonist's forefather: "Moia iudeiskaia gordost' pela" ("My Judaic pride sang," line 422). However, Bagritskii does use the adjective *evreiskii* elsewhere in *February*. In one instance, he employs something of a cliché, "evreiskii mal'chik" ("a Jewish boy"), as he relates his experiences in the military service: "Still not cured of stooping my shoulders— / The company's dodger, a Jewish boy . . ." (123–124); in contrast to "evreiskii mal'chik," "iudeiskii mal'chik" ("a Judaic boy") would not have been a cliché if used in its stead.[70] The adjective *evreiskii* also occurs in the protagonist's depiction of the oppressive (from his point of view) atmosphere of his childhood home:

Above the blackness of our dwelling,
Above the notorious Jewish smoke
Of goosefat cracklings, above the cramming
Of tedious prayers, bearded faces
In family pictures. . . .
(80–84)

Could it be that in deliberately employing the words *iudei* and *iudeiskii*, the poet sought to make a distinction between the Judaic historical, religious, and cultural heritage, which his protagonist embraces as an adult, and Jewish daily life (*byt*) in the Pale of Settlement, the life his protagonist recalls scornfully? Note that in the post-revolutionary monologue, the image of the Judaic forefather with "grey spirals of earlocks" and a "square beard" invites a comparison with the Jewish "bearded faces" in the "family pictures" of the protagonist's childhood. The bearded ancestors are fundamentally the same; what has changed is the tone and thrust of Bagritskii's discourse. Indeed, Bagritskii's protagonist proudly portrays his Judaic ancestor as wearing traditional garb, a fox fedora and a long caftan. He loftily reaffirms his link with the millennial heritage of the Jewish people.

I find it absolutely remarkable that Bagritskii created this image of a Jewish forefather in 1933–34, following a decade and a half of a sweeping campaign against Judaism and traditional Jewish life in the Soviet Union.[71] Given that Soviet ideologues were increasingly unwilling to hear the word *Judaic* (the word *Jewish* was less of a taboo), it should not strike one as surprising that *February* was reprinted only twice between 1936 and 1964. Although *February* was reluctantly returned to the Bagritskii canon following Khrushchev's Thaw, attacks on it continued, climaxing again in the late 1970s with the rise of the Russian national right.

5. Jewish Self-Hatred, Russian Anti-Semitism, and Bagritskii's Judaic Theme

Among the charges leveled against Bagritskii by his Russian nationalist detractors, those of the poet and essayist Stanislav Kuniaev speak most explicitly of their great uneasiness with Bagritskii's handling of the problem of a dual Russian-Jewish identity. Kuniaev delivered his infamous Bagritskii speech on December 21, 1977, in a panel discussion entitled "Klassika i my" (literally means "Classics and We"). Held at a large auditorium of the Central House of Writers in Moscow, with almost a thousand people present in the audience, the discussion was supposed to afford its fifteen participants a chance to debate the place of Russian classical literature in Soviet culture as a whole and in their own works. Organizers of the event used the "Noah's ark" approach, inviting speakers of various colors and stripes within the Soviet cultural establishment: liberals and conservatives, Slavophiles and Westernizers, Communists and non-Communists, traditionalists and avant-gardists.[72] Leaders of the emerging Russian cultural right—the precursors of the Pamiat´ movement and today's post-Soviet ultranationalists—used this opportunity to mount a show of force. Among the speakers representing Russian ultranationalist circles was critic Petr Palievskii, who is known to have called Osip Mandelstam a "Kikeish boil on the pure body of Tiutchev's poetry" (Fedor Tiutchev was a major nineteenth-century Russian poet).[73] Also speaking was the éminence grise of the Russian cultural right, Vadim Kozhinov, most recently the author of a treatise in defense of the Black Hundreds and a monograph containing a revisionist and falsifying interpretation of the Jewish Holocaust.[74] In his recent memoir, Kuniaev called the "Classics and We" discussion "our first mutiny" (nash pervyi bunt).[75]

The pretext for Kuniaev's attack on Bagritskii was a collection of reminiscences about the poet, edited by his widow and published in 1973.[76] Kuniaev discussed several works by Bagritskii, including February and The Lay of Opanas, and offered his interpretation of Bagritskii's entire career in Russian letters. Later he tried to publish an expanded version of his remarks in the form of an essay entitled "Legenda i vremia" ("Legend and Time"), but no Soviet magazine would print it because of its openly anti-Semitic thesis. It circulated in samizdat and appeared in the West, in the Israeli Russian-language journal Dvadtsat´ dva ("Twenty Two").[77] Kuniaev's remarks about Bagritskii were reported and partially reprinted in Russian émigré journals in Europe and America and stirred up a polemic.[78] Readers may be surprised by my fascination with someone who has become—not only in the eyes of the students of the Jewish question but also in those of today's Russian intelligentsia—synonymous with anti-Semitism itself. I realize that a detailed summary of Kuniaev's ideas stands a chance of lending his argument further credence. However, I feel strongly that the goebbelses of the world—goebbelses both large and small, both past and present—ought to be studied and understood rather than silenced and ignored. Kuniaev belongs to the ideological leadership of a growing ultranationalist trend in post-Soviet Russia, and I hope that my analysis of his ideas will not only elucidate the past of Russia's Jewish question but also help forecast its future.

Kuniaev aimed to show that Bagritskii the poet was an alien trespasser in the fields of Russian poetry. His most inflammatory remarks concerned the poem "Origin" (the poem's English translation was provided in chapter 1):

With terrifying consistency and pathos, [Bagritskii] renounced not only the everyday living [byt] in general, the everyday living alien to him, but also the shtetlness of his native origins [*rodnoi emu po proiskhozhdeniiu mestiachkovosti*]. He pronounced such damnations about it that no diehard reactionary [*mrakobes*] would even think of. . . . The poet remains faithful to a non-acceptance of eternal forms of life, and with fearless cruelty he renounces his origins [*otrekaias' ot svoego proiskhozhdeniia*].[79]

An ominous irony reverberates in Kuniaev's tirade as he assesses Bagritskii's attitudes toward his Jewish "origins" to be more derogatory than those of anti-Semites and—in the essay based on his talk—of the members of the Black Hundreds (*chernosotentsy*). Kuniaev styles himself as a guardian of the purity of the Russian poetic tradition, which Bagritskii allegedly transgressed by hating and disavowing his ancestors. Kuniaev juxtaposes Bagritskii's poetic sensibility with those of two major Russian poets of Jewish origin, Afanasii Fet (1820–1892) and Osip Mandelstam, both of whom satisfy his criteria of cultural "Russianness." Furthermore, Kuniaev even speaks of the "touching" shtetl characters of the classic of Yiddish literature Sholom Aleikhem, from whom, as Kuniaev alleges, Bagritskii might have but did not learn to love his own Jewish people.[80] As a matter of record, in a 1978 conversation with David Shrayer-Petrov, a Russian poet and novelist who is Jewish, Kuniaev vehemently denied charges of "vulgar anti-Semitism," insisting instead that he was "defending Russian poetry."[81] In his recent memoirs, Kuniaev also claimed that "what blood flowed in his friends' veins" made no difference to him—referring to his late friend Ernst Portniagin, a poet whose mother was Russian and father Jewish.[82] What is one to make of Kuniaev's position?

In *Jewish Self-Hatred: Anti-Semitism and the Hidden Language of the Jews* (1986), Sander L. Gilman foregrounds a model of how assimilated Jews relate to their ethnic, religious, and cultural heritage. Jewish thinkers and historians of Jewish past and present have long pondered the subject of assimilation and acculturation in Diaspora, and Theodor Lessing's landmark study of 1930, *Der judische Selbsthass* ("*The Jewish Self-Hatred*," 1930), articulated the concept of a "Jewish self-hatred" to the reading public.[83] Following in Lessing's footsteps and drawing largely on the history of Jews in Germany, Gilman argues in his study that an assimilated Jew or, as in several of his key case studies, a converted ex-Jew constructs a new identity by performing a ritual of abnegating the Jewish past. The concept of Jewish self-hatred suggests that an ex-Jew must undo his former identity—constructed upon the millennia of Jewish religion, culture, and history—in order to fashion himself as an adequate member of gentile society, a society that is at best neutral to the Jew and at worst violently anti-Semitic.

What an uncanny and unlikely intersection of viewpoints! Is Kuniaev in effect using Bagritskii's works to foreground a model of Jewish self-hatred that is similar to Gilman's? Gilman argues that the German Jews—Ludwig Börne, Heinrich Heine, or Karl Marx, to take three of his case studies—entered the mainstream of German culture in the nineteenth century after having performed rituals of hatred against their Jewish ancestry. While the degree and intensity of their selfrenunciations varied, the discourse of Jewish self-hatred appears to have been a prerequisite for their passage into a new, Christianized or secularized identity in the gentile world. How could it be that a Jewish-American scholar of German-Jewish cultural history and a Soviet (and post-Soviet) ideologue of Russian anti-Semitism described phenomena that, mutatis mutandis, seem quite kindred? Why was Eduard Bagritskii compelled to direct hostility and scorn at the Jewish milieu that had birthed him? Consider these lines from "Origin," the poem that Kuniaev employed to advance his thesis:

Parents?
But aging in the twilight,
Hunchbacked, knotty, and wild,
Rusty Jews fling at me
Their stubbly fists.
(46–50)

Were these lines composed because as a Soviet Jew, by the end of the 1920s, Bagritskii had undergone a "conversion"? Did such a Soviet conversion—where Marxism-Leninism took the place of the Christian faith—amount to a ritual of Jewish self-hatred? Was Bagritskii, after all, trying to reproduce a Soviet rhetoric on nationalities in which an act of Jewish self-hatred was almost expected en route to becoming a *Homo soveticus Judaeus*?

On the cold, breezy morning of May 26, 1997, I met Kuniaev in the editorial offices of *Nash sovremennik* (*"Our Contemporary"*), a monthly review of culture and politics that has become a flagship of Russian anti-Semitism under his editorship. It has now been more than two years since I saw Kuniaev, and the time has come to make our conversation public; Kuniaev himself has since told his version of the "Bagritskii affair" in his memoirs. Below is an excerpt of our exchange about Jewish identity in Russian culture, which has been translated into English:[84]

Maxim D. Shrayer: Why did Bagritskii become the object of such a direct attack?
Stanislav Kuniaev: Because he formulated these ideas with the most cruel consistency, and in particular in *February*.[85]
MDS: When did you first read *February*?
SK: I read *February* seriously and started thinking about it some time in the mid-1960s.
MDS: And what was your impression?
SK: I started thinking about the fact that among talented Russian poets in the twentieth century, there are those who possess a mighty Jewish mentality, a Jewish revolutionary mentality, I would say, rather than a Jewish religious mentality. . . .

MDS: You probably read Tarasenkov's well-known essay, published in 1950, "On National Traditions and Bourgeois Cosmopolitanism," where for the first time—

SK: —oh, I do not really remember what it said. I know that it exists, and I must have read it, but back then everything was said in such an Aesopean language, so approximately, that it did not produce an impression on me.[86]

MDS: The long poem *February* was subjected to exorcism in that article.

SK: From what point of view?

MDS: From all points of view. From both the official Communist Party position and from that of a Russian chauvinist and anti-Semite. But it is also remarkable that of all works [by Russian-Jewish authors], *February* became the object of such an attack. And later Shafarevich in his *Rusophobia* also attacked *February*. . . .

SK: You see, in *February* is expressed in the most concentrated fashion the rapturous joy of a Jewish revolutionary youth at the collapse of life, a collapse which revolutionary Jewry sought to destroy.

MDS: Fine, let us pause for a minute and turn to the facts. You said [earlier] that the [protagonist] had an inferiority complex. What, in your view, are the reasons behind it? I believe *that* is the question. Do you recall what happens there?

SK: Perfectly well.

MDS: He was rejected by a student from a *gymnasium* solely because he was Jewish.

SK: No, actually there is nothing about that. She rejected him because he was unattractive, because he walked around in those ill-fitting jackboots, because he was not her equal socially. If, let us suppose, he had been an attractive and well-groomed young man from the Jewish elite, she might not have rejected him. He was rejected based on social, not national, criteria. . . .[87] No-no-no! He comes from insufficient means compared to the girl from the *gymnasium*.

MDS: What about this: "I never loved properly . . . / A little Judaic boy"?

SK: So that is his complex, not hers [Kuniaev laughs viciously].

MDS: . . . You have also said that [the protagonist] becomes a revolutionary. . . . Other critics from your camp have treated the poem as a hymn to Jewish revolution. But the facts of the poem do not support such a statement.

SK: Well, he is in charge of a unit of sailors.

MDS: Yes, but in the capacity of a deputy commissar of [the militia, created by] the Provisional Government. . . . The events take place between the February and October Revolutions, and it would be absolutely inaccurate to call him some sort of a Jewish Bolshevik commissar. This is against the facts. . . . The activity [of the protagonist's unit] is not revolutionary. They are fighting criminals and smugglers, they look for gangsters, and it is interesting that they look for Jewish gangsters, i.e., their activities are not at all aimed at the [Russian people].

SK: I am not interested in the outward form of their activity but in the inner self-consciousness of this Jewish boy.

MDS: What does this mean?

SK: Well, in those monologues . . . "I would've given much for my Judaic fore-father. . . ."[88] This is the apogee of the entire poem.

MDS: And so what, actually, surprises you so much? I think it is natural for any person to address one's forefathers—

SK: —yes, but this triumph results in his regarding himself a man of power, and not merely rejoicing at his liberation.

MDS: And so what is wrong with that?

SK: In that case he should take responsibility for the power that is in his hands.

MDS: . . . Fine, what if a Russian person invoked the names of Prince Igor´ or Dmitrii Donskoi, how different would that be from what we have in the poem?

SK: Well, at least, it would be natural in Russia. . . . Russia is the country of Dmitrii Donskoi.

MDS: . . . This Jewish youth has no other country. Russia is his country to the same extent. There are no hints here—as there are none in Bagritskii's own life—that the protagonist sees himself outside of or apart from Russia.

SK: [Kuniaev speaks about "Jewish commissars" from Lev Trotsky to Bagritskii's characters.]

MDS: You juxtapose Bagritskii and Mandelstam. You say that Bagritskii is some sort of an anomaly in Russian poetry: "Such a complex could not be and never was a part of Russian poetry."[89] How is one to understand this?

SK: Literally. Russian classical poetry is Pushkin's testament: "And [I] called for mercy toward the fallen."[90] . . . I mean a complete lack of this Pushkin-ian humanism, or Dostoevskian humanism, whichever you like, of this Christian humanism. To a certain degree it was always alive in Russia; it is present in [Sergei] Esenin's poetry, despite Esenin's extremism in many of his works.[91]

MDS: . . . You also said that even the most vicious anti-Semites did not write about Jews as Bagritskii did. Do you really believe that is the case? Do you really think that Bagritskii was a self-hating Jew?

SK: To a certain extent, yes. This is the "collapse of humanism."[92]

MDS: I would very much like to know your interpretation of the ending, since it contains keys to the understanding of the events described.

SK: Bagritskii's ending will become clear when the Last Judgment takes place. Let us wait a bit.

MDS: That would not work for me. To put it simply, what is Bagritskii saying here? He has offered her the money; she has refused the money; they are engaged in sexual intercourse. . . . And then [he pronounces his closing monologue]. Do you recall: "I take you to avenge the world / From which I couldn't break away."

SK: This is the very anti-Pushkinian, "avenging the world."

MDS: . . . This may be anti-Pushkinian, but we are now . . . discussing this concretely, either as a statement by a Jewish boy or as Bagritskii's own prophecy.

SK: "Avenging the world" is an anti-Christian statement or, to narrow the focus of our conversation, anti–Russian Orthodox; but saying "anti–Russian Orthodox" would be expecting too much of Bagritskii, whereas an anti-Christian notion of the world is certainly here.

MDS: . . . But on what ground should you expect it to be Christian? [The protagonist] is a Jew, and a "Judaic boy." Why . . . do you expect a Christian notion of the world from him?

SK: Because he wishes to be a Russian poet.

MDS: First of all, the poem's protagonist does not wish—

SK: —no, but Bagritskii wishes to be a Russian poet, after all. He wished to, but nothing came of it, in contrast to Mandelstam.

MDS: Why do you say "nothing came of it"?

SK: Because one cannot be in the lap of Russian poetry while wishing to avenge the world.[93]

MDS: I categorically disagree with what you are saying. This is a solely subjective criterion. Bagritskii has had such a tremendous impact on contemporary poetry in Russia that one cannot just dispose of him—

SK: —this influence has come to naught, like water through sand. It was an influence in its time. And Mandelstam has not disappeared like water through sand.

MDS: . . . Could you tell me what Bagritskii meant by this: "Maybe my night seed / Will fertilize your desert"?

SK: Let us think about it together.

MDS: . . . I think that this is a dream of creating harmony between the Russian and Jewish currents in Russian history. This is a dream, if you wish, of a harmonious synthesis, which would lead to the blurring of all boundaries, i.e., to the formation of a Russian-Jewish identity.

SK: But this is a utopia.

MDS: In my view, this is a beautiful utopia. . . . I do not understand why it infuriated you so much?

SK: What infuriated me is that this utopia is based on an absolute conviction, that [Russia] must go through bloodshed, and there is no other way.[94]

MDS: What about Blok's long poem *Dvenadtsat'* ["*The Twelve*," 1919]?

SK: Blok in this case acts more as an historian than as a poet.

MDS: Do you not remember, the whole point there is that Russia must go through bloodshed and redeem itself in order to enter a new historical phase. I think the ending of *The Twelve* is very telling . . ., especially if you claim that Bagritskii the Jew wrote of "avenging the world," while Blok did not.

SK: No, Blok's is slightly different [confusion and long silence]. Blok's is different. Remember, in Blok's [ending] scoundrels are marching—

MDS: —with Christ!

SK: We do not know that.

MDS: Well, then we do not know anything! I think it is quite clear.[95]

SK: Blok pieced it all together [*u Bloka vse eto prisobacheno*], so to say, in a sweep of inspiration—the last stanza; whereas the people [in the last stanza] are horrible.

MDS: [Ivan] Bunin wrote that Blok rhymed *pes* ["dog"] and *Khristos* ["Christ"], which just maddened him, but this is a literary fact, and you cannot ignore it. Why doesn't Blok infuriate you more than Bagritskii?

SK: In Blok's poem, everything is balanced historically. Bagritskii is admiring all that, whereas Blok, perhaps, is horrified by it.

MDS: I think Bagritskii is jubilant over the fact that anti-Jewish restrictions were finally abolished, that [his protagonist] is finally an equal citizen of Russia.

SK: Even for such a talent as Bagritskii's [*dlia takogo talanta, kak Bagritskii*][96] . . . this thought is shallow. It is too shallow.

MDS: Why? There are facts, the Kishinev pogrom, the Beilis trial—

SK: —too shallow . . . to give birth to such a prominent poem. Shallow, shallow. A political and judicial fact can never be the foundation of such a nearly religious, messianic mentality.[97]

MDS: . . . The one who has suffered a pogrom always speaks a different language than the one who will never suffer one. This [persecution of the Jews in Czarist Russia] is a crucial factor in the first half of the poem. And I am not at all surprised that in *February*, his last work, Bagritskii turned to this subject.

SK: As concerns the pogroms, this is a very complicated issue, surrounded by much mythology and lying. [Kuniaev goes on to speak about "exaggerated numbers" of pogrom victims.]

MDS: So, to return to [your reasons for speaking about Bagritskii in 1977], you decided to cross the t's and dot the i's, right?

SK: My task was to explain the historical situation.

MDS: What if you were to address the same subject today?

SK: I would write the same, but with greater historical argumentation, with more objectivity and calmness. . . .[98]

MDS: I have always felt that this is [Bagritskii's] swan song, his last testament, in which he expresses the dream of one who is both a Jew and a Russian poet and who sees no contradiction in that. Apparently you see some contradiction there, [as though] the two were incompatible.

SK: They are incompatible only within the space of Russian culture.

MDS: Really?

SK: Bagritskii's extreme, or shall we put it directly, nationalistic views, are incompatible with Russian culture.

Following the meeting and conversation with Kuniaev, I rode to the airport in a beat-up Soviet-era car with my best friend Maksim, whose Jewish grandfather Israel married a Russian woman of merchant stock, Olimpiada, had two children by her, and loved and adored her his whole life. As we slowly moved in late-morning traffic toward Pushkin Square past the old Moscow Circus down the Orchard Ring, I kept asking myself as I still do today: Is it possible to negotiate between Gilman's view of Jewish self-hatred, which offers a historian's warning against the dangers of Jewish assimilation, and Kuniaev's charges, which in their inspired anti-Semitic flight attempt to eliminate Bagritskii from the history of Russian literature? Was, after all, Bagritskii a self-hating Jew in terms either Gilman's or Kuniaev's? To decide, I propose to examine briefly the dynamics of Bagritskii's Jewish theme as well as the place of Jewishness in Bagritskii's life from the early 1920s, before he moved from Odessa to Moscow, until his death in Moscow in 1934.

Prior to 1923, no explicitly Jewish motifs can be found in Bagritskii's works. In 1923, while working on the staff of a local newspaper in the southern city of Nikolaev, Bagritskii composed and published a bellicose and weak poem scorning traditional Jewish life.[99] Entitled "Na bitvu s bogom" ("Join the Battle with God") in keeping with official Communist slogans, the poem draws a forlorn picture of Jewish religious life during the czarist period:

> The trumpet blares in a desolate synagogue,
> And decrepit congregants walk
> Across bushes, down a grassless path,
> Barely moving, bent, crawling.[100]

The poem tries to imply, not without logical contradictions, that Judaism could not and did not ease the suffering of the Jews, whereas the Revolution and Soviet power liberated them from both the oppressive strictures of faith and the persecution by the czarist regime. This argument was in fact commonplace in Soviet writings on the Jewish question. Consider the middle section of the poem:

> And the ancient god of legends and hymns
> Is nothing now. He is wind, smoke, and ashes.

His emaciated shadow walks by,
He melts in bare sand like a cloud.
The time of strength and freedom has come,
An exploited slave has spread his shoulders.
And, having forgotten the years of suffering, those
Who were abandoned, poor and weak, now rise.[101]

After moving to Moscow, Bagritskii published his best known work, the epic poem *Duma pro Opanasa* ("The Lay of Opanas," 1926). It featured the Communist knight Iosif Kogan (in 1932, Bagritskii would write an opera libretto based on his epic poem).[102] Commissar Kogan dies by the hand of the Ukrainian peasant Opanas, a Red Army deserter fighting in the anarchist army of Nestor Makhno.[103] A visceral anti-Semite, Opanas refers to Kogan as "Kogan-zhid" ("Kogan the Yid") and wears a fur coat that had previously belonged to a rabbi whom Opanas murdered. In contrast to Opanas's marked anti-Semitism, Kogan is only nominally a Jew. He belongs to a series of Communist characters in early Soviet fiction whose distinct Jewish traits are their phenotypical features, telling last name, and stern loyalty to the Revolution and the Party (compare with Levinson in Aleksandr Fadeev's novel *Ragrom* ["The Rout," 1927] or Margulis in Valentin Kataev's *Vremia, vpered* ["Time, Forward," 1932]).[104] While Kogan identifies himself only as a Communist, Opanas regards him primarily as a "Yid" who stands in the way of peasant happiness in the Ukraine. Despite a measure of stereotyping in the depiction of a Ukrainian chieftain, Bagritskii's epic poem is superb at exploring and exposing linkages between Jewish participation in the Revolution and the Civil War and explosions of anti-Semitism among the peasant masses caught in the gears of history.[105]

Reminiscing about the years following the publication of *The Lay of Opanas*, the writer Sergei Bondarin recalled a telling incident. Around 1929, Bagritskii's son Vsevolod had to start elementary school. Bagritskii was known for his Bohemian lifestyle and his lack of respect for official documents and bureaucracy, and his son did not even have a birth certificate.[106] Bagritskii, as Bondarin—his friend from Odessa years—recalled, joked about registering the nationality of his son as "Czech" in the school papers. Why "Czech"? The father of Bagritskii's wife was an Austrian Czech who was born in Vienna and moved to Russia in 1894, where he was a music professor until his death in 1933. He married an ethnic Russian woman, and their three half-Russian/half-Czech daughters were raised Russian Orthodox, although they did carry their father's foreign name, "Suok."[107] In Soviet terms, nationality stood for one's ethnic origins and was generally determined on the basis of one's parents' nationalities. It was therefore expected that Vsevolod Bagritskii would be registered as either "Jew" (*evrei*)—after his father—or "Russian" (*russkii*)—after his mother—the latter if his parents chose the common and increasingly encouraged route of assimilation.[108] An obvious explanation for Bagritskii's joke would be that Bagritskii's wife was of Czech stock. However, Lidiia Suok came from a Russianized family and admittedly regarded herself as Russian, and the decision to list Vsevolod as "Czech" would have hardly been a display of his mother's sense of a Czech national identity. Another possibility would be that Bagritskii as a Jew believed that the mother's origin determines a child's identity. Anecdotal as this episode may appear to Western readers today, it may also signal that even during his most "Soviet" period of the late 1920s, Bagritskii both feared that his son would fall victim to anti-Semitism and had doubts about the dominant pattern of Russianization and assimilation of the Soviet Jews. In the passport of Vsevolod Bagritskii, issued in 1940 when he had turned eighteen, his nationality was registered as "Russian" (see illustration 18).

After the tremendous success of *The Lay of Opanas* and after joining the Russian Association of Proletarian Writers (RAPP), Bagritskii wrote "Proiskhozhdenie" ("Origin," 1930), a militant monologue of a Soviet Jew at odds with his familial past and upbringing. One of Bagritskii's most brilliant and tragic poems, "Origin" testifies to a profound crisis of its author's identity. It tells a terrifying story of a Jewish childhood and youth in which things went amuck every step of the way. From the moment of his circumcision, the protagonist sees "rusty Jews" who "cross the blades of their slanted beards" over his cradle. Remarkably, and despite the continuous efforts of his kinsmen to "dry him out with matzos" and to "deceive him with the candle," the Jewish youth retains his capacity to question his condition and to protest. This inborn gift, which he terms "Jewish disbelief" (*evreiskoe neverie*), impels him to flee. His escape recalls that made by the protagonist of Babel's story "Awakening." Compare Bagritskii's "I'm abandoning my old bed: 'Shall I go? Yes, I'll go!'" and Babel's "[my grandmother] held me tightly by the hand, so that I should not run away. She was right. I was thinking of escape."[109] Does one find a discourse of Jewish self-hatred in "Origin"? Was Bagritskii emulating the Soviet rhetoric on nationalities? Yes and no. Descriptions such as this sketch of a Jewish girl would make many readers cringe:

Love?
But what about lice-eaten braids;
A jutting collar bone;
Pimples; a mouth, greased with herring;
And a horsey curve of the neck?
(41–45)

What redeems "Origin" is the realization that even in his militant protest against—as well as his de-aestheticizing of—the traditional Jewish life, the protagonist preserves a Jewish mind-set. The expression "Jewish disbelief" as a vehicle of self-discovery, occurs twice throughout the poem. Emblematically Jewish is the protagonist's restlessness, his unceasing questioning of himself and his milieu.

Although the protagonist rejects much of the heritage of Jewish communal living in the Pale of Settlement, he will never become a "rook . . . not knowing his kin" (line 55). In an essay on Jewish self-hatred among Russian-Jewish authors, Shimon Markish pointed out a striking similarity between Bagritskii's world of child's fantasy—a Jewish shtetl world "turned inside out"—and that of Marc Chagall's paintings. Central to Markish's interpretation of "Origin" is the "Jewish skepticism that puts into question both the solidness of the habitual (and fiercely rejected!) world, and its capacity to change, and especially for the better. This is the very same skepticism which expressed itself most perfectly in Heine."[110]

A partial early draft of "Origin" also suggests that beneath the surface of the irascible rhetoric directed against the provincial world of Jewish everyday living lies a quest to reconcile the poet's Jewish past and his Soviet present:

Where are you, my world! . . .
I walked to my people. But turning black in the twilight,
Hunchbacked, knotty, and wild,
Rusty Jews flung at me
Their stubbly fists. . . .
Pariah! How will I disobey the stricture,
How will I then conflate in my existence
This restless [dry] land
And my angry loneliness?[111]

There is fragile ambiguity in the words "my people"—Jews of Bagritskii's past or Soviet people of his present. There is also a metaphorically formulated yet distinct desire to "combine" Jewishness and ex-Jewishness. Finally, there is in the draft a measure of skepticism concerning the success of the Soviet assimilationist project.

While steadily rising to the top of the young Soviet literature (the funeral issue of *Literary Gazette* called him "krupneishii sovetskii poet" ["a most prominent Soviet poet"]; see illustration 17[112]), Bagritskii never abandoned Jewish topics or disavowed his Jewish origin. In autobiographical notes and remarks from the 1930s, Bagritskii did not fail to mention his growing up in a Jewish family, although not without embarrassment for his parents' "petit bourgeois" status and the philistine milieu of his childhood.[113] In 1928–30, he masterfully translated the Yiddish poet Itzik Fefer into Russian. Rather Soviet in their treatment of history, Fefer's poems about the transformed Ukraine share with Bagritskii's their abhorrence of the Jews' prerevolutionary past and their idealization of the Soviet present.[114] These poems recall the times when masses of Ukrainian Jews fell victim to the pogromists, to "fires" of Khmel´nyts´kyi and "knives" of Mazepa and Gonta. Hopeful about the future of Soviet Jews, Fefer's poems that Bagritskii rendered in Russian speak with love and sadness about the former shtetl-dwellers and with warmth of the disappearing world of the Pale of Settlement.

Somewhere between 1928 and 1932, Bagritskii underwent a transformation, resulting in both a more critical reflection on the Bolshevik revolutionary project and an increased emphasis on Jewish themes in his works. What may have affected these changes? There were, of course, the horrors of the First Five-Year Plan and the collectivization of agriculture, of which Bagritskii must have been at least partly informed; his friends included Nikolai Aseev, Isaac Babel, Vladimir Lugovskoi, Il′ia Sel′vinskii, and other writers who regularly traveled and had firsthand knowledge of what really went on. Due to his severe asthma, Bagritskii hardly left his home during the last three years of his life. And yet, I cannot imagine that he did not know about the rapid increase of popular anti-Semitism in the late 1920s and early 1930s.[115] It was, after all, reported in the Soviet papers; consider the February 1929 *Pravda* editorial "Attention to the Struggle against Anti-Semitism."[116] The Soviet Prime Minister M. I. Kalinin wrote essays and made speeches against anti-Semitism. Books such as M. Gorev's *Against Anti-Semites* (1928) or Iu. Larin's *Jews and Anti-Semitism in the USSR* (1929) were released by central publishing houses and circulated. Of particular interest in this connection is *The Unvanquished Enemy: A Collection of Literary Works against Anti-Semitism*, edited by V. Veshnev and published in 1930 by Federatsiia, the publishing house where Bagritskii worked as a consulting—and from 1931, the chief—poetry editor. Works by famous authors of the Imperial and Soviet periods, both Jewish and non-Jewish, appeared in the collection. Bagritskii's own *The Lay of Opanas* was anthologized alongside works by Vladimir Korolenko, Aleksandr Serafimovich, Isaac Babel ("Story of My Dovecote"), S. An-sky, Semen Iushkevich, Aleksandr Fadeev (an excerpt from *The Rout*), and others. None other than Emelyan Yaroslavsky (Russian pseudonym of M. I. Gubel′man), head of the League of Militant Godless and Stalin's would-be official biographer, wrote an introduction to the volume. In Yaroslavsky's introductory essay, anti-Semitism was treated in terms of Marxist historiography as a notorious remnant of Russia's czarist and capitalist past. Yaroslavsky quoted a long passage from Lenin's speech, "Anti-Jewish Pogroms" (1919):

> Animosity toward the Jews takes firm hold only there, where the bondage of capitalists and landowners keeps workers and peasants in hopeless darkness. . . . It is not the Jews who are the enemies of the workers, the enemies of the workers are the capitalists of all countries. Among the Jews there are working people—they make up their majority. They are our brothers in being exploited by capital, they are our comrades in the struggle for socialism. Among the Jews there are kulaks, exploiters, capitalists, just as there are among all of us. . . . Wealthy Jews, like wealthy Russians—like the rich in all countries and in alliance with one another—suppress, exploit, divide the workers. Shame on accursed czarism that tormented and persecuted the Jews! Shame on those who plant seeds of hatred toward other nations! Long live the fraternal trust and the fighting alliance of all nations in their struggle to overthrow capitalism.[117]

Notwithstanding Lenin's words and the Marxist-Leninist introduction that claimed that anti-Semitism would disappear in the Soviet Union, the literary works from the 1880s–1920s collected in *The Unvanquished Enemy* conveyed a stringent sense of anti-Semitism's uninterrupted stride across Russia's past and into her present—the Soviet present. All of the above surely left the Bagritskii of the early 1930s with a bitter feeling of betrayed revolutionary universalist ideals and made him question the Soviet rhetoric on Jewish identity. His last years, culminating in *February*, were marked by a utopian quest for a harmonious synthesis between a fundamentally Judaic definition—religious, historical, and cultural—of a Jewish identity and a fundamentally Soviet—ahistorical, ethnic (and supraethnic)—construction of the self. When Israeli critic Mikhail Vainshtein referred to Bagritskii's latter years as those of "gaining sight" (*prozrenie*),[118] he must have had in mind the Sophoclean image from *Oedipus at Colonus*. Toward the end of the tragedy, the self-blinded king says this as he acquires inner vision:

I am driven
By an insistent voice that comes from God.
Children, follow me this way: see, now
I have become your guide, as you were mine!
Come: do not touch me: let me alone discover
The holy and funereal ground where I
Must take this fated earth to be my shroud.[119]

Memories of his Jewish past, now rekindled by the news of the growth of anti-Semitism in the Soviet Union, gnawed at Bagritskii's heart. Following his anti-Jewish rebellion and attempted self-sanitization of the early and mid-1920s, in the last years of his life the poet turned increasingly to the problem of Jewish identity. In "Papirosnyi korobok" ("A Box of Cigarettes," 1927)—an insomniac's imagined conversation with his young son—Bagritskii puts the issue of origin and identity and the idea of genetic, blood kinship at the poem's passionate conclusion:

Rise, Vsevólod, and be in charge of everything,
Stand up under the autumn sky!
I know: you were born with pure blood,
You stand at the threshold of joyous times![120]

One notes the Old Russian stress in the name Vsevolod (pronounced "Vsévolod," not "Vsevólod," in modern Russian) as well as the archaic verb *volodat´* (here, "to be in charge"—see the Russian text in the appendix), and one asks this question: What is "pure blood"?[121] Slavic? Jewish? Soviet? Somehow devoid of ethnic markers and "pure" in an internationalist sense?

No other text of the early 1930s attests to Bagritskii's confronting the problem of a Russian-Jewish identity as does the lyrical poem "Razgovor s synom" ("Conversation with My Son," 1931). Just as in the long poem *February*, "Conversation with My Son" opens on a boulevard in Odessa:

I walk on the boulevards. Whistle
In light trees. The alley is humming.[122]

These lines clearly anticipate the opening of *February*:

Here I am again on this land.
                              Again
I walk under the young plane trees.

Revisiting his hometown, Bagritskii invites his teenage son to look back at the conditions under which the Jews lived during the czarist period. Bagritskii's focus is a pogrom; his description is reminiscent of Babel's "Story of My Dovecote":

In red shirts, in long cloth jackets,
Red-haired grain merchants, stumping mud,
Carry an icon on a clean towel,
And a corpulent merchant falls smack
Into mud and stretches his hands greedily,
A simian civil servant crosses his forehead,
Ferocious old women push through to kiss the icon.
Feather from eiderdowns, like a flock of doves.
The street is flung open . . . And wild
Screaming hovers over the universe: "Kill!"[123]

The czarist period is here identified with a pogromist incitement to "kill the Jews," usually followed by a call to "save Russia" *(bei zhidov—spasai Rossiiu)*. In contrast to the czarist past, Bagritskii idealizes and embellishes the Soviet present, portraying it as forever free of pogroms and anti-Semitism. At the same time, and despite the poem's focus on the legacy of Russian anti-Semitism, it fails to mention the word *Jew* or its cognates or equivalents. Bagritskii refers to "*my*" (Russian for "we"), an ambiguous entity that can mean several things simultaneously: the poet himself and his son Vsevolod (a would-be poet, later killed in World War II), the Soviet Jews as a group, and all the Soviet people:

The world of these crowds is ours forever. . . .
[. . .]
My son! The same inspiration
Now scorches us.

The poem metonymically links memories of pogroms and the rise of fascism in Europe[124]:

Where a pogrom passed, growling . . .
We carry on broad shoulders
A thirst for victory and an awesome weight.
Although the animals rear up on coats of arms,
And platoons march in black shirts . . .
Although the attack plane at furious dawn
Is marked with a black fascist sign. . . .

Bagritskii counterbalances the references to fascism (note Bagritskii's foresight; this was written in 1931) with an image of workers gathering under a red flag. He concludes the poem with this pronouncement:

The time will come—and we shall walk,
My son, you and I, along the roads of the world,
Brothers from the East alongside
Brothers of the liberated planet.[125]

Who are the mysterious "brothers from the East" (or the Orient—both readings of the Russian noun *Vostok,* here capitalized by Bagritskii, are possible)? Does this phrase stand for people of the Soviet Union, geographically east of Western Europe? Perhaps, although in light of the poem's Jewish theme, this could also be Bagritskii's Soviet euphemism for the Jews? And if so, does this express his dream of an international brotherhood that would eliminate all national, religious, and racial boundaries in the Soviet Union and worldwide?

In the long poem *Posledniaia noch´* ("*The Last Night,*" 1932), Bagritskii speaks tenderly of the Jewish Sabbath. As elsewhere in his later poems set in Odessa, the imagery recalls that of Babel's *Odessa Stories:*

I passed by Jewish houses.
I heard the fierce snoring
Of movers sleeping on their carts;
Through the windows I saw
Sabbath in a purple wig
Walking with a candle.[126]

The last three lines brilliantly draw an image of the descending Friday night (the Bride of Sabbath?) as an Orthodox Jewish woman, wearing a wig and holding a Sabbath candle. The poem is set in Odessa on the eve of World War I and portrays a seventeen-year-old literary cousin of the protagonist in *February. The Last*

Night—here meaning the last night of both peace and the protagonist's old iden-
tity—anticipates *February* in several ways, and it is time to return to Bagritskii's
last work.[127]

6. Conclusion: Has He "Made Her Wilderness Like Eden"?

What was Bagritskii's view of the future of Jews in Soviet Russia? To determine
this view, I propose to examine closely the final scene of *February*. This scene
completes the making of Bagritskii's *discourse of Jewish pride*, a discourse that I
have so termed in contrast to the discourse of Jewish self-hatred, which has been
investigated in research on European Jewry by Gilman and others. The discourse
of Jewish pride has been the main target of Kuniaev's intemperate statements
about Bagritskii and other Russian-Jewish writers.

The Jewish protagonist, now a proud deputy commissar of the militia during
the interim period of summer–fall 1917, leads a unit of sailors in a raid on an
underground bordello. Breaking into the bordello at night, the crime fighters
arrest three legendary Jewish gangsters.[128] To his astonishment, the protagonist
finds his former beloved in bed with one of them. How ironic: the same beauti-
ful Russian girl who rejected him before the February Revolution because he was
Jewish now sells her body to figures of the Jewish underworld. In fact, the speech,
manners, and names of the gangsters (Semka Rabinovich, Pet´ka Kambala, and
Monia Brilliantshchik, all anglicized in my translation of the poem) resemble
those of Benia Krik and Babel's other Jewish gangsters.[129]

In 1936, Bagritskii's editor, Fedor Levin, reminisced about visiting the poet
not long before his death. Bagritskii spoke to him about the creation of *February*:

> I am writing a long poem. The poem is about myself, about the old world. Almost
> everything is truly the way it happened to me. . . . All of this happened exactly how
> I write about it, the *gymnasium* student and the search. I only made up a little bit.
> . . . But that was necessary for the concept. First of all, the gangsters were not there.
> Secondly, when I see this [girl] I have been in love with, who has now become [a]
> prostitute, in the poem I make everyone leave and I jump into her bed. That is, so
> to speak, my break-up with the past, a revenge. In actuality I was so embarrassed and
> confused that I did not know how to get myself out of there.[130]

In admitting to the autobiographical nature of most of the poem, Bagritskii
stressed the fictionality of the sexual scene. At the same time, in her analysis of
the testimonies of various relatives, friends, and associates of the poet, Monika
Spivak quotes a source confirming that Bagritskii had been in love with a woman
who later became a prostitite.[131] One should also bear in mind that Bagritskii had

a reputation as a mystifier and virtuoso liar, and recent archival research by Spivak has shown that on more than one occasion Bagritskii may have fictionalized his past.[132] The question of whether or not the conclusion of *February* has its sources in Bagritskii's biographical past has relevance for this discussion, especially because some of Bagritskii's detractors have tried to identify the protagonist of the poem directly with its creator.

Spokespeople of Soviet and post-Soviet Russian nationalism have used the final scene as proof of the author's "foul, nationalistic, decadent" position. As Tarasenkov put it in 1950: "*February* ends with a disgusting scene of the 'hero's' raping a prostitute. Bagritskii interprets this violence as the 'self-affirmation' of the Jew who was oppressed before the revolution. *February* is a deeply corrupt work. . ."[133] And now Kuniaev's 1977 remark, which was repeated almost verbatim in his memoir twenty years later: "The long poem ends with a liquidation of a bordello, during which the lyrical hero meets among the prostitutes the *gymnasium* student after whom he had pined as a young man, and greedily rapes her [*zhadno nasiluet ee*]."[134]

Let us examine in detail the exchange between the protagonist, formerly a "little Judaic boy," and the prostitute,[135] the one "whose nightingale glances / And flight of shoes across slippery asphalt" had so anguished him before the February Revolution:

"Remember me?" but she didn't speak,
Weightless hands covering
Her pale face.
        "Now you remember?"
Still more silence.
        Angry, I blurted out,
"How much do you want for the hour?"
Quietly, not parting her lips, she said,
"Have pity . . . I don't want the money. . . ."
(560–566)

There is no question that by offering money for sex to the young woman he once loved, the protagonist acts toward her with the youthful brutality of one who now has power and control. Moreover, by throwing the money at the woman, Bagritskii's protagonist is in effect denying his love for her, confirming again his earlier assertion that he could not "love properly." He wants to hurt her, to humiliate her, to treat her as a prostitute. He also wants to treat her the way the criminals he has just arrested—the arrogant and proud Jewish gangsters—treat Russian prostitutes. Recall Babel's "How It Was Done in Odessa":

You can spend the night with a Russian woman, and the Russian woman will be satisfied with you. You are twenty-five years old. If heaven and earth had rings attached to them, you would seize hold of those rings and pull heaven down to earth. And that is why he [a prominent Jewish gangster] is the King, while you are nothing.[136]

   While the behavior of the protagonist during the exchange with his former beloved is crude and direct, it is the young woman's response that harbors greater subtlety and is therefore prone to misreading. Again, I wish to emphasize that I am conducting an analytical reading in order to determine the exact meaning of the final episode. I have given this matter a lot of thought and am well aware of the extremely sensitive nature of this sexual scene, especially so for the female reader. From the outset, the protagonist has established the conventional and limited terms of his relationship with the prostitute by asking how much she charges. Why, as a prostitute who sells her body for money in a bordello and has just done so with a Jewish gangster, does she not want to take the money from the main character? She does *not*—and this is critical for the alleged charges of rape—say to the protagonist something like this: "Have pity and let me be," or even this: "I did it with him but won't do it with you." Rather, she tells him that she does not want the *money* ("ne nado deneg"). If her plea for mercy (*Pozhalei menia* = "Have pity") indeed refers to the money part, why does she not want his money? Is it because she feels completely in the protagonist's power? Is it because she recognizes the protagonist and now hopes to recompense him for the pain and humiliation she had previously inflicted upon him? Or is it a strange mixture of inborn aristocratic pride and acquired circumstantial humility that govern her behavior here? Could it also be that she tries to separate their pre-February past, in which she was a privileged Russian girl and he an oppressed Jewish boy, from their present, in which she as a prostitute is expected to sleep with him or anyone else for money? Recall an earlier scene, where she rejects her Jewish suitor and threatens to seek the help of the police. Consider also the transitional, lyrical passage, where the protagonist himself speaks about the changing shape of the world. It is indeed a world turned upside down after the Revolution, and in this new, upended world she is a prostitute and he a policeman. At the same time, if "Have pity" is the prostitute's plea only for mercy and compassion, why does she bring up the money at all? Why does she not simply say "Have pity" without ever mentioning the payment?

   While constructing *February*'s final, non-autobiographical scene, Bagritskii carefully weighed every word of the dialogue. He did not want to embellish the protagonist. He portrayed him as capable of romantic cruelty and arrogant boorishness toward the woman he had once loved:

I tossed her the money.
                    I threw myself down—
Not pulling off my boots, not taking off the holster
Or unbuttoning my shirt—
Right into the mess of feathers, into the blanket
Under which all my predecessors
Had throbbed and sighed, into the somber

Muddled flow of visions,
Screams and unencumbered movements,
Into darkness and awesome light. . . .
(567–575)

Writing with disarming confessionalism, Bagritskii does not seek to justify his protagonist's cruelty. The overall logic of the poem's plot presents sexual intercourse with his former beloved as a rite of passage for the protagonist, the completion of his Russian-Jewish identity. However, the circumstances under which his love is consummated debase this very love, deprive it of the loftiness and grace it possessed in the earlier parts. Still, it is one thing to accuse Bagritskii's main character of cruelty—and cruelly he did act—and a totally different one is to charge him with rape. In my view, the poem's evidence does not support such a charge. The prostitute says to the protagonist that she does not want his *money*. She never says that she will not have *sex* with him—although such a response would be quite plausible even at this point given her past rejections of the timid protagonist.

I hold that Tarasenkov's and Kuniaev's interpretations of *February* are flawed even in terms of today's understanding of "rape" in Western democracies, an understanding that rests on the "no means no" concept. Although some readers may chose to disagree, I believe there is no crime of rape here. In fact, in an earlier variant of the text, Bagritskii even toyed with the idea of a bargaining exchange between his protagonist and the acerbic prostitute. The considered line, which Bagritskii crossed out in his notebook, follows line 565 in the published text: "Quietly, not parting her lips, she said: 'As an acquaintance, I will charge you only fifty'" ("Po znakomstvu s vas vsego poltina").[137] In the manuscript, Bagritskii also considered and crossed out the form *otdavaisia* in lines 576–579 of the protagonist's monologue (*otdavaisia* is the singular imperative of the verb *otdavat´sia*, the verb that frequently refers to a voluntary sexual submission: to give oneself to someone).[138] These are further indications that, even in the variants, Bagritskii never allowed the possibility of his protagonist's raping his former love. This point is central to the reception of *February*, because in leveling charges of rape against Bagritskii's Jewish protagonist, his detractors have implied that the alleged rape of an ethnic Russian woman by a Jewish man bears ritualistic significance, religious, historical and cultural. Such a charge is familiar to students of anti-Semitism and racism.

History knows numerous cases in which an ethnic, religious, or racial majority has charged members of an oppressed minority group with raping women of the majority group. In American history, as is evident from historical, sociological, and juridical studies and such well-publicized cases as the Scottsboro boys trial and the Leo Frank trial, African American and Jewish men have been falsely accused of raping European American and Christian women, respectively.

In claiming that African American (and Jewish) men have a massive urge to rape European American (and Christian) women, prejudiced ideologues and politicians fail to make a crucial distinction. On the one hand, there is a theoretical anthropological model positing that sex with a woman from a majority group may constitute a rite of passage for a member of an oppressed minority. On the other hand, to take the well-researched matter of interracial rape in America, there is an actual racist assumption that an African American man experiences an urge to *rape* a European American woman, an assumption that is certainly not supported by legal and sociological evidence.[139] Both in the case of interracial rape in America and in that of the rape of an ethnic Russian woman by a Jewish man, prejudiced polemicists make a faulty and biased leap from the theoretical model, in which sexual intercourse awards an ethnically, racially, or religiously oppressed man a full sense of equality, to a criminal accusation, which replaces sexual intercourse with rape, a criminal act. Ideologues of Soviet and post-Soviet Russian anti-Semitism would thus find a similarity between the situation described in Bagritskii's *February*—the summer of 1917 following the granting of equal rights to the Jews of the Russian Empire—and the periods in American history (when false charges of interracial rape rose dramatically) following the postbellum emancipation of slaves in the 1860s and the desegregation of the South and the civil rights movement in the late 1950s and 1960s. In his officially sanctioned essay of 1950, Tarasenkov charged that Bagritskii's Jewish protagonist "participated in the revolution only in order to affirm his racial full worth [*rasovuiu polnotsennost*]."[140] Some twenty-five years later, in his essay based on his speech at the Central House of Writers in 1977, Kuniaev likewise interpreted the sex scene as a rape of Russia by a Jew. He insisted that in Russian poetry

> Eduard Bagritskii is the only completely developed poet of the openly Romantic, ideal Zionism that does not differentiate between ideas of messianism and pragmatic cruelty. He perceives the Russian revolution under the sign of tribal nationalism [*plemennogo nationalizma*], only as a liberation and rebirth of Jewishness, as a transition to its new life, hence his rejection of his native shtetlness which he hates, hence, of course, a simultaneous complete denial of the national humanistic traditions of Russian poetry.[141]

Is not Kuniaev trying to have it both ways with Bagritskii's Jewish identity? Within two versions of the same diatribe of 1977 (and also twenty years later in a recorded interview and in his own memoir), Kuniaev simultaneously charges Bagritskii with being a Zionist and a self-hating Jew. Not only does he reproduce a vintage 1970s official Soviet rhetoric on Judaism, Jewish history, and the state of Israel, but he continues to do so even in the post-Soviet period. In order to malign Bagritskii's legacy, Kuniaev also advances a thesis that mimics and turns on its head the one that Jewish thinkers have introduced in pondering Jewish history and culture in Diaspora.

This is the most fundamental difference between the Western arguments about Jewish self-hatred (Theodor Lessing, Hans Mayer, Sander L. Gilman, and others) and those by Stanislav Kuniaev and his cohorts in Russia: the former seek to explain (and in some cases to prevent) Jewish assimilation, whereas the latter attempts to excommunicate Jews from Russian cultural history by claiming that their "spirit" is not part of the Russian classical tradition and of Christianity. Moreover, and contrary to what Kuniaev alleges, Bagritskii wishes precisely for an internationalist Russia undivided into Jews and Russians. He is the opposite of a Jewish nationalist (or a Zionist), however perverted Kuniaev's Soviet understanding of these terms may be.[142]

In addition to his failure to read Bagritskii's text closely, Kuniaev (and other voices in this intolerant chorus) also grossly distort the meaning and message of the closing monologue. In the monologue, the protagonist speaks about the meaning of sexual intercourse between a liberated Jew and his former Russian beloved, now a prostitute:

I am taking you because my age
Was shy, because I am so bashful,
Because of the shame of my homeless ancestors,
Because a chance bird twitters!

I take you to avenge the world
From which I couldn't break away!

Let me into your empty womb,
Where grass cannot take hold,
Maybe my night seed
Will fertilize your desert.[143]

There'll be rainfalls, southern winds will blow,
Swans will make again their calls of passion.
(576–587)

While elements of brutality, ever short of the crime of rape, certainly play a part in the final scene of *February*, in my view this monologue does redeem Bagritskii's protagonist in eyes of the reader. As the Italian scholar Danilo Cavaion aptly put it, "The act of brutality finds justification, human and historical, profound and constituting a definite passage to the world of tomorrow, a violent redemption of a past full of violence [il riscatto violento da un passato pieno di violenza]."[144] In these twelve lines of blank trochaic pentameter, two lines short of a sonnet, the protagonist recounts the entire history of the making of his Russian-Jewish identity. He recalls his timidity and humiliation as a Jewish boy. He remembers the persecution of the Jews, the Pale of Settlement, and other anti-Jewish restrictions in Imperial Russia. He then speaks of the way he tried to escape the narrow Jewish world of his childhood and raw youth, first through the realm of exotic birds and later through the aestheticized world of his Russian beloved. Real social escape, however, was not possible until the February 1917 Revolution. Sexual intercourse with his former Russian beloved is the modicum of the protagonist's revenge upon and liberation from the prerevolutionary world of legal Jewish inequality and popular anti-Semitic prejudice. Recall the heart-rending pogrom scene in Babel's "The Story of My Dovecote," where an ethnic Russian woman says about the Jews: "Their seed [*semia*] ought to be destroyed."[145] The ending of *February* speaks of fertilizing the "desert" of Russia—both the beloved and the prostitute—with Jewish seed in the hopes that Russian-Jewish children will be born. Why, otherwise, would Bagritskii end the poem with a promise of rainfalls? Over millennia of human civilization, rain has been regarded as "God's sperm," a universal symbol of fertility and fertilization of the earth by the sky.[146] As for the swans' cries of love, the significance of this image is twofold. On the one hand, the "trumpeter swan"—sounding its plaintive song before his death—symbolizes a person's last words or works. On the other, this is a prophecy of grace, beauty, and purity.[147]

An American historian of Jews in the Soviet Union, Nora Levin, wrote that

> Bolshevism attracted marginal Jews, poised between two worlds—the Jewish and the Gentile—who created a new homeland for themselves, a community of ideologists bent on remaking the world in their own image. . . . Having abandoned their own origins and identity, yet not finding, or sharing, or being fully admitted to Russian life (except in the world of the party), the Jewish Bolsheviks found their ideological home in revolutionary universalism.[148]

Compare these remarks with a comment by Bagritskii's contemporary, the Odessan writer Zinadia Shishova (Brukhnova): "Bagritskii came to the Revolution as one comes to his native home. A hobo and a romantic, he came in, sat down, threw his derby down and asked for bread and salt pork fat [*khleba i sala*, a deliberate image of nonkosher, non-Jewish, Slavic food]."[149] Despite his love affair with the Russian Revolution, Bagritskii was never a marginal Jew. Yes, he did indeed write a number of poems that displayed allegiance to the Bolshevik doctrine—such as his verses about the Industrial Party trial of 1930, "O chem oni mechtali" ("What They Dreamt About"). But Bagritskii never did become a Bolshevik or a self-sanitized Jew of the sort that Nora Levin speaks of in the passage I quoted earlier. After his move in 1925 from Odessa to Moscow, and until his death, he retained a bond with Jewish culture, splendidly translating Yiddish poetry (Itzik Fefer, Peretz Markish). Friends of Bagritskii's reminisced that the poet routinely peppered his Russian with Yiddish expressions and gesticulated in a manner that an ethnic Russian would associate with being Jewish.[150] In his daily life, Bagritskii never shed the skin of an Odessan Jew from Market Street. The writer Valentin Kataev, who was instrumental in bringing Bagritskii to

Moscow from Odessa, recalled this example of Bagritskii's use of Judaic heritage in his Russian speech: "[Bagritskii would say] 'I give you my word, Ben Emunos [Hebrew expression, literally means "son of honesty"],' and he could not help but add a Jewish oath. . . ."[151] The prosaist Konstantin Paustovskii reminisced about the way Bagritskii, whose birth name was Dziubin, explained his background: "One should say this: 'Bagration Bagritskii, the last descendant of the princely Caucasian-Polish dynasty from the Judaic tribe of Dziub [*kniazheskogo kavkazsko-pol'skogo roda iz iudeiskogo kolena Dziuba*]."[152]

Semen Lipkin, who was close to Bagritskii in the late 1920s, told me about Bagritskii's affinity for and identification with the Jewish past. "He had this book about some Jew in the Middle Ages," Lipkin reminisced, "who said that he came from someplace far away, someplace where two Jewish tribes had survived . . . it was in a novel . . . and he was a representative of this [Jewish] state."[153] Given what we know about Bagritskii and his time, it is not very difficult to recognize the book to which the nearly nonagenarian Lipkin refers as Max Brod's famous novel *Reübeni, Fürst der Juden: Ein Renaissanceroman* (*"Reubeni, Prince of the Jews: A Novel of the Renaissance"*), first published in German in 1925. Two years after its original publication, Brod's novel came out in Moscow in the Russian translation—one year prior to the English translation and two years earlier than the Hebrew edition.[154] The subject of the False Messiah David Reubeni (or Reuveni, ca. 1490–ca. 1535), Jewish adventurer and mystic, has inspired a number of Jewish authors, including the Yiddish writers David Pinski and David Bergelson (both have written plays about Reubeni). And it is hardly surprising that Bagritskii was so taken with both the historical Reubeni and Max Brod's novel about him, the first part of which is set in Prague, and the second mainly in Rome and in Portugal in the first third of the sixteenth century. Born in Khaibar, Central Arabia, Reubeni arrived in Rome in 1524 falsely claiming to be the ambassador from his brother, King Joseph Reubeni, ruler over a mighty (fictitious) kingdom of the descendants of the tribe of Reuben, one of the ten lost tribes of Israel. (This mysterious Jewish kingdom, modeled after the ancient state of Israel, is referred to in Brod's novel as "the wilderness of Chabor"; its description in Brod's novel seems to be informed by the history of Khazaria.) Intent on liberating Palestine to deliver the oppressed Jews of Europe to it, Reubeni convinced Pope Clement VII to endorse his plan of an allied military action by European powers and the Jewish state of Chabor against the Ottoman Empire. Reubeni's mission eventually failed, and Charles V, Emperor of the Holy Roman Empire, had Reubeni delivered to the hands of the Spanish Inquisition.[155] According to Lipkin, "Bagritskii loved [Brod's novel about Reubeni] and said time and again: 'And what if it's true?'"

In her unpublished chronicle of Bagritskii's life and work, Bagritskii's wife recorded that in the winter of 1926–27—about the same time as that of his fascination with the story of David Reubeni—Bagritskii was also very taken with

the poem "Levivot" ("Dumplings," 1902) by the great Hebrew poet Saul Tcher-
nichowsky (1875–1943). Bagritskii liked to read it aloud in the splendid Rus-
sian translation by Vladislav Khodasevich.[156] This long idyll describes one
morning in the life of Gitl, an old Jewish woman living somewhere in the
Ukrainian part of the Pale. Gitl wakes up with a craving for cheese dumplings.
A Ukrainian neighbor, Domakha, comes by to see Gitl, and the two of them
talk of the erosion of religious faith among both Ukrainians and Jews. As she
makes her dumplings, Gitl ruminates about the loss of Jewish traditions and
assimilation. Her thoughts travel to the time when her beloved granddaughter
Raizele was still a child. Later Gitl's son moved to a city where Raizele attended
a *gymnasium*, and for a while a volume of Pushkin occupied a place of honor
next to the girl's Jewish prayer books. Gitl recalls her granddaughter as a
teenager attending a Russian school where Jews had to study catechism and
other "alien" disciplines. She thinks about her granddaughter's sense of animos-
ity toward the ones who "forced her to worship alien holy objects." Several years
after finishing school, Raizele became a revolutionary. At the end of Tcherni-
chowsky's poem, as the dumplings cook in the boiling water, the mailman brings
old Gitl a letter from Raizele, who has been arrested and awaits trial at the SS.
Peter and Paul Fortress in St. Petersburg.

I find the episodes of Bagritskii's reading and admiring Russian translations of
Brod's *Reubeni, Prince of the Jews*, and Tchernichowsky's "Dumplings" to be hid-
den clues to his own dual Russian-Jewish identity. Moreover, this Hebrew poem
about the pains of Jewish assimilation and the reasons Russian Jews went into the
Revolution could serve as a perfect epigraph to Bagritskii's whole career.

A self-questioning Jew and a poet, Bagritskii was a universalist who dreamed
of a Russia free of anti-Semitism or any other interethnic boundaries. He mixed
discourses of Jewish self-hatred and Jewish pride to create a free and happy home
for himself in the world of Russian letters.[157] In the notebook where Bagritskii
composed *February*, he also kept a list of phone numbers and addresses of those
writers with whom he was close in his last days. It is a poignant document, a pre-
cious little page in the history of early Soviet literature, where the writers' Slavic
and Jewish names neighbor each other: "[Shmuel] Halkin 5–47–64; [Isaac] Babel
9–56–44; [Mark] Kolosov 1–98–02; [Nikolai] Ushakov, Kiev, Neranovich Street
21–20; [Nikolai] Aseev 5–51–31; [Vladimir] Lugovskoi 73–72."[158] Having found
this home in Russian-language poetry, Bagritskii was able to embark on a path,
however utopian, toward an ideal Soviet society, where Jews would need no dis-
course of their own.

In a 1925 preface to a projected collection of works by Odessan writers—the
book was never published—Babel said this about Bagritskii:

> He smells like mackerel that my mother has just fried in sunflower oil. He smells like
> stew made of Black Sea fish, which the fishermen of Little Fountain cook right on

The Poetics and Politics of Russian-Jewish Identity 93

the aromatic sand in the twelfth hour of the irrepressible day in July. Bagritskii is full of purple moisture like a watermelon that in the remote days of our youth he and I would break open against the bollards of the Pratique Harbor.[159]

One of Bagritskii's closest friends and the last writer to see him alive, Babel contributed a two-page memoir of Bagritskii to the ill-fated 1936 memorial volume.[160] Ten years had passed since the 1925 introduction, and how strikingly different was the tone of Babel's remarks:

> The fame of François Villon from Odessa earned [Bagritskii] love, but did not earn trust. And thus: his tales of hunting have become a prophecy, and his childishness has become wisdom, because he was a wise man, conjoining a member of the Komsomol with Ben Akiva [Joseph Ben Akiva (ca. 40—135 C.E.), great Talmudic scholar, Jewish leader, and martyr].[161]

In the essay, Babel also said that "on his way toward becoming a member of Communist society, Bagritskii went farther than many others. . . ."[162] Some forty years later, the editors of the 1973 volume of reminiscences about Bagritskii added two more sentences in place of the ellipses. In these lines, Babel further champions his art of suggestiveness: "I catch myself thinking that the paradise of the future, the Communist paradise, will consist of Odessites, resembling Bagritskii [*iz odessitov, pokhozhikh na Bagritskogo*], of loyal, intelligent, joyful friends, devoid of self-interest."[163] Like black diamonds, Babel's remarks radiate a tragic, luminous irony for posterity.

Since the late 1940s, Bagritskii's Soviet and post-Soviet detractors have regarded the ending of *February* as a "symbol of Russia's fertilization with Judeo-Messianic semen [*iudeisko-messianskim semenem*]."[164] A scenario of a "Judeofied" Russia is their worst fear incarnate, synonymous in their minds with their country's "un-Russianing" and devastation. From the vantage point of the end of the twentieth century, Bagritskii's idealistic hope for a fertilization of the Russian "desert" with Jewish "seed" has proven to be an unfruitful dream. The grass did not take hold. Russia has aborted her Jewish children. Fortunately for him, Bagritskii died too early to see the execution of the leading Yiddish writers in 1952, the Doctor's plot of 1953, the abominable Soviet anti-Israeli policy in the 1960s–1980s with its rhetorical equation of Zionism with fascism, the persecution of the Jewish Refuseniks, the rise of the anti-Semitic Pamiat´ movement, and the current outbreak of post-Soviet Judeophobia.

In closing, and in honoring Bagritskii's gift to Russian poetry, I would also like to celebrate his contribution to the treasury of Jewish thought. Bagritskii's unfulfilled prophecy at the end of *February* shows nevertheless that he was keenly aware of the spiritual and historical mission of the Jews. Reading the protagonist's final monologue, one cannot help but think of its biblical intonation and imagery, and particularly of two chapters in the book of Isaiah. In Isaiah 35:1–2, the Jewish Prophet promises his people that

the arid desert shall be glad,
The wilderness shall rejoice
And shall blossom like a rose.
It shall blossom abundantly,
It shall receive the glory of Lebanon,
The splendor of Carmel and Sharon.
They shall behold the glory of the Lord,
The splendor of our God.[165]

Bagritskii's reliance on Isaiah highlights the complexity of his literary pedigree: Russia's great poets, from Aleksandr Pushkin to Hayyim Nahman Bialik, have leaned upon the words of this ancient Prophet in voicing their own visionary testaments. It also suggests, I believe, that Bagritskii was not a Jewish messianist in the conventional sense of this term. Rather, his universalist vision of Jewish history as articulated in the ending of *February* amounts to the following: Jews are a constant source of vital energy for humankind, and their discrete genes will live on in the children of assimilating Jews. Expressed less than a decade before the Holocaust, Bagritskii's romantic viewpoint conflates both the enduring Judaic idea of Jews as divinely chosen to carry out a historical mission and a short-lived Soviet ideal of Jews living in harmony with other nations. Later, in Isaiah 51:3, the Prophet brings forth an image of a transformed wilderness:

Truly the Lord has comforted Zion,
Comforted all her ruin;
He has made her wilderness like Eden,
Her desert like the Garden of the Lord.
Gladness and joy shall abide there,
Thanksgiving and the sound of music.[166]

An image of a beautified desert crowns Bagritskii's last poem, but not the history of Russia's Jews.

CHRONOLOGY

~

Eduard Bagritskii—
His Life and Works

Information from the following: papers of E. G. Bagritskii at IMLI and papers of E. G. Bagritskii, L. G. Bagritskaia, and V. E. Bagritskii at RGALI; L. G. Bagritskaia, comp., *Eduard Bagritskii. Vospominaniia sovremennikov*; M. Bozhatnik, ed., "Maloizvestnye stikhi Eduarda Bagritskogo"; S. Bondarin, "Sud´by i stikhi"; S. Bondarin, "Eduard Bagritskii"; E. Bonner, *Dochki-materi*; E. A. Dinershtein, ed., "Pis´ma [Eduarda Bagritskogo]"; L. H. Kowalski, "Eduard Bagritsky: A Biographical Sketch"; L. H. Kowalski, "Eduard Bagritsky: Life and Poetry"; *Literaturnaia gazeta*, February 18, 1934 (Bagritskii funeral issue); E. P. Liubareva and S. A. Kovalenko, eds., *Eduard Bagritskii. Stikhotvoreniia i poemy*; V. Narbut, ed., *Eduard Bagritskii. Al´manakh*; M. Spivak; A. Tarasenkov, ed., *Russkie sovetskie pisateli. Poety. Bibliograficheskii ukazatel´*, vol. 2; K. Zelinksii, "Odna vstrecha u M. Gor´kogo (Zapis´ iz dnevnika)."

1895

November 3 (October 22). Bagritskii is born Eduard Godelevich Dziubin (Dziuban) in Odessa, to a middle-class Jewish family. His parents were Ida Dziubin (née Shapiro) and Godel´ Dziubin (Dziuban). Bagritskii's Jewish patronymic was subsequently Russianized and became "Georgievich." Bagritskii's father worked in retail. Bagritskii was his parents' only child.

1905

Fall. Bagritskii enters Zhukovskii School. He does poorly in all subjects except language/literature and history. He soon develops a lifelong professional passion for birds and fish.

October. Czar Nicholas II issues the October Manifesto, promising reforms and a legislative Duma. A wave of ferocious anti-Jewish pogroms ensues, chiefly in the southern and southwestern provinces, including Bagritskii's native city of Odessa.

1907

Bagritskii comes down with bronchitis, which leads to a complication resulting in lifelong bronchial asthma.

1908

Bagritskii makes his earliest attempt at writing poetry. He contributes to the school literary journal.

1913

Bagritskii transfers to the School of Land Surveying (*zemlemernoe uchilishche*). He debuts with two poems, signed "Eduard D.," in the collection *Akkordy* (*"Chords"*). He meets and befriends Anatolii Fioletov (b. Natan Shor), a gifted poet and cult figure among Odessa's young literati; Fioletov probably served as a prototype of the student in the scene of the police station takeover in *February*.

1914

January 16 and 19. Vladimir Maiakovskii reads at the Odessa Russian Theater; his reading has a tremendous impact on young Bagritskii.

Summer before World War I. Critic Petr Pil'skii organizes two readings in which Bagritskii participates.

July 30 (17). Russia enters World War I.

Bagritskii briefly serves in Odessa's branch of PTA (Petersburg Telegraphic Agency) as an editor.

1915

Bagritskii graduates from the School of Land Surveying.

Bagritskii contributes poems to two collections of new writing, with a cubo- and ego-futurist slant: *Serebrianye truby* (*"Silver Trumpets"*) and *Avto v oblakakh* (*"Automobile in the Clouds"*), both published in Odessa. He adopts a pen name, "Eduard Bagritskii," although he still signs some of his publications with alternative pseudonyms, including "Desi" and "Nina Voskresenskaia." He begins contributing to local newspapers, including *Iuzhnaia mysl'* (*"Southern Thought"*), where his exemplary early poem, "Autumn," is printed.

1916

Bagritskii contributes to the collection *Sed'moe pokryvalo* (*"The Seventh Coverlet"*). He meets and befriends a number of young writers: Sergei Bondarin, Vera Inber, Valentin Kataev, Vladimir Narbut, Iurii Olesha, Lev Slavin, Zinaida Shishova, and others.

1917

March 12 (February 27). The February Revolution occurs.

March 15 (2). Czar Nicholas II abdicates.

Spring–Summer. Bagritskii works in the militia, established by the Provisional Government in place of the czarist police. His poems appear in the collection *Chudo v pustyne* (*"Miracle in the Desert"*).

October. Bagritskii joins General Baratov's military expedition to Persia. In the expedition, he works as a record keeper.

November 6–7 (October 24–25). Bolshevik coup d'état occurs.

1918

Early February. Bagritskii returns to Odessa from Persia.

Spring. Bagritskii enlists in the Red Army special guerrilla regiment named after VTsIK (abbreviation of All-Union Central Executive Committee) and participates in the military actions against Nestor Makhno's anarchist army.

Bagritskii starts contributing to Odessan newspapers, including *Izvestiia* (*"News"*), *Moriak* (*"The Seaman"*), *Zritel'* (*"The Spectator"*), and others. His earnings from literary publications in the newspapers constituted a major part of his meager income in 1919–24. He ends cocaine addiction that began around 1917.

1919

February. Bagritskii's major early poem "Ia sladko iznemog ot tishiny i snov . . ." ("I have sweetly languished from silence and dreams . . .") appears in the Odessan newspaper *Ogon'ki* (*"Little Lights"*).

April. Bagritskii joins the First Red Cavalry Army; later he works as a political officer in the Special Sniper Brigade. He composes political propaganda, leaflets, and agitational verse.

April 13. Bagritskii's father dies of stomach cancer at age sixty-one.

October 8. General Denikin's troops march into Odessa.

1920

Spring. Bagritskii returns to Odessa. He works for BUPE, the Ukrainian division of IuGROSTA (Southern-Russian Telegraph Agency). His boss is the poet Vladimir Narbut.

Bagritskii marries Lidiia Gustavovna Suok (1896–1972). Lidiia Bagritskaia's two sisters were also married to writers, Ol'ga to Iurii Olesha, Serafima first to Vladimir Narbut, then to Viktor Shklovskii. After her husband's death in 1934, Lidiia Bagritskaia was arrested in July of 1937 and spent over fifteen years in the Gulag. Following her release and rehabilitation, she did much to promote her late husband's legacy, including compiling and coediting a collection of reminiscences about Bagritskii, which was published in 1973.

Fall. Bagritskii serves as military correspondent of Agitational Train "III International."

1921

Bagritskii writes the long poem *Traktir* (*"The Inn"*).

Spring. Bagritskii makes a trip to Voznesensk on assignment for IuGROSTA.

August 7. Poet Aleksandr Blok dies. Blok was one of Bagritskii's main Russian masters.

August 24. Poet Nikolai Gumilev is executed. Gumilev had an impact on Bagritskii's early verse.

1922

April 19. Bagritskii's son, Vsevolod Eduardovich Bagritskii, is born. A poet, Vsevolod Bagritskii was killed in World War II on February 26, 1942.

Bagritskii supervises a creative writing workshop of workers at a railroad repair shop. He contributes to Odessan newspapers and journals.

Fall. Bagritskii travels to Moscow for the first time.

1923

Bagritskii writes and publishes in newspapers two monologues of Til Eulenspiegel, based on Charles de Coster's novel, one of Bagritskii's favorite books.

Bagritskii publishes in newspapers renditions of Robert Burns's "John Barleycorn," Thomas Hood's "Song of the Shirt," and Sir Walter Scott's "Brignall Banks" (excerpt from *Rokeby,* entitled "Razboinik" ["The Robber"] in Bagritskii's version).

August–October. Bagritskii lives in the southern city of Nikolaev and contributes to the local newspaper, *Krasnyi Nikolaev* (*"Red Nikolaev"*), where he also serves as managing editor.

1924

During a visit to Odessa, at a public reading Vladimir Maiakovskii attacks Bagritskii's poems for their idealism and references to "knights and Chablis wine." Odessan publications temporarily stop printing Bagritskii's poetry, which in part affects his decision to move to Moscow.

Bagritskii's asthma worsens, and he spends most of his time indoors, inhaling cough suppressant.

Bagritskii's stillborn daughter is born. Isaac Babel participates in the funeral.

April–May. Bagritskii travels to Moscow.

1925

February–March. Bagritskii visits Moscow and stays with the writer Konstantin Paustovskii.

March. Bagritskii returns to Odessa from Moscow and contracts pneumonia for the third time. His major poem "Ballada ob arbuze" ("Ballad about a Watermelon") appears in *Krasnaia nov'* (*"Red Virgin Soil"*) (vol. 3, 1925) and becomes a literary event in Moscow. In the collection *Iugo-Zapad* (*"South-West,"* 1928) and in subsequent editions, the poem appeared under the title "Arbuz" ("The Watermelon").

Spring–Summer. Bagritskii moves to Moscow with his family and settles in Kuntsevo, then a suburb, renting rooms in a private home.

Bagritskii's major poem "Verses about a Nightingale and a Poet," and his version of Sir Walter Scott's "Brignall Banks" are published in *Red Virgin Soil* (vol. 8, 1925).

Circa end of 1925. Bagritskii joins Pereval ("The Pass"), a literary group of fellow travelers under the leadership of the critic Aleksandr Voronskii. He begins contributing regularly to the group's journal, *Red Virgin Soil*. The group's members included Ivan Kataev, Abram Lezhnev, Petr Pavlenko, Mikhail Prishvin, and others. The Pass was dissolved in 1932, along with other independent literary associations.

Winter. Bagritskii travels to Vologda in the north of Russia. He reads at a local college.

1926

Bagritskii leaves The Pass and joins Literaturnyi Tsentr Konstruktivistov ("Literary Center of Constructivists"), whose members also included Vera Inber, Aleksandr Kviatkovskii, Vladimir Lugovskoi, Il'ia Sel'vinskii, Kornelii Zelinskii, and others. Bagritskii's affiliation with constructivists was based on shared ideas about art as well as his personal friendships with several of the group's members.

May–July. Bagritskii completes his major epic poem *Duma pro Opanasa* (*"The Lay of Opanas"*) and publishes an abridged version in *Komsomol'skaia pravda* (*"Komsomol Truth"*), then the full text in *Red Virgin Soil* (vol. 10, 1926).

July 1926. Bagritskii journeys to Odessa for a few days.

1927

Bagritskii publishes his major poems "Ot chernogo khleba i vernoi zheny . . ." ("From black bread and a faithful wife . . ."), in *Red Virgin Soil* (vol. 1, 1927), "Kontrabandisty" ("The Smugglers"), in *Red Virgin Soil* (vol. 3, 1927), and "Ptiselov" ("The Fowler"), in *Red Virgin Soil* (vol. 5, 1927).

Bagritskii contributes his major poem "Spring" to volume 1 of the collection *Zemlia i fabrika* (*"Earth and Factory"*).

Bagritskii makes a trip to the Polesie region of Belorussia; he reads in Minsk.

November. Bagritskii delivers a lecture at the Moscow Polytechnical Museum. The lecture, "Poetry of Our Days," is introduced by poet and critic Georgii Shengeli.

1928

Bagritskii's first poetry collection, *Iugo-Zapad* (*"South-West"*), is published to much critical acclaim. Reproductions of Dürer's engravings appear on the covers of the first edition. The print run is three thousand copies.

February. Part 1 of the poem "Triasina" ("The Swamp") appears in the journal *Novyi Mir* (*"New World"*).

April. Bagritskii travels to Odessa to visit his mother and give a poetry reading.

August. Bagritskii journeys to the north of Russia, to the Archangel'sk Province.

Fall. Bagritskii makes trips to Ivanovo and Briansk to read poetry.

December. The cycle "Cyprinus carpio" is published in *Novyi mir* (vol. 12, 1928). Bagritskii makes a trip to Leningrad with Nikolai Khardzhiev; he stays in the Astoria Hotel.

1929

Bagritskii contributes major poem "TBC" to volume 6 of *Zemlia i fabrika* (*"Earth and Factory"*).

Fall. Bagritskii travels to Kolomna and Riazan´ with poet Aleksei Surkov and novelist Aleksandr Fadeev.

1930

Bagritskii leaves the Literary Center of Constructivists and joins RAPP (Russian Association of Proletarian Writers), a literary organization then vying for total hegemony of Soviet literature. Bagritskii's move was motivated largely by a desire to avoid criticism and to secure housing in Moscow.

The second edition of *South-West* is published.

December 1. Bagritskii publishes an occasional political poem "O chem oni mechtali" ("What They Dreamt About") on the subject of the Prompartiia trial (trial of the Industrial Party) in *Rabochaia Moskva* (*"Working Moscow"*).

December. Bagritskii publishes his major poem "Proiskhozhdenie" ("The Origin") in *Novyi mir* (vol. 11, 1930).

End of year. Bagritskii publishes "Vesna, veterinar i ia" ("Spring, the Vet and I") in *Krasnoe slovo* ("Red Word") (vol. 11, 1930). He makes a trip to Mordovia.

Bagritskii's book of illustrated children's poems *Sobolinyi sled* (*"Sable's Track"*) is published by GIZ (State Publishing House).

Bagritskii coedits with Aleksandr Fadeev a collection of literary works by Tartar authors (*Al'manakh tatarskoi literatury*, Moscow, 1930).

1931

Bagritskii moves to Moscow, to a writers' building at 2 Kamergerskii pereulok [proezd MKhATa], apt. 9, tel. 4–82–78.

Bagritskii contributes eleven translations to a Russian-language volume of the Yiddish poet Itzik Fefer.

Bagritskii's book of illustrated children's poems *Zvezda mordvina* (*"The Mordvinian's Star"*) is published by Molodaia Gvardiia.

Summer. Bagritskii assumes the responsibilities of chief poetry editor at Federatsiia. For the next two years, he writes numerous in-house reports and edits many collections of poetry by younger authors.

1932

Bagritskii adapts songs from Ben Johnson's *Volpone* for Iurii Zavadskii's Theater. The production premieres on 11 January 1932.

Bagritskii publishes a trilogy of long poems, *Posledniaia noch'* (*"The Last Night"*), *Chelovek iz predmest'ia* (*"Man from the Suburb"*), and *Smert' pionerki* (*"Death of a Young Pioneer Girl"*) in *Red Virgin Soil* (vol. 10, 1932).

Bagritskii's second collection, *Pobediteli* (*"The Victors"*) is published by GIKhL (State Publishing House of Literature).

Bagritskii's third collection, *Posledniaia noch'* (*"The Last Night"*), is published by Federatsiia.

Commissioned by the V. I. Nemirovich-Danchenko Musical Theater, Bagritskii writes an opera libretto based on his work *The Lay of Opanas*. The composer Vissarion Shebalin was commissioned to write the music, and B. Mordvinov was to direct the production. The production was abandoned following Bagritskii's death, and the literary libretto came out posthumously in 1935.

Bagritskii's volume of *Collected Poems, 1918–1932*, is published by Federatsiia.

July. Bagritskii becomes a member of the editorial board of the leading literary review, *Literaturnaia gazeta* (*"Literary Gazette"*).

October 26. Meeting takes place at Maxim Gorky's house between Soviet writers and Stalin and other government and military leaders. Bagritskii, asthmatic and short of breath, reluctantly reads *Man from the Suburb*. At the meeting, Stalin famously calls writers "engineers of human souls" while discussing the role and place of writers in the Soviet state.

1933

By the time of his death, Bagritskii acquires a reputation of a poem doctor and literary mentor to younger poets and is inundated with visits and manuscripts by young and unknown authors. He writes many of them letters of recommendation and assists in getting their poetry published.

Bagritskii writes the radioplay *Taras Shevchenko* about the Ukrainian national poet.

A chapbook of Bagritskii's selected poems is published by Zhurgazob˝edinenie (Association of Journals and Newspapers).

Bagritskii prepares a volume of his collected poems, which was published posthumously in 1934 (*Odnotomnik*).

An illustrated edition of *The Lay of Opanas* is issued by Molodaia gvardiia.

End of year. Bagritskii starts his last work, the long poem *February*, which was published posthumously in 1936. He travels to Leningrad with poet Vera Inber. A recording of Bagritskii's voice is made by the Soviet Radio Committee. Bagritskii recites *Death of a Young Pioneer Girl* and "Chitatel´ v moem voobrazhenii" ("The Reader as I Imagine Him").

1934

February 16. Bagritskii dies of pneumonia at the Pirogov Street branch of the Kremlin Hospital and is given an official funeral. Isaac Babel is one of the last people to speak with Bagritskii at his deathbed. Soviet Minister of Defense K. Voroshilov orders a Red Army squadron to escort his coffin. Bagritskii's brain is deposited at the Institute of the Brain alongside Lenin's and Maiakovskii's.

August 1934. First Congress of Soviet Writers convenes in Moscow.

Notes

Notes to Introduction (pages 1 to 19)

1. Lidiia Ginzburg, "Vstrechi s Bagritskim," in *Den' poezii. Leningrad* (Leningrad: Sovetskii pisatel', 1966), 63.

2. Selected studies of Bagritskii's life and poetry include Vsevolod Azarov, "Put' k 'Pobediteliam' (K chetyrekhletiiu so dnia smerti Eduarda Bagritskogo)," *Zvezda* 2 (1938): 175–84; idem, "U istokov pesni," *Znamia* 2 (1947): 159–65; idem, "Bagritskii i sovremennost'" (po neopublikovannym materialam)," *Novyi mir* 7 (1948): 201–14; idem, "Iz vospominanii o Bagritskom (lichnost' i masterstvo)," *Russkaia literatura* 2 (1976): 151–58; Revol'd Banchukov, "Odessa—Kuntsevo—vechnost'," *Vestnik*, 21 December 1999, 46–50; Natal'ia Bank, "'My poimany oba, my oba—v setiakh! . . .': Slovo v pamiat' i zashchitu poeta Eduarda Bagritskogo," *Neva* 11 (1995): 202–6; S[ergei] Bondarin, "Eduard Bagritskii," *Novyi mir* 4 (1961): 130–43; I.M. Bespalov, "Poeziia Eduarda Bagritskogo," in *Stat'i o literature* (Moscow: Gosudarstvennoe izdatel'stvo khudozhestvennoi literatury, 1959), 151–88; Danilo Cavaion, "Ebracità come memoria oscura (Eduard Bagrickij)," in *Memoria e poesia: Storia e letteratura degli ebrei russi nell'età moderna* (Rome: Carucci editore, 1988), 159–289; A. Evgen'ev and B. Runin, "Eduard Bagritskii (K piatiletiiu so dnia smerti)," *Novyi mir* 2 (1939): 253–67; I. Grinberg, *Eduard Bagritskii* (Moscow/Leningrad: GIKhL, 1940); Luba Halat Kowalski, "Eduard Bagritsky: Life and Poetry" (Ph.D. diss., Bryn Mawr College, 1966); idem, "Eduard Bagritsky: A Biographical Sketch with Three Unpublished Letters," *Russian Literature Triquarterly* 8 (1974): 472–81; idem, "Eduard Bagritsky: A Selected Bibliography," *Russian Literature Triquarterly* 8 (1974): 540–42; Herbert Krempien, "Nachwort," in Eduard Bagritzki, *Vom Schwarzbrot und von der Treue der Frau* (Berlin: Verlag Volk und Welt, 1971), 161–72; Stanislav Kuniaev, "Legenda i vremia," *Dvadtsat' dva* 14 (September 1980): 136–55; M[ikhail] Kuzmin, "Eduard Bagritskii," *Literaturnaia gazeta*, 17 May 1933, 3; A[bram] Lezhnev, "E. Bagritskii," in *Literaturnye budni* (Moscow: Federatsiia, 1929), 127–61; E.P. Liubareva, "Tak li nado tolkovat' Bagritskogo?" *Voprosy literatury* 9 (1960): 67–70; idem, *Eduard Bagritskii* (Moscow: Sovetskii pisatel', 1964); idem, "Eduard Bagritskii," in Eduard Bagritskii, *Stikhotvoreniia i poemy* (Moscow: Sovetskii pisatel', 1964), 5–46; Arkadii L'vov, "Vernost' i otstupnichestvo Eduarda Bagritskogo," in *Utolenie pechal'iu: Opyt issledovaniia evreiskoi mental'nosti* (New York: Vremia i my, 1983), 73–129; D[mitrii] Mirskii, "Tvorcheskii put' Eduarda Bagritskogo," in *Eduard Bagritskii. Al'manakh*, ed. Vladimir Narbut (Moscow: Sovetskii pisatel', 1936), 5–23; Alice Stone Nakhimovsky, "Bagritsky and Mandelshtam," in idem, *Russian-Jewish Literature and Identity* (Baltimore: Johns Hopkins University Press, 1992), 20–28;

Lev Ozerov, "Mir otkrytyi nastezh´. . . ." in *Masterstvo i volshebstvo: Kniga statei* (Moscow: Sovetskii pisatel´, 1972), 207–17; A.I. Prokhorov, "E. Bagritskii v poslednii period tvorchestva (1928–1934 gg.)," *Uchenye zapiski Piatigorskogo pedagogicheskogo instituta* 11 (1956): 183–217; Wendy Rosslyn, "The Path to Paradise: Recurrent Images in the Poetry of Eduard Bagritsky," *Modern Language Review* 71.1 (January 1976): 97–105; idem, "Bagritskii's *Duma pro Opanasa:* The Poem and Its Context," *Canadian-American Slavic Studies* 11.3 (Fall 1977): 388–405; idem, "The Unifying Principle of Bagritsky's 'Yugo-Zapad'," *Essays in Poetics* 4.1 (1979): 20–34; idem, "Eduard Georg´evich Bagritskii," in *Reference Guide to Russian Literature*, ed. Neil Cornwell (London: Fitzroy Dearborn, 1988): 132–33; I. Rozhdestvenskaia, *Poeziia Ed. Bagritskogo* (Leningrad: Khudozhestvennaia literatura, 1967); Vera Sandomersky [Dunham], "Bagritsky, Edouard (1895–1934)," in *New Directions Anthology of Prose and Poetry*, ed. James Laughlin (Norfolk, Conn.: New Directions, 1941), 521–22; A. Selivanovskii, "Eduard Bagritskii," *Novyi mir* 6 (1933): 210–27; Mikhail Sinel´nikov, "Ptitselov: K stoletiiu Eduarda Bagritskogo," *Moskovskie novosti* (29 October–5 November 1995): 25; Andrei Siniavskii, "Eduard Bagritskii," in *Istoriia russkoi sovetskoi literatury*, vol. 1 (Moscow: Izdatel´stvo AN SSSR, 1958), 397–420; Marc Slonim, *Soviet Russian Literature: Writers and Problems, 1917–77*, 2nd ed. (New York: Oxford University Press, 1977), 132–33; M.L. Spivak, "Eduard Bagritskii: Memuary dlia sluzhebnogo pol´zovaniia, ili posmertnaia diagnostika genial´nosti," *Literaturnoe obozrenie* 5/6 (1996): 198–207; and 1 (1997): 34–60; Gleb Struve, *Russian Literature under Lenin and Stalin* (Norman: University of Oklahoma Press, 1971), 191–92; Boris Thomson, "Bagritskii's *February*," in *Lot's Wife and the Venus of Milo: Conflicting Attitudes to the Cultural Heritage in Modern Russia* (Cambridge: Cambridge University Press, 1978), 83–97; E. [D.] Troshchenko, "O poslednikh proizvedeniiakh Bagritskogo," in *Stat´i o poezii* (Moscow: Sovetskii pisatel´, 1962), 33–47; V.A. Tsybenko, *Eduard Bagritskii (Ocherk tvorchestva)*, ed. A.A. Volkov (Novosibirsk: Novosibirskii gosudarstvennyi pedagogicheskii institut, 1970); Mikhail Vainshtein, "'Otnyne ia drugoi . . .' (Illiuzii i prozrenie Eduarda Bagritskogo)," in *A list´ia snova zeleneiut . . . (Stranitsy evreiskoi russkoiazychnoi literatury)* (Jerusalem: Kakhol´-Lavan, 1988), 133–56; and I.L. Volgin, "Eduard Bagritskii," in Eduard Bagritskii, *Stikhotvoreniia i poemy* (Moscow: Pravda, 1987), 5–20.

A selection of thirty letters by Bagritskii sent to various addressees, including his wife, his mother, and his literary colleagues and disciples, has been published by E.A. Dinershtein; see E.A. Dinershtein, ed., "Pis´ma [Eduarda Bagritskogo]," in *Literaturnoe nasledstvo* 74 (Moscow: Nauka, 1965): 435–66.

Reminiscences of Bagritskii have appeared in two volumes. See Vladimir Narbut, ed., *Eduard Bagritskii. Al´manakh* (Moscow: Sovetskii pisatel´, 1936), where a useful chronology of Bagritskii's life is found on pp. 145–47; and L.G. Bagritskaia, comp. and ed., *Eduard Bagritskii: Vospominaniia sovremennikov* (Moscow: Sovetskii pisatel´, 1973); see also Sergei Bondarin, "Sud´by i stikhi," *Literaturnaia Rossiia*, 5 February 1965, 9; idem, "V gostiakh u vnukov," in *Parus plavanii i vospominanii* (Moscow: Sovetskaia Rossiia, 1971), 194–210; Ginzburg; Valentin Kataev, "Vstrecha," in *Sobranie sochinenii v deviati tomakh*, vol. 1 (Moscow: Khudozhestvennaia literatura, 1968), 419–427; and idem, *Almaznyi moi venets* (Moscow: Sovetskii pisatel´, 1979); in Kataev's book Bagritskii appears under the name *ptitselov* ("bird catcher"; "fowler"); Arkadii Shteinberg, *K verkhov´iam* (Moscow: Sovpadenie, 1997): 303–4.

A bibliography of Bagritskii's works published prior to 1977 is found in An[atolii] Tarasenkov, gen. ed., *Russkie sovetskie pisateli. Poety. Bibliograficheskii ukazatel´*, vol. 2 (Moscow: Kniga, 1978), 202–53.

The following English translations of Bagritskii's poetry have been published: Vera Sandomersky, trans., "Silence and Dreams"; "Smugglers"; "Verses about a Poet and Lady

Romanticism"; "Origin"; "Song of Ustine"; "Black Bread," in James Laughlin, ed., *New Directions Anthology of Prose and Poetry* (Norfolk, Conn.: New Directions, 1941), 526–34; Maurice Bowra, trans., "The Fowler"; "A piece of black bread and faithful wife . . . ," in Maurice Bowra, ed., *A Second Book of Russian Verse* (London: Macmillan, 1948), 141–43; "My Honeyed Languor," "Black Bread," "Spring, the Vet, and I," in Avram Yarmolinsky, ed., *A Treasury of Russian Verse* (New York: Macmillan, 1949), 229–33; "The Bird-Catcher" and "The Smugglers," in Vladimir Markov and Merril Sparks, eds., *Modern Russian Poetry* (London: MacGibbon and Kee, 1966), 672–81; Luba Halat Kowalski, trans., "Verses about a Nightingale and a Poet" and "Insomnia," *Russian Literature Triquarterly* 8 (1974): 65–68; "I am pleasantly exhausted . . ." and "The Water-melon," in Dimitri Obolensky, ed., *The Heritage of Russian Verse* (Bloomington: Indiana University Press, 1976), 401–5.

The papers of E.G. Bagritskii are deposited at the manuscript division of the Institute of World Literature (IMLI) and the Russian State Archive of Literature and the Arts (RGALI), both of Moscow. In IMLI, look under *Fond* 33, "Bagritskii Eduard Georgievich." In RGALI, look under *Fond* 1399, where the papers of Bagritskii's wife, Lidiia Gustavovna Bagritskaia, are also deposited. The papers of Bagritskii's son, the poet Vsevolod E. Bagritskii, are also deposited at RGALI, *Fond* 2805.

3. Monika Spivak recently published a highly provocative study of Bagritskii's legend, based on the materials of the Institute of the Brain (Moscow). Following the poet's death in 1934, his brain was deposited there alongside the brains of V.I. Lenin, Vladimir Maiakovskii, and other dignitaries of the early Soviet period in order to be studied. A group of Bagritskii's friends and relations were also interviewed with the purpose of compiling a detailed profile of his personality. These records have survived in an archive and were aptly analyzed in Spivak's two-part article; see Spivak, "Eduard Bagritskii."

4. For a concise study of Maiakovskii's career, see Victor Terras, *Vladimir Mayakovsky* (Boston: Twayne, 1983).

5. See, for instance, A.I. Prokhorov's comments: "A true hymn to the arriving socialist life, to the triumphant youth is Bagritskii's very best long poem, *Death of a Young Pioneer Girl*"; Prokhorov, 211; see also Prokhorov, 211–17.

6. See, for instance, a telling description of *The Lay of Opanas* in a Soviet encyclopedia of 1947: S.I. Vavilov et al., eds. *Bol'shaia sovetskaia entsiklopediia. Soiuz sovetskikh sotsialisticheskikh respublik* (Moscow: OGIZ SSSR, 1947), 1488.

7. In 1933, Mikhail Kuzmin wrote a very favorable essay about Bagritskii's poetry; see Kuzmin. Semen Lipkin reminisced about Kuzmin's visiting Bagritskii in Kuntsevo and admiring his poetry; see Semen Lipkin, *Kvadriga* (Moscow: Knizhnyi sad/Agraf, 1997), 267.

8. For a useful study of modernism in Russia at the time of the Revolution, see Victor Erlich, *Modernism and Revolution: Russian Literature in Transition* (Cambridge: Harvard University Press, 1994).

9. Eduard Bagritskii, *Stikhotvoreniia i poemy*, ed. E.P. Liubareva and S.A. Kovalenko (Moscow: Sovetskii pisatel', 1964), 93. Unless specified, all quotations from Bagritskii's works are from this Biblioteka poeta edition, hereafter cited as "Bagritskii."

10. See Edward J. Brown, *Mayakovsky: A Poet in the Revolution* (Princeton: Princeton University Press, 1973), 370.

11. "Eduard Bagritskii," *Literaturnaia gazeta*, 18 February 1934, 1.

12. "Pafos i mechta revoliutsii," *Literaturnaia gazeta*, 18 February 1934, 1.

13. "Glubokii udar sovetskoi poezii," *Literaturnaia gazeta*, 18 February 1934, 2.

14. Viktor Shklovskii, "O serdtse," *Literaturnaia gazeta*, 18 February 1934, 2. Shklovskii mistakenly reports Bagritskii's age as thirty-seven, instead of thirty-nine.

15. Kornelii Zelinskii, "O druge," *Literaturnaia gazeta*, 18 February 1934, 2; see also idem, "Odna vstrecha u M. Gor′kogo (Zapis′ iz dnevnika)," *Voprosy literatury* 5 (1991): 144–70.

16. See the title of Vsevolod Azarov's introduction, "Pevets molodosti" ("Singer of Youth"), in Eduard Bagritskii, *Ptitselov. Stikhi i poemy* (Moscow: Gosudarstvennoe izdatel′stvo detskoi literatury, 1960), 3. Another case in point is I. Rakhtanov's introduction presenting a children's version of Bagritskii's Soviet legend; see Eduard Bagritskii, *Zvezda mordvina* (Moscow: Detskaia literatura, 1972), 3–4.

17. See, for instance, Benjamin Pinkus, *The Jews of the Soviet Union: The History of a National Minority* (Cambridge: Cambridge University Press, 1988), 145–59.

18. Daniil Danin, who edited a 1948 volume of Bagritskii's works, was persecuted during the anti-Semitic (anti-"cosmopolitan") campaign of 1949–53; see Pinkus, 158.

19. "Za ideinuiu chistotu sovetskoi poezii," *Literaturnaia gazeta*, 30 July 1949, 2.

20. Ibid.

21. Ibid. Just two years earlier, in an encyclopedic article devoted to literature and the arts in the Soviet Union, Bagritskii's *The Lay of Opanas* was listed among "the finest achievements of Soviet poetry"; see S.I. Vavilov et al., eds., 1488.

22. Ibid.

23. The students of Bagritskii who were criticized in the two newspaper articles were S. Ivantsova, for an article about Bagritskii; Vsevolod Azarov, for a 1938 essay and an introduction to a volume of Bagritskii's poems published in Odessa in 1949; and Anatolii Tarasenkov, for an introduction to a 1948 collection of Pervomais′kyi's poems in Russian.

24. See Anatolii Tarasenkov, "O natsional′nykh traditsiiakh i burzhuaznom kosmopolitizme," *Znamia* 1 (1950): 152–64. Note that Tarasenkov's anti-Semitic zeal might have had something to do with his trying to rehabilitate himself in the eyes of the Soviet ideological leadership; see S.[A.] Tregub, "Vozvyshaiushchii primer" in *Zhivoi s zhivymi. Sbornik statei* (Moscow: Sovetskii pisatel′, 1949), 171–80.

25. Tregub, 171–80.

26. Ibid., 178.

27. Ibid., 176.

28. See Eduard Bagritskii, *Stikhi i poemy*, ed. Vs. Azarov (Moscow: Gosudarstvennoe izdatel′stvo khudozhestvennoi literatury, 1956). See an upbeat review of the volume in a central newspaper: Bor[is] Bobovich, "Odnotomnik Eduarda Bagritskogo," *Komsomol′skaia pravda*, 21 October 1956, 3; see also a review where a seven-year gap in the publication of Bagritskii's works is acknowledged: V. Afanas′ev, "Kommentarii k kommentariiam," *Literaturnaia gazeta*, 8 December 1956, 3.

29. See Prokhorov's long essay attempting a balanced view of Bagritskii's development into "a poet of emerging socialism." See also E. P. Liubareva's article in which she defends Bagritskii against crude and tendentious sociological interpretations: Liubareva, "Tak li nado tolkovat′ Bagritskogo?"

30. See P.S. Vykhodtsev, ed., *Istoriia russkoi sovetskoi literatury*, 2nd ed. (Moscow: Vysshaia shkola, 1974), 134.

31. Bagritskii, 68.

32. Roman Jakobson, "On a Generation that Squandered Its Poets," in *Language in Literature*, ed. Krystyna Pomorska and Stephen Rudy (Cambridge: Belknap Press of Harvard University Press, 1987), 274. Jakobson's essay originally appeared in Russian in Berlin as "O pokolenii, rastrativshem svoikh poetov" (1931).

33. Vera Sandomersky [Dunham], "A Note on Soviet Poetry," in Laughlin, ed., 519.

34. Leonid Znakomy and Dan Levin, "A Decade of Soviet Poetry," in Laughlin, ed., 624.

35. Alexander Kaun, *Soviet Poets and Poetry* (Berkeley: University of California Press, 1943; reprint, Freeport, N.Y.: Books for Libraries, 1968).
36. Struve, 191.
37. Slonim, *Soviet Russian Literature*.
38. Renato Poggioli, *The Poets of Russia, 1890–1930* (Cambridge: Harvard University Press, 1960), 320.
39. Ibid., 321.
40. The quote comes from Pasternak's long autobiographical essay *Liudi i polozheniia* (*"People and Positions"*); see Boris Pasternak, *Vozdushnye puti* (Moscow: Sovetskii pisatel´, 1982), 460.
41. Bagritskii, 349. The poet and essayist Il´ia Kutik, who spent a number of years as a member of Arsenii Tarkovskii's household, reports that "Verses about a Poet and Lady Romanticism" was one of Tarkovskii's favorite poems of all times and that Tarkovskii often quoted the lines about Gumilev. Il´ia Kutik, e-mail communication to Maxim D. Shrayer, 13 December 1999, Evanston, Ill., to Boston.
42. At the First Congress of Soviet Writers, the poet Aleksei Surkov spoke of Bagritskii as the herald (*glashatai*) of revolutionary humanism and drew on the example of "TBC"; see Prokhorov, 201.
43. Vladimir Maiakovskii, *Polnoe sobranie sochinenii*, vol. 10 (Moscow: Gosudarstvennoe izdatel´stvo khudozhestvennoi literatury, 1958), 18.
44. Although Natal´ia Bank also notes that the source of these lines is not the poet but rather Dzerzhinskii, she refers to Bagritskii's formulation as "one of the most cruel and memorable" ones in Soviet literature; additionally, she identifies direct parallels between Bagritskii's lines and two other famous formulations: Maxim Gorky's article "If the Enemy Does Not Surrender, He Should Be Destroyed" (1930) and Maiakovskii's ". . . i tot, kto segodnia poet ne s nami, / tot—protiv nas" (". . . and the one who does not sing with us today— / sings against us") from the poem "Mr. 'People's Artist'" ("Godpodin 'Narodnyi artist'"; 1927); see Bank, 203; and Maiakovskii, vol. 8, 122.
45. Bagritskii, 126.
46. Victor Terras, *A History of Russian Literature* (New Haven: Yale University Press, 1991), 553.
47. M.L. Spivak, "Eduard Bagritskii," 5/6 (1996): 198–207; 1 (1997): 34–60.
48. Sinel´nikov. See also Bank.
49. Tomas Venclova, "Chuvstvo perspektivy. Razgovor Tomasa Ventslovy s Iosifom Brodskim," *Strana i mir* 3.45 (1988): 150.
50. On Russian literary constructivism, see Edward Możejko, "Russian Literary Constructivism: Towards a Theory of Poetic Language," in *Canadian Contributions to the VIII International Congress of Slavists*, ed. Z. Folejewski et al. (Ottawa: Canadian Association of Slavists, 1978), 61–70; and Rainer Grübel, "Russkii literaturnyi konstruktivizm," *Russian Literature* 17 (1985): 9–20.
51. Iaroslav Smeliakov, *Postoianstvo* (Moscow: Sovetskii pisatel´, 1991), 5.
52. Boris Kornilov, *Stikhotvoreniia i poemy* (Leningrad: Sovetskii pisatel´, 1960), 10–11.
53. I am grateful to Evgenii Vitkovskii (Moscow)—poet, translator, editor, and scholar—for sharing with me his expertise and the contents of his archive. In 1978, after having meticulously studied Tarlovskii's papers at RGALI, Vitkovskii put together and published a samizdat two-volume edition of Tarlovskii's oeuvres; see Mark Tarlovskii, *Sobranie stikhotvorenii*, 2 vols., ed. by Evgenii Vitkovskii (samizdat edition, Moscow: 1978), Archive of Evgenii Vitkovskii; in this edition, the text of *Veselyi strannik* occupies pp. 197–263. See also Evgenii Vitkovskii, "Koshelek na mostovoi," manuscript, 3 pp.

54. Quoted in Sinel´nikov and confirmed during a telephone interview with Aleksandr Mezhirov, 12 May 1998, Boston to Portland, Oreg.

55. Shteinberg, 304.

56. Viktor Bokov, tape-recorded interview with Maxim D. Shrayer, 8 January 1998, Peredelkino, outside Moscow.

57. Bagritskii, 73. The Russian *v´iun* refers to the freshwater fish known in English as "loach." It is derived from the verb *vit´sia*, meaning "to wind," "to twist." The English translation does not do justice to Bagritskii's complex metaphor.

58. Viktor Krivulin, tape-recorded interview with Maxim D. Shrayer, 14 January 2000, St. Petersburg.

59. A number of Bagritskii's poems belonged to a standard repertoire of that very Soviet and presently disappearing genre of poetic declamation. Soviet schoolchildren routinely learned several of Bagritskii's poems by heart and recited them at various official events. However, even the inclusion of those "official" poems was problematic. The poet Viktor Krivulin recalls reciting one of Bagritskii's poems, "Razgovor s komsomol´tsem N. Dement´evym" ("Conversation with Komsomol Member N. Dement´ev," 1927), which Krivulin deems "rather silly" (*dovol´no-taki duratskoe*), at the height of the "Pasternak affair" (1958), and being dragged off the stage because the poem's refrain lists the names of the poets "Tikhonov, Sel´vinskii, Pasternak" as the best poets of his generation; see Viktor Krivulin, *Okhota na mamonta* (St. Petersburg: Russko-Baltiiskii informatsionnyi tsentr, 1998), 29. Further commenting on this scene, Krivulin said this: "This was . . . a form of 'protest ideology.' . . . This was at the time when Pasternak was being ostracized, of his Nobel Prize, and I read [Bagritskii's poem] precisely because the name of Pasternak sounded in it . . ."; tape-recorded interview with Maxim D. Shrayer, 14 January 2000, St. Petersburg. The great complexity of the reception of Bagritskii's poetry is also illustrated by a poem by Ian Satunovskii, "Pomniu LTsK—literaturnyi tsentr konstruktivistov . . ." ("I remember LTsK—the literary center of constructivists . . ."), written in 1966 but not published in Russia (as also the majority of Satunovskii's writings) until the end of the Soviet period; see Ian Satunovskii, *Khochu li ia posmertnoi slavy* (Moscow: Biblioteka al´manakha "Vesy," 1992), 61.

60. Il´ia Kutik, e-mail communications to Maxim D. Shrayer, 6 December 1999 and 13 December 1999, Evanston, Ill., to Boston. Kutik wrote to me that Joseph Brodsky once described Aleksei Parshchikov's poetry the following way: "He wants to outdo Bagritskii with metaphors." Kutik has stated that, in his own development, Bagritskii's *The Lay of Opanas* and Bagritskii's renditions of Robert Burns's poetry have been the most important of all of Bagritskii's works. Kutik also reported that Bagritskii's "From black bread and faithful wife . . ." and "Spring" have been extremely popular among the members of his literary group (that is, the metametaphorists/metarealists).

61. Semen Lipkin, *Kvadriga* (Moscow: Knizhnyi sad/Agraf, 1997), 268. Lev Losev strikes a similar note, charging Bagritskii with having "depicted suffering, violence, cruelty . . . without compassion, without horror or wrath"; see Losev's introduction to Evgenii Shvarts's memoirs: "Memuary E. L. Shvartsa," in Evgenii Shvarts, *Memuary*, ed. Lev Losev (Paris: La presse libre, 1982), 12–13.

62. Semen Lipkin and Inna Lisnianskaia, tape-recorded interview with Maxim D. Shrayer, 11 January 2000, Peredelkino, outside Moscow.

63. There are suggestions that Bagritskii might have associated himself with General Denikin's Voluntary Army and entered Odessa on a white horse in 1919. The Russian-Jewish émigré writer Arkadii L´vov reports an account of this by Lev Slavin, an Odessan writer and friend of Bagritskii's youth; see L´vov, "Vernost´ i otstupnichestvo Eduarda

Bagritskogo," 113. L'vov confirmed this account to me during a telephone interview, 10 March 1998, Boston to Fort Lee, N.J. I have great reservations concerning this suggestion. It is not unlikely that Slavin meant 1918, not 1919, and confused General Denikin's "White" Army with the remains of General Baratov's expedition.

64. Bagritskii, 7. Here is Prokhorov's comment on Bagritskii's poem "Origin": "Bagritskii drew a truthful picture of his origins, depicting the suffocating world of Jewish pre-revolutionary petite bourgeoisie from the vantage point of the builders of socialism" (202; see also Prokhorov, 205). Lev Slavin's self-hating remarks about Bagritskii's Jewish origins are found in Eduard Bagritskii, *Izbrannoe* (Moscow: Detskaia literatura, 1970), 7.

65. See Nakhimovsky, 20–28.

66. For recent discussions of the place of Judaism and Jewishness in Mandelstam's career, see chapters 4 "(Judaic Chaos")" and 6 ("Jewish Creation") of Clare Cavanagh's *Osip Mandelstam and the Modernist Creation of Tradition* (Princeton: Princeton University Press, 1995); and Mikhail Epstein's essay "Judaic Spiritual Traditions in the Poetry of Pasternak and Mandelstam," trans. from the Russian by Ruth Rischin, *Symposium* 52.4 (Winter 1999): 205–31. Seminal remarks on Mandelstam's Jewishness are also found in Gregory Freidin's *A Coat of Many Colors: Osip Mandelstam and His Mythologies of Self-Representation* (Berkeley: University of California Press, 1987); and in Alice Stone Nakhimovsky's chapter "Bagritsky and Mandelshtam," in Nakhimovsky, 20–28.

67. Cavanagh, 201.

68. The quote is from Tsvetaeva's *Poema kontsa* (*"Poem of the End,"* 1924).

69. Simon [Shimon] Markish, "Eshche raz o nenavisti k samomu sebe," *Dvadtsat' dva* 16 (December 1980): 184–85.

70. For a classic study of the ideological and historical roots of ethnic relations in the Soviet Union, see Richard Pipes, *The Formation of the Soviet Union: Communism and Nationalism, 1917–1923*, rev. ed. (Cambridge: Harvard University Press, 1997).

Notes to Chapter 1 (pages 21 to 43)

1. See Eduard Bagritskii, "Fevral'. Poema. Varianty. Chernovoi avtograf," IMLI im. A.M. Gor'kogo, Otdel rukopisei, f. 33, op. 1, ed. khr. 423; hereafter *"February* IMLI." A general description of the manuscript of *February* by its two editors, V. Trenin and N. Khardzhiev, is found in Vladimir Narbut, ed., *Eduard Bagritskii. Al'manakh* (Moscow: Sovetskii pisatel', 1936), 143–44.

2. The *dol'nik* of *February* has been described and compared to *dol'niki* of Akhmatova and Maiakovskii in A.N. Kolmogorov and A.V. Prokhorov, "O dol'nike sovremennoi russkoi poezii," *Voprosy iazykoznaniia* 1 (1964): 75–94.

3. See Robert Paul Browder and Alexander F. Kerensky, eds., *The Russian Provisional Government, 1917*, vol. 1 (Stanford: Stanford University Press, 1961), 218.

Notes to Chapter 2 (pages 45 to 94)

1. Note that Bagritskii wrote and published three different texts under the title *Fevral'*: a 1923 short poem ("Temnoiu volei sud'biny . . ."); a 1926 short poem ("Gudela zemlia ot moroza i v'iug . . ."); and the 1934 long poem here under principal consideration.

2. Isaak Babel to Lidiia Bagritskaia, 21 September 1935, postcard in Isaak Babel´, *Sochineniia*, vol. 1, ed. A.N. Pirozhkova (Moscow: Khudozhestvennaia literatura, 1991), 347; the original is in RGALI, *Fond* 1399, opis´ 2, ed. khr. 111.

3. Babel´, *Sochineniia*, vol. 2, 263. Babel's sketch was first published in Vladimir Narbut, ed., *Eduard Bagritskii*. *Al´manakh* (Moscow: Sovetskii pisatel´, 1936), 160–62; and appears in Babel´, *Sochineniia*, in the same form as in Narbut; compare also L.G. Bagritskaia, comp. and ed., *Eduard Bagritskii: Vospominaniia sovremennikov* (Moscow: Sovetskii pisatel´, 1973), 400–1, where the text is several lines longer and the editorial/censorial corruption has been undone.

4. See *February* IMLI.

5. See Eduard Bagritskii, *Sobranie sochinenii v dvukh tomakh*, vol. 1, ed. I. Utkin (Moscow: Goslitizdat, 1938–39). (Volume 2 never appeared.)

6. See RGALI, *Fond* 1399, opis´ 1, ed. khr. 17. The folder contains the bound galley proofs of volume 2 with notes and corrections by L.G. Bagritskaia, I. Utkin, V. Narbut, and K. Zelinskii as well as censors' stamps and signatures. For a very useful study of Soviet censorship, see Herman Ermolaev, *Censorhip in Soviet Literature, 1917–1991* (Lanham, Md.: Rowman & Littlefield, 1997).

7. Materials pertaining to L.G. Bagritskaia's arrest, penal servitude in the Gulag, and subsequent rehabilitation are found in RGALI, *Fond* 1399, op. 2, ed. khr. 192; see, in particular, L.G. Bagritskaia's letter to I.V. Stalin of 17 May 1939 and her letter to K.E. Voroshilov of 29 April 1954; see also Luba Halat Kowalski, "Eduard Bagritskii: A Selected Bibliography," *Russian Literature Triquarterly* 8 (1974): 477; and Sergei Bondarin, "Sud´by i stikhi," *Literaturnaia Rossiia*, 5 February 1965. Lidiia Gustavovna Bagritskaia (née Suok) had two sisters who were married to writers, Ol´ga to Iurii Olesha, Serafima first to Vladimir Narbut, then to Viktor Shklovskii. Elena Bonner, who was close to Bagritskii's son, Vsevolod, in the 1930s, tells about the three Suok sisters and the arrest of Bagritskii's wife in her memoir, *Dochki-materi* (Moscow: Progress/Litera, 1994), 196, 220–21, 243, 255, 260–63, and passim.

8. In the Bagritskii funeral issue of *Literaturnaia gazeta*—the leading cultural review where Bagritskii had been a member of the editorial board in his latter years—Nikolai Aseev, Osip Brik, and Semen Kirsanov printed a call to put together and publish what would later become *Eduard Bagritskii*. *Al´manakh* (1936); see "Almanakh pamiati Bagritskogo," *Literaturnaia gazeta*, 18 February 1934, 2. Bagritskii died some six months prior to the First Congress of Soviet Writers, and the issue of *Literaturnaia gazeta* dedicated to his funeral accurately reflects his prominent position in early Soviet literature on the eve of its final institutionalization.

9. See Eduard Bagritskii, *Stikhotvoreniia*, ed. I. Grinberg (Leningrad: Sovetskii pisatel´, 1940); *Izbrannoe*, ed. D. Danin (Moscow: Sovetskii pisatel´, 1948); *Stikhotvoreniia i poemy*, ed. E.P. Liubareva and S.A. Kovalenko (Moscow: Sovetskii pisatel´, 1964) (hereafter cited as "Bagritskii"); *Stikhotvoreniia i poemy* (Minsk: Nauka i tekhnika, 1983); *Stikhotvoreniia i poemy*, ed. S.A. Kovalenko (Moscow: Moskovskii rabochii, 1984); and *Stikhotvoreniia i poemy*, ed. I.L. Volgin (Moscow: Pravda, 1987).

Examples of editions where *February* was not included follow below: *Izbrannoe* (Minsk: Gosudarstvennoe izdatel´stvo pri SNK BSSR, 1941); *Poemy i stikhi* (Moscow: Pravda, 1947); *Stikhi i poemy*, ed. Vs. Azarov (Moscow: Gosudarstvennoe izdatel´stvo khudozhestvennoi literatury, 1956); *Stikhotvoreniia i poemy* (Moscow: Gosudarstvennoe izdatel´stvo khudozhestvennoi literatury, 1958); *Stikhi i poemy*, ed. Vs. Azarov (Ufa: Bashkirskoe knizhnoe izdatel´stvo, 1972); *Izbrannoe*, ed. N. Kriukov (Petrozavodsk: Kareliia, 1975); and *Stikhi i poemy* (Moscow: Khudozhestvennaia literatura, 1976). Note also a volume of Bagritskii's poems in Yiddish translation where *February* was not included: *Ois-geveilte lider un poemes*, trans. Ia. A. Zeldin (Moscow: Melukhe-farlag der emes, 1940).

10. See S.[A.] Tregub, *Zhivoi s zhivymi*. *Sbornik statei* (Moscow: Sovetskii pisatel', 1949), 179; and Anatolii Tarasenkov, "O natsional'nykh traditskiiakh i burzhuaznom kosmopolitizme," *Znamia* 1 (1950).

11. Bagritskii crossed out these lines in the manuscript: "I shall tell her about the most important thing . . . / About a boy, who grew up on Bazarnaia Street"; see *February* IMLI, 15.

12. Anatolii Naiman, *Rasskazy o Anne Akhmatovoi* (Moscow: Khudozhestvennaia literatura, 1989); the memoirs were originally published in *Novyi mir* 1–3 (1989); the episode is also mentioned in Naiman's essay "Paladin poezii," *Russkaia mysl'* (30 April–6 May 1988): 14.

13. Dmitrii Bobyshev, e-mail communication to Maxim D. Shrayer, 21 November 1999, Champaign, Ill., to Boston. See also the published text of my conversation with Bobyshev about Jewish themes in Russian poetry; Maksim Shraer [Maxim D. Shrayer], "Poeziia i evreistvo," *Nash Skopus* 18 (2000): 7–12.

14. Discussions of *February* are few. In Russian, see Pavel Antokol'skii, *Puti poetov* (Moscow: Sovetskii pisatel', 1965), 287–89, cf. Bagritskaia 7–9; Vsevolod Azarov, "Put' k 'Pobediteliam' (K chetyrekhletiiu so dnia smerti Eduarda Bagritskogo)," *Zvezda* 2 (1938): 178–79; I. Grinberg, *Eduard Bagritskii* (Moscow/Leningrad: GIKhL, 1940): 155–59; Stanislav Kuniaev, "Legenda i vremia," *Dvadtsat' dva* 14 (September 1980); E.P. Liubareva, *Eduard Bagritskii* (Moscow: Sovetskii pisatel', 1964), 172–94; Arkadii L'vov, "Vernost' i otstupnichestvo Eduarda Bagritskogo," in *Utolenie pechal'iu: Opyt issledovaniia evreiskoi mental'nosti* (New York: Vremia i my, 1983), 81–83, 122–29; D[mitrii] Mirskii, "Tvorcheskii put' Eduarda Bagritskogo," in Narbut, 19–20; I. Rozhdestvenskaia, *Poeziia Ed. Bagritskogo* (Leningrad: Khudozhestvennaia literatura, 1967), 301–3; Tarasenkov, "O natsional'nykh traditsiiakh i burzhuazhom kosmopolitizme," 152–64; and Mikhail Vainshtein, "'Otnyne ia drugoi . . .' (Illiuzii i prozrenie Eduarda Bagritskogo)," in *A list'ia snova zeleneiut . . . (Stranitsy evreiskoi russkoiazychnoi literatury)* (Jerusalem: Kakhol'-Lavan, 1988), 154–56. In English, see Luba Halat Kowalski, "Eduard Bagritskii: Life and Poetry" (Ph.D. diss., Bryn Mawr College, 1966), 215–19; and Alice Stone Nakhimovsky, "Bagritsky and Mandelshtam," in idem, *Russian-Jewish Literature and Identity* (Baltimore: Johns Hopkins University Press, 1992), 23–24. The only in-depth analysis of the poem by a Western critic is a section in Danilo Cavaion's book; see Danilo Cavaion, "Ebracità come memoria oscura (Eduard Bagrickij)," in *Memoria e poesia: Storia e letteratura degli ebrei russi nell'età moderna* (Rome: Carucci editore, 1988), 251–66; see also Boris Thomson's esoteric critique of the poem in his *Lot's Wife and the Venus of Milo: Conflicting Attitudes to the Cultural Heritage in Modern Russia* (Cambridge: Cambridge University Press, 1978), 83–97.

15. A.V. Blium's recent study investigates the ways the Soviet censorial machine exercised control over the treatment of the Jewish question in literature; see A.V. Blium, *Evreiskii vopris pod sovetskoi tsenzuroi, 1917–1991* (St. Petersburg: Peterburgskii evreiskii universitet, 1996).

16. Cavaion, 251.

17. Mirskii, "Tvorcheskii put' Eduarda Bagritskogo," 18–20.

18. Andrei Siniavskii, "Eduard Bagritskii," in *Istoriia russkoi sovetskoi literatury*, vol. 1 (Moscow: Izdatel'stvo AN SSSR, 1958), 406, 410–11, 419.

19. See Grinberg, 157–59; and Antokol'skii, 288–89. In his introduction to a 1964 edition of Bagritskii's poetry that did not include *February*, Grinberg speaks of *February* as a raw, unfinished work that should not have been published; see Bagritskii, *Stikhi i poemy*, ed.

P. Viacheslavov (Moscow: Khudozhestvennaia literatura, 1964), 31. Prokhorov was adamant about the publication of *February*, also treating it as unfinished drafts that should never have been published; see A.I. Prokhorov, "E. Bagritskii v poslednii period tvorchestva (1928–1934 gg.)," *Uchenye zapiski Piatigorskogo pedagogicheskogo instituta* 11 (1956): 217.

20. Liubareva, *Eduard Bagritskii*, 194.

21. Rozhdestvenskaia, 301–2.

22. Tarasenkov, "O natsional'nykh traditsiiakh i burzhuaznom kosmopolitizme." Echoes of Tarasenkov's essay can be heard in the conclusion to Prokhorov's article: "In places bourgeois nationalism can be heard in the poem" (217). Kuniaev's speech about Bagritskii was part of a panel discussion that took place on December 21, 1977, at the Central House of Writers in Moscow. Sections of Kuniaev's speech circulated in samizdat press in the Soviet Union and appeared in the West, first in *Grani*; see "Klassika i my," *Grani* 114 (1979): 126–55; then in *Poiski*; see "Klassika i my," *Poiski* 2 (1980): 65–88. The speech was reprinted in the journal *Moskva* 1 (1990): 183–200; 2 (1990): 169–80; and 3 (1990): 186–96. A longer essay based on Kuniaev's speech was also published in the Israeli journal *Dvadtsat' dva*; see Kuniaev, "Legenda i vremia."

23. Igor' Shafarevich, "Rusofobiia," *Nash sovremennik* 11 (1989): 171; see also Shafarevich, "O rusofobii," *Vremia i my* 104 (1989): 161–62. *Rusofobiia* was widely circulated in Soviet samizdat in the mid-1980s.

24. See Stanislav Kuniaev, "Nash pervyi bunt" (ch. 3 of his *Poeziia. Sud'ba. Rossiia*), *Nash sovremennik* 3 (1999): 175–91; and idem, "Russko-evreiskoe Borodino" (ch. 4 of his *Poeziia. Sud'ba. Rossiia*), *Nash sovremennik* 4 (1999): 169–97. I take pleasure in recording my debt to scholars and critics who have previously written about Russian-Jewish identity and its representation in Soviet literature and culture. It would take both a long bibliography and a separate publishing forum to acknowledge all the contributions to the study of Russian-Jewish culture and identity, and I regret that I am unable to do it here: Vera Alexandrova, "Jews in Soviet Literature," in *Russian Jewry, 1917–1967*, ed. Gregor Aronson et al. (New York: Thomas Yoseloff, 1969), 300–327; Carol J. Avins, "Jewish Ritual and Soviet Context in Two Stories by Isaac Babel," in *American Contributions to the Twelfth Congress of Slavists*, ed. Robert A. Maguire and Alan Timberlake (Bloomington, Ind.: Slavica, 1998), 11–20; Jakub Blum, "Soviet Russian Literature," in *The Image of the Jew in Soviet Literature: The Post-Stalin Period* (New York: Ktav Publishing House, 1984), 3–97; Cavaion; Clare Cavanagh, ch. 4 ("Judaic Chaos") and ch. 6 ("Jewish Creation") of *Osip Mandelstam and the Modernist Creation of Tradition* (Princeton: Princeton University Press, 1995); Shmuel Ettinger, "The Position of Jews in Soviet Culture: A Historical Survey," in *Jews in Soviet Culture*, ed. Jack Miller (New Brunswick, N.J.: Transaction, 1984), 1–21; Maurice Friedberg, "Jewish Contributions to Soviet Literature," in *The Jews in Soviet Russia since 1917*, 3rd ed., ed. Lionel Kochan (Oxford: Oxford University Press, 1978), 217–25; idem, "Jewish Themes in Soviet Russian Literature," in Kochan, ed., 197–216; idem, "The Jewish Search in Russian Literature," *Prooftexts: A Journal of Jewish Literary History* 4.1 (January 1984): 93–105; Zvi Gitelman, "The Evolution of Jewish Culture and Identity in the Soviet Union," in *Jewish Culture and Identity in the Soviet Union*, ed. Yaacov Ro'i and Avi Beker (New York: New York University Press, 1991), 3–24; I. Kisin, "Razmyshleniia o russkom evreistve i ego literature," *Evreiskii mir* 2 (1944): 164–72; A. Kobrinskii, "K voprosu o kriteriiakh poniatiia 'russko-evreiskaia literatura,'" *Vestnik evreiskogo universiteta v Moskve* 5 (1994): 100–114; Nora Levin, *The Jews in the Soviet Union since 1917: Paradox of Survival*, 2 vols. (New York: New York University Press, 1988); L'vov, *Utolenie pechal'iu*; Simon [Shimon] Markish, "Eshche raz o nenavisti k samomu sebe," *Dvadtsat' dva* 16 (December 1980): 177–91; idem, "The Example of

Isaak Babel," in *What Is Jewish Literature?*, ed. Hana Wirth-Nesher (Philadelphia: Jewish Publication Society, 1994), 199–215; Nakhimovsky; Ruth Rischin, "The Most Historical of People: Yushkevich, Kuprin and the Dubnovian Era," in *The Short Story in Russia, 1900–1917*, ed. Nicholas Luker (Nottingham, Eng.: Astra, 1991), 23–52; Ephraim Sicher, "The Jewishness of Babel'" in Jack Miller, ed., *Jews in Soviet Culture* (New Brunswick, N.J.: Transaction, 1984), 167–82; idem, *Jews in Russian Literature after the October Revolution: Writers and Artists between Hope and Apostasy* (Cambridge: Cambridge University Press, 1995); Mark Slonim, "Pisateli-evrei v sovetskoi literature," *Evreiskii mir* 2 (1944): 146–64; Josephine Woll, "Russians and 'Russophobes': Antisemitism on the Russian Literary Scene," *Soviet Jewish Affairs* 19.3 (1989): 3–21; Leon I. Yudkin, "In the Eye of the Revolution: Russia," in *Jewish Writing and Identity in the Twentieth Century* (New York: St. Martin's, 1982), 59–77; Vladimir Zhabotinskii, "O 'evreiakh i russkoi literature,'" in Vladimir Zhabotinskii, *Izbrannoe* (Jerusalem: Biblioteka-Aliia, 1978), 61–68; and Steven J. Zipperstein, *The Jews of Odessa: A Cultural History, 1794–1881* (Stanford: Stanford University Press, 1985).

26. Useful observations about Babel's childhood stories are found in Carol A. Luplow, "Isaak Babel' and the Jewish Tradition: The Childhood Stories," *Russian Literature* 15 (1984): 255–78.

27. Bagritskii intended *February* to be the first in a second trilogy of long poems, following an earlier trilogy, completed by and published in 1932 under the title *Posledniaia noch'* ("*The Last Night*") and comprising *Chelovek iz predmest'ia* ("*The Man from the Suburbs*"), *Posledniaia noch'* ("*Last Night*"), and *Smert' pionerki* ("*Death of a Young Pioneer Girl*"); see Babel', *Sochineniia*, vol. 2, 561; Narbut, 143; Rozhdestvenskaia, 301; and Bagritskii, 529.

28. For historical background on Odessa in the first decade of the twentieth century, see Patricia Herlihy, *A History of Odessa* (Cambridge: Harvard University Press, 1986); Alexander Orbach, *New Voices of Russian Jewry: A Study of the Russian-Jewish Press of Odessa in the Era of Great Reforms, 1860–1871* (Leiden: Brill, 1980); and Zipperstein.

29. On the South-Western school, see V[iktor] Shklovskii, "Iugo-zapad," *Literaturnaia gazeta*, 5 January 1933, 3.

30. Isaac Babel, *Collected Stories*, trans. David McDuff (Harmondsworth, Eng.: Penguin, 1994), 32.

31. See "Birds," in *The Herder Dictionary of Symbols* (Wilmette, Ill.: Chiron, 1994), 22–23.

32. Babel, *Collected Stories*, 27.

33. In the time described in Babel's story, pigeon breeding represented an activity that lay outside the sphere of traditional Jewish occupations, be they entrepreneurial or intellectual. In terms of Judaic law, a skepticism toward the activity of pigeon breeding may have a foundation in Leviticus 19:19: "You shall not let your cattle mate with a different kind; you shall not sow your field with two kinds of seed; you shall not put on cloth from mixture of two kinds of material"; see *Tannakh: The Holy Scriptures* (Philadelphia: Jewish Publication Society, 1988), 186. The issue of whether or not pigeon breeding is proscribed in traditional Jewish thought stems from the commentary on this broad prohibition in *The Babylonian Talmud, Seder Zera'im, Kil'ayim*, ch. 8: "It is prohibited to use a behemah with a behemah [of another species], or a hayyah with a hayyah [of another species], or a behemah with a hayyah, or a hayyah with a behemah, or an unclean beast with an unclean beast [of another species], or a clean beast with a clean beast [of another species], or an unclean beast with a clean beast, or a clean best with an unclean beast" (*The Babylonian Talmud: Seder Zera'im*, trans. and ed. Rabbi I. Epstein [London: Soncino, 1948]).

While there appear to be no direct halakhic prohibitions against pigeon breeding, Mishna Sanhedrin 3:3 lists those who race or breed doves among those individuals who are disqualified from serving as judges and appearing as witnesses in legal proceedings; such individuals are considered to be morally suspect. I am grateful to Ruth Rischin for her having drawn my attention to this matter, and to Ruth Langer for posting a query on my behalf on H-JUDAIC (H-NET Jewish Studies List) as well as for her help with researching this subject. I alone am responsible for the results of the investigation.

34. Babel, *Collected Stories*, 33.

35. Ibid., 26.

36. Ibid., 38.

37. Ibid.

38. Ibid., 39.

39. In an early poem, "Golubi" ("Pigeons/Doves," 1922), one of Bagritskii's least successful texts, pigeons/doves function as traditional symbols of peace.

40. Babel, *Collected Stories*, 41.

41. Ibid.

42. See Kh. N. Bialik, "Mladenchestvo," trans. Viacheslav Ivanov, in *Evreiskaia antologiia: Sbornik molodoi evreiskoi poezii*, ed. V.F. Khodasevich and L.B. Iaffe (Berlin: Izdatel'stvo S.D. Zal'tsman, 1922), 77–79. Incidentally, Viacheslav Ivanov's own autobiographical cycle, *Mladenchestvo* ("*Infancy*," 1918), may have left a trace in the prerevolutionary episodes of *February*.

43. Babel, *Collected Stories*, 29.

44. Ibid., 65.

45. Ibid.

46. Ibid., 44; Babel', *Sochineniia*, vol. 1, 156.

47. Osip Mandelstam, *The Noise of Time*, trans. Clarence Brown (San Francisco: North Point, 1986), 85; O.E. Mandelstam, *Sobranie sochinenii*, ed. G.O. Struve and B.A. Filippov, vol. 2 (Moscow: Terra, 1991), 66.

48. For a discussion of Blokian motifs and images in Bagritskii's oeuvre, see E.P. Liubareva, *Almaz gorit izdaleka . . . : Blokovskie traditsii v sovetskoi poezii* (Moscow: Sovetskii pisatel', 1987), 110–30, 145–48; Azarov, "Put' k 'Pobediteliam,'" 178; Antokol'skii, 289; and Bagritskii, *Stikhotvoreniia i poemy*, ed. Volgin, 10–11. On Blok's importance in Bagritskii's life, see Bagritskaia, 115–20, 141, 406. Note also that Bagritskii authored a poem about Blok, "Aleksandru Bloku" ("For Aleksandr Blok," 1922). V. Narbut said about Bagritskii that his "command of versification was on a par with Blok's"; see M.L. Spivak, "Eduard Bagritskii: Memuary dlia sluzhebnogo pol'zovaniia, ili posmertnaia diagnostika genial'nosti," *Literaturnoe obozrenie* 1 (1997): 56.

49. Antokol'skii (289) mentions a connection to Blok's "The Unknown Lady." Azarov ("Put' k 'Pobediteliam,'" 178) and Bondarin (Bagritskaia, 406) speak of an echo of Blok's *Vozmezdie* ("*Retribution*") in *February*.

50. Aleksandr Blok, *Sobranie sochinenii*, vol. 2 (Moscow/Leningrad: Gosudarstvennoe izdatel'stvo khudozhestvennoi literatury, 1960–63), 185–86.

51. Blok, vol. 3, 241.

52. See "Nightingale," in *Herder Dictionary of Symbols*, 22–23. In "Verses about a Nightingale and a Poet," Bagritskii called love for nightingales his "profession."

53. Blok, vol. 3, 242.

54. Among the pre–Silver Age Russian sources of *February*, I find very significant Pushkin's *Tsygany* ("*The Gypsies*," 1827) and Lermontov's *Mtsyri* (1840).

55. *February* IMLI.

56. Robert Paul Browder and Alexander F. Kerensky, eds., *The Russian Provisional Government, 1917*, vol. 1 (Stanford: Stanford University Press, 1961), 211–12; see also Alexander Kerensky, *The Crucifixion of Liberty*, trans. G. Kerensky (New York: Krauss Reprint, 1972), 82.

57. Browder and Kerensky, eds., 211–12.

58. The last verse of the passage ("Peace is far away . . .") is reminiscent of Blok's meditation on Russia's destiny, the cycle "Na pole Kulikovom" ("On the Kulikovo Field," 1908): "I vechnyi boi! Pokoi nam tol´ko snitsia / Skvoz´ krov´ i pyl´ . . ." ("And the eternal battle! Peace is but a dream / Through blood and dust . . .); Blok, vol. 3, 249.

59. See Browder and Kerensky, eds., 218–21.

60. For a very useful overview of the 1946–53 campaign against "Jewish nationalism," see Benjamin Pinkus, *The Jews of the Soviet Union: The History of a National Minority* (Cambridge: Cambridge University Press, 1988), 145–61; and Nora Levin, *Jews in the Soviet Union*, vol. 1, 512–25; vol. 2, 527–50.

61. See "Redaktor," *Literaturnaia gazeta*, 18 February 1934, 2. Additionally, in 1939 Tarasenkov also published a review of the first of the projected two volumes of Bagritskii's works; see A.K. Tarasenkov, "Pervyi tom sochinenii Eduarda Bagritskogo," in *Stat´i o literature*, vol. 1 (Moscow: Gosudarstvennoe izdatel´stvo khudozhestvennoi literatury, 1958), 227–35. Tarasenkov's review already contains the germs of his subsequent attack on Bagritskii.

62. Tarasenkov, "Pervyi tom sochinenii Eduarda Bagritskogo," 159.

63. *February* IMLI, 33. This has been one of the principal sore spots in the *February* criticism. Several critics, both Soviet and Western, speak of the poem as though it describes the Bolshevik Revolution. For a typical Soviet reading, see Liubareva, *Eduard Bagritskii*, where the protagonist is said to be "working in the Odessa Cheka" (193). L´vov, *Utolenie pechal´iu*, 86, is right on target in his polemic with Soviet Bagritskii-bashers, who have purposely obliterated a distinction between the February and October Revolutions, merely speaking of "Revolution."

64. Tarasenkov, "Pervyi tom sochinenii Eduarda Bagritskogo," 159. S.[A.] Tregub holds a similar position in his book *Zhivoi s zhivymi*.

65. Here and hereafter, all quotes are from Vladimir Maiakovskii, "Fevral´," in *Polnoe sobranie sochinenii*, vol. 8 (Moscow: Gosudarstvennoe izdatel´stvo khudozhestvennoi literatury, 1958), 53–55.

66. *February* IMLI, 29.

67. Bagritskii, 300.

68. D. Zaslavskii, *Evrei v SSSR* (Moscow: Izdatel´stvo "Emes," 1932).

69. Prokhorov, 217.

70. I will not discuss here the prosodic constraints of Bagritskii's *dol´nik* in *February*; I am, of course, aware of the fact that as compared to *evréiskii, iudéiskii* has one extra syllable before the stress, which—from a metrical standpoint—in some cases may not make the two words each other's perfect substitutes in a line of Bagritskii's *dol´nik*.

71. See Levin, vol. 1, 68–119.

72. The text of the discussion apparently circulated in samizdat in the late 1970s and early 1980s. It was published in the Soviet Union in 1990 in the conservative monthly review *Moskva* ("Moscow"); see "Klassika i my." Although the preface to the 1990 publication of "Klassika i my" in *Moskva* states that the "stenogram of the discussion is being published from a tape recording and without abridgment" (*Moskva* 1 [1990]: 183), I believe that the speeches were subjected to some editorial embellishment. In addition, in a disclaimer published after the third (!) installment of "Klassika

i my," the editors explained that they were missing the final tape with the concluding remarks by Kuniaev and P. Palievskii, and they apologized for not printing a complete text (*Moskva* 3 [1990]: 196).

73. Reported by Markish, "Eshche raz o nenavisiti k samomu sebe," 180.

74. Vadim Kozhinov, *Zagadochnye stranitsy istorii XX veka* (Moscow: Prima B, 1995); idem, *Rossiia. Vek XX (1939–1964): Opyt bespristrastnogo issledovaniia* (Moscow: Algoritm, 1999).

75. See Kuniaev, "Nash pervyi bunt."

76. See Bagritskaia.

77. Kuniaev, "Legenda i vremia."

78. See M. Kheifets, "Nashi obshchie uroki," *Dvadtsat´ dva* 14 (September 1980): 156–66; Viktor Boguslavskii, "V zashchitu Kuniaeva," *Dvadtsat´ dva* 16 (December 1980): 166–76; Markish, "Eshche raz o nenavisiti"; R[aisa] Lert, "Vyskazannoe i nedoskazannoe. Kommentarii k diskussii," *Poiski* 2 (1980): 89–113 (this essay was subsequently reprinted in her collection *Na tom stoiu* [Moscow: Moskovskii rabochii, 1991], 193–218); L´vov, "Vernost´ i otstupnichestvo"; see also Lev Losev, "Memuary E. L. Shvartsa," in Evgenii Shvarts, *Memuary*, ed. Lev Losev (Paris: La presse libre, 1982), 12–13.

79. "Klassika i my," *Moskva* 1 (1990): 194; cf. Kuniaev, "Legenda i vremia," 146–47.

80. Kuniaev, "Legenda i vremia," 147.

81. See David Shraer-Petrov [David Shrayer-Petrov], "Serp i molot: Kuniaev i Shkliarevskii," in *Moskva zlatoglavaia* (Baltimore: Vestnik Information Agency, 1994), 289.

82. Kuniaev, "Nash pervyi bunt," 177.

83. Theodor Lessing, *Der judische Selbsthass* (Berlin: Judischer Verlag, 1930). Also invaluable for the study of Jewish self-hatred is Hans Mayer's *Aussenseiter* (1975), translated into English as *Outsiders;* see Hans Mayer, "Jewish Self-Hate," ch. 22 in *Outsiders: A Study in Life and Letters* (Cambridge: MIT Press, 1982), 357–63.

84. Stanislav Kuniaev, tape-recorded interview with Maxim D. Shrayer, 26 May 1997, Moscow.

85. By "these ideas," Kuniaev presumably means Jewish nationalism; he repeats almost verbatim his comment from the 1977 discussion, "Klassika i my" ("Classics and We") and from his essay "Legenda i vremia," ("Legend and Time").

86. In Tarasenkov's article, *February* and Bagritskii's Jewishness are discussed in direct and unequivocally hateful terms; Kuniaev here tries to disassociate himself from Tarasenkov.

87. Note that although Kuniaev's argument here is to view the girl's rejection of the Jewish protagonist as based on class, and not ethnic considerations, he never doubts the fact that she is Slavic, and not Jewish.

88. Quoting from memory, Kuniaev adds the word *Judaic* to line 424 of Bagritskii's verse.

89. "Klassika i my," *Moskva* 1 (1990): 194; cf. "Klassika i my," *Poiski* 2 (1980): 73.

90. The last line of the penultimate stanza of Pushkin's Horatian poem "Pamiatnik" ("The Monument," 1836). Pushkin was one of Bagritskii's cultural idols, and Bagritskii thought and wrote of him throughout his life; see, for instance, his poem about Pushkin's duel, "Pushkin" (1923); "O Pushkine" ("About Pushkin," 1924); see also "Odessa" (1923). A number of studies have traced Pushkinian themes and subtexts in Bagritskii's works; see, for instance, Vsevolod Azarov, "Pushkinskaia tema v tvorchestve E. Bagritskogo," *Literaturnyi sovremennik* 1 (1937): 169–71; and V.A. Tsybenko, *Eduard Bagritskii (Ocherk tvorchestva)*, ed. A.A. Volkov (Novosibirsk: Novosibirskii gosudarstvennyi pedagogicheskii institut, 1970), 77–80.

91. Kuniaev wants to fashion Esenin as Bagritskii's ethnic and ideological antipode. At the same time, as he must have known from the 1973 volume of reminiscences (which he cites elsewhere), Bagritskii himself held Esenin in high esteem. Kuniaev refers

to the 1973 volume in his speech; see "Klassika i my," *Poiski* 2 (1980): 69; cf. "Klassika i my," *Moskva* 1 (1991): 190. On Esenin in Bagritskii's life, see Bondarin's remark in Bagritskaia, 141. In addition, one finds textual parallels between Esenin's and Bagritskii's poems, including *February*. Cf. Bagritskii's "A ne shliat´sia po nocham, kak syshchik, / Ne vryvat´sia v tikhie semeistva / V poiskakh nevedomykh banditov" (*February*, lines 506–508) and Esenin's "Ne zlodei ia i ne grabil lesom, / Ne rasstrelival neschastnykh po temnitsam" ("Ia sebia obmanyvat´ ne stanu . . .," ["I shall not lie to myself . . . ," 1922]); see Sergei Esenin, *Sobranie sochinenii v piati tomakh*, vol. 2 (Moscow: Khudozhestvennaia literatura, 1966), 119.

92. The reference is to Blok's 1919 essay "Krushenie gumanizma" ("The Collapse of Humanism"), which, incidentally, has nothing to do with the subject matter; Kuniaev uses Blok's expression out of sheer convenience and thereby evokes an unwanted comparison; see Blok, vol. 6, 93–115.

93. Kuniaev uses the expression "v lone russkoi poezii" ("in the lap of Russian poetry"); although this is a cliché, the underlying sexual connotation of *lono* ("vagina") may be intentional.

94. Kuniaev seems to have forgotten his own programmatic poem, "Dobro dolzhno byt´ s kulakami" ("The good must have fists," 1962).

95. This is the ending of Blok's *The Twelve*: "V belom venchike iz roz— / Vperedi— Isus Khristos" ("In a wreath of white roses / Jesus Christ [marches] onward ahead of them."

96. The stress is on "such"; Kuniaev here means "for such a Jewish revolutionary mentality."

97. Kuniaev earlier refers to Bagritskii's "Jewish revolutionary mentality" as opposed to "Jewish religious mentality," and he now contradicts himself.

98. Kuniaev tried to do just that in his memoir of 1999.

99. M. Bozhatkin, ed., "Maloizvestnye stikhi Eduarda Bagritskogo," *Raduga* 6 (1970): 90–91, 96–97.

100. Ibid., 96–97.

101. Ibid., 97.

102. See Bagritskii, 157–202. The opera production was abandoned following Bagritskii's death, although the libretto was published in 1935.

103. For an illuminating study of the epic poem's poetics, see Wendy Rosslyn, "Bagritskii's *Duma pro Opanasa*: The Poem and Its Context," *Canadian-American Slavic Studies* 11.3 (Fall 1977): 388–405.

104. See Nakhimovsky, 24.

105. Henry Abramson, in a recent book, shows the Ukrainian-Jewish relations during the Revolution and Civil War to have been a great deal more complex and polyvalent than it is customary to think; see Henry Abramson, *A Prayer for the Government: Ukrainians and Jews in Revolutionary Times, 1917–1920* (Cambridge: Ukrainian Research Institute/Harvard University Press, 1999).

106. Reported by L´vov, "Vernost´ i otstupnichestvo Eduarda Bagritskogo," 73, 86–87; on Vsevolod Bagritskii's absence of a birth certificate, see Spivak, 1 (1997): 50.

107. See L.G. Bagritskaia's letter to K.E. Voroshilov, 29 April 1954, RGALI, Fond 1399, op. 2, ed. khr. 192. Elsewhere, Bagritskaia referred to her father's nationality as "German"; see "Avtobiografiia," RGALI, Fond 1399, op, 2, ed. khr. 194.

108. For an illuminating discussion of the statistics of Jewish assimilation in the early Soviet period, see Pinkus, 135–37; see also Levin, vol. 1, 266–68.

109. Babel, *Collected Stories*, 67.

110. Markish, "Eshche raz o nenavisti k samomu sebe," 185–86.

111. Bagritskii, 487.

112. *Literaturnaia gazeta*, 18 February 1934, 1.

113. See "Bagritskii (Dziubin Eduard Georgievich)," in *Sovetskie pisateli. Avtobiografii*, vol. 3 (Moscow: Khudozhestvennaia literatura, 1966), 34, 35, 36.

114. I[tsik] Fefer, *Sbornik stikhov* (Moscow/Leningrad: Gosudarstvennoe izdatel´stvo khudozhestvennoi literatury, 1931), 68–9, 70–71, 78–96; Itsik Fefer, *Izbrannoe* (Moscow: Sovetskii pisatel´, 1957), 49; see also Bagritskii, 428–36. Mirskii claimed in 1935 that another translator of Yiddish poets into Russian utilized Bagritskii's poetic experience; see D[mitrii] Mirskii, "Evreiskie poety," *Literaturnaia gazeta*, 4 December 1935, 9. In the preface to the 1957 edition of Fefer's poems, Antokol´skii listed Bagritskii among Fefer's teachers, also including Maiakovskii, Heine, and Dem´ian Bednyi. Vainshtein (153–54) briefly discusses Bagritskii's translations of Fefer's poetry.

115. On the increase of anti-Semitism in the Soviet Union in the 1920s and early 1930s, see Levin, vol. 1: 259–81; see also M. Gorev, *Protiv antisemitov* (Moscow/Leningrad: Gosudarstvennoe izdatel´stvo, 1928); Iu. Larin, *Evrei i antisemitizm v SSSR* (Moscow: Gosudarstvennoe izdatel´stvo, 1928).

116. See "Vnimanie bor´be s antisemitizmom," *Pravda*, 19 February 1929, 1.

117. V. Veshnev, ed., *Neodolennyi vrag: Sbornik khudozhestvennoi literatury protiv antisemitizma* (Moscow: Federatsiia, 1930), 20–21. A series of gramophone records of Lenin's speeches was produced in 1919–21. My translation of Lenin's speech follows the text as it is quoted in Yaroslavsky's introductory essay, 5–21. A slightly different English translation is found in Hyman Lumer, ed., *Lenin on the Jewish Question* (New York: International Publishers, 1974), 135–36.

118. Vainshtein.

119. Sophocles, *Oedipus at Colonus*, trans. Robert Fitzgerald, in Sophocles, *The Oedipus Cycle: An English Version* (New York: Harcourt, Brace & World, 1949), 158–59.

120. Bagritskii, 105.

121. See L´vov, "Vernost´ i otstupnichestvo Eduarda Bagritskogo," 86–87.

122. Bagritskii, 391.

123. Ibid., 392.

124. Vainshtein, 145.

125. Bagritskii, 393.

126. Ibid., 138.

127. See Cavaion's illuminating examples of textual parallels between *The Last Night* and *February; Cavaion*, 253.

128. This section of *February* reveals parallels with Velimir Khlebnikov's long poem *Nochnoi obysk* (*"Night Search"*), written in 1918 but not published until 1930. Thomson compares the two texts in his *Lot's Wife and the Venus of Milo*, 77–97.

129. Liubareva, *Almaz gorit izdaleka*, 147.

130. Narbut, 375–76; cf. Bagritskaia, 319.

131. See Spivak 1 (1997): 45.

132. See Spivak; see especially Spivak 1 (1997): 44–48.

133. Tarasenkov, "O natsional´nykh traditsiiakh i burzhuaznom kosmopolitizme," 158.

134. "Klassika i my," *Moskva* 1 (1990): 194; cf. Kuniaev, "Legenda i vremia," 149.

135. Alexander Zholkovsky's remarkable analysis of the topos of prostitution in late nineteenth- and early twentieth-century literature, mainly French and Russian, is found in A.K. Zholkovskii and M.B. Iampol´skii, *Babel´/Babel* (Moscow: Carte Blanche, 1994), 317–69.

136. Babel, *Collected Stories*, 244–45.

137. *February* IMLI, 40.

138. Ibid., 41.

139. I have examined a representative sample of literature on the subject of black–white and Jewish–non-Jewish rape in America. The studies that have proven to be most helpful include Kristin Bumiller, "Rape as a Legal Symbol: An Essay on Sexual Violence and Racism," *University of Miami Law Review* 42 (September 1987): 75–91; Lynn A. Curtis, *Violence, Race, and Culture* (Lexington, Mass.: Heath, 1975); Nick Davies, *White Lies: Rape, Murder, and Justice Texas Style* (New York: Pantheon, 1991); Leonard Dinnerstein, "The Fate of Leo Frank," *American Heritage* (October 1996): 99–109; Gary D. LaFree, "Male Power and Female Victimization: Toward a Theory of Interracial Rape," *American Journal of Sociology* 88:2 (1982): 311–28; Deb Friedman, "Rape, Racism and Reality," *Quest* 1.1 (Summer 1979): 40–52; Sandra Gunning, *Race, Rape, and Lynching: The Red Record of American Literature, 1890–1912* (New York: Oxford University Press, 1996); Calvin C. Hernton, *Sex and Racism in America* (New York: Grove Weidenfield, 1965); Gerald Horne, "When Race and Gender Collide: The Martinsville Seven Case as a Case Study of the 'Rape-Lynch' Controversy," in *Challenging Racism and Sexism: Alternatives to Genetic Explanations*, ed. Ethel Tobach and Betty Rosoff (New York: Feminist Press, 1994), 211–28; Martha A. Myers, "The New South's 'New' Black Criminal: Rape and Punishment in Georgia, 1870–1940," in *Ethnicity, Race, and Crime: Perspectives across Time and Place*, ed. Darnell F. Hawkins (Albany: State University of New York Press, 1995), 145–66; and Gunnar Myrdal, *An American Dilemma* (New York: Harper, 1944).

140. Tarasenkov, "O natsional'nykh traditsiiakh i burzhuaznom kosmopolitizme," 159.

141. Kuniaev, "Legenda i vremia," 149–50.

142. One should keep in mind that in the Soviet 1960s through 1980s, the term *Zionist* and its derivatives were frequently used to connote any "Jewish cause," not only ideas associated with the creation of the state of Israel and with Jewish repatriation to it; *anti-Zionist* (*anti-sionistskii*) was a Soviet rhetorical smoke screen draping not only the official hostility toward Israel but also anti-Jewish sentiments at large; see William Korey, *The Soviet Cage: Anti-Semitism in Russia* (New York: Viking, 1973); idem, *Russian Anti-Semitism, Pamyat, and the Demonology of Zionism* (Chur, Switz.: Harwood Academic Press, 1995). See also R[aisa] Lert, "Vyskazannoe i nedoskazannoe. Kommentarii k diskussii," *Poiski* 2 (1980): 89–113; idem, *Na tom stoiu* (Moscow: Moskovskii rabochii, 1991); and L'vov, "Vernost'" i otstupnichestvo Eduarda Bagritskogo," 75, 85–87, 124–29.

143. In the manuscript, an earlier variant is crossed out: "Prinimai menia v pustye nedra / Iz kotorykh vyrosti ne smeet / Ni trava, ni kust, pokrytyi rzhav'iu" ("So let me in your empty womb / From which would not dare grow / Grass or bush, covered with rust"); see *February* IMLI, 41.

144. Cavaion, 255. It is puzzling, to say the least, that Boris Thomson charges Bagritskii's protagonist with rape without even attempting a discussion of this problematic issue; see Thomson, 86.

145. Babel, *Collected Stories*, 38.

146. See "Rain," in *Herder Dictionary of Symbols*, 155. In Babel's story "Sashka Khristos" ("Sashka Christ") from the *Red Cavalry* cycle, a beggar woman says to a man she has just had intercourse with: "Rain on an old woman. . . . I'll give you two hundred *poods* to the *desyatina*. . . ."; see Babel, *Collected Stories*, 139. I am grateful to Thomas Seifrid for bringing this detail to my attention.

147. See "Swan," in *Herder Dictionary of Symbols*, 188–89.

148. Levin, vol. 1, 49; Pinkus (57) comes to similar conclusions.

149. Bagritskaia, 70.

150. See Zinaida Shishova's recollections in Bagritskaia, 58–70, esp. 65–69; see Spivak, 1 (1997): 53.

151. Kataev, *Almaznyi moi venets* (Moscow: Sovetskii pisatel', 1979), 52; see also Shishova's examples of Bagritskii's use of Yiddishisms, Bagritskaia, 69.

152. Bagritskaia, 112.

153. Semen Lipkin and Inna Lisnianskaia, tape-recorded interview with Maxim D. Shrayer, 11 January 2000, Peredelkino, outside Moscow.

154. See Max Brod, *Reübeni, Fürst der Juden: Ein Renaissanceroman* (Munich: K. Wolff, 1925); idem, *Reubeni, kniaz' iudeiskii*, trans. B. Zhukhovetskii (Moscow: Gosudarstvennoe izdatel'stvo, 1927; reprint, Jerusalem: Biblioteka "Aliia," 1974); idem, *Reubeni, Prince of the Jews: A Tale of the Renaissance*, trans. Hannah Waller (New York: Knopf, 1928); and idem, *Reuveni sar ha-Yehudim: Roman*, trans. Yitshak Lamdan (Tel Aviv: Shtibel, 1929).

155. See "Reubeni, David," *Evreiskaia entsiklopediia*, vol. 13, ed. A. Garkavi and L. Ketsenel'son (St. Petersburg: Obshchestvo dlia Nauchnykh Evreiskikh Izdanii/Izdatel'stvo Brokgauz-Efron, n.d. [1906–1913]; reprint, Moscow: Terra, 1991, 447–50); "Reuveni, David," *Encyclopedia Judaica*, vol. 14 (New York: Macmillan, 1971), 114–16; and "Reubeni, David," in Mordecai Schreiber, ed., *The Shengold Jewish Encyclopedia* (Rockville, Md.: Shengold, 1998), 218.

156. See "Khronika zhizni i tvorchestva E.G. Bagritskogo," RGALI, *Fond* 1399, op. 2, ed. khr. 53. Lidiia Bagritskaia indicates that her husband read from the 1923 Berlin edition of Khodasevich's anthology of Jewish poets; see Vladislav Khodasevich, ed. and trans., *Iz evreiskikh poetov* (Berlin: Izdatel'stvo Z.I. Grzhebina, 1923), where the Russian translation of Saul Tchernichowsky's "Dumplings" is entitled "Vareniki" and is found on pp. 39–46.

157. L'vov ("Vernost' i otstupnichestvo Eduarda Bagritskogo," 80–81) speaks of Bagritskii's love-hate, hate-love relationship with his own Jewishness.

158. *February* RGALI.

159. See typescript with L.G. Bagritskaia's introductory note explaining the source of the preface; RGALI, *Fond* 1399, op. 2. I translated the original's "ukha iz bychkov" as "stew made of Black Sea fish"; the taxonomic name of *bychok* is Gobius. Little Fountain (Malyi Fontan) is an area in Odessa. Practique Harbor is a common translation of Prakticheskaia Gavan'.

160. S[ergei] Bondarin, "Eduard Bagritskii," *Novyi mir* 4 (1961): 143.

161. Narbut, 160; cf. Babel', *Sochineniia*, vol. 2, 362. Babel characterized himself as a "great master" of the genre of silence in his speech at the First Congress of Soviet Writers in 1934; see Babel', *Sochineniia*, vol. 2, 381.

162. Narbut, 161.

163. Bagritskaia, 401.

164. Kuniaev, "Legenda i vremia," 150.

165. *Tannakh*, 689–90; cf. the Russian Orthodox Bible, *Bibliia* (Moscow: Izdanie Moskovskoi Patriarkhii, 1992), 705.

166. *Tannakh*, 728; cf. *Bibliia*, 718.

Works Cited

Works by Eduard Bagritskii (selected editions)

Duma pro Opanasa. Moscow: Molodaia gvardiia, 1933 [illustrated edition].
Duma pro Opanasa. Libretto opery. Moscow: Gosudarstvennoe izdatel'stvo khudo-
  zhestvennoi literatury, 1935.
Iugo-Zapad. Moscow: Zemlia i fabrika, 1928 (2nd ed., 1930).
Izbrannoe. Minsk: Gosudarstvennoe izdatel'stvo pri SNK BSSR, 1941.
Izbrannoe. Edited by D. Danin. Moscow: Sovetskii pisatel', 1948.
Izbrannoe. Edited by Ia. Gorodskoi. Odessa: Oblastnoe izdatel'stvo, 1949.
Izbrannoe. Moscow: Detskaia literatura, 1970.
Izbrannoe. Edited by N. Kriukov. Petrozavodsk: Kareliia, 1975.
Izbrannye stikhi. Moscow: Federatsiia, 1932.
Oisgeveilte lider un poemes [in Yiddish]. Translated by Ia.A. Zeldin. Moscow: Melukhe-
  farlag der emes, 1940.
Pobediteli. Moscow: Gosudarstvennoe izdatel'stvo khudozhestvennoi literatury, 1932.
Poemy i stikhi. Moscow: Pravda, 1947.
Posledniia noch'. Moscow: Federatsiia, 1932.
Ptitselov. Stikhi i poemy. Moscow: Gosudarstvennoe izdatel'stvo detskoi literatury, 1960.
Sobolinyi sled. Moscow: GIZ, 1930.
Sobranie sochinenii v dvukh tomakh. Vol. 1. Edited by I. Utkin. Moscow: Goslitizdat,
  1938–39. [Volume 2 never appeared.]
Stikhi. Moscow: Zhurgazob''edinenie, 1933.
Stikhi i poemy. Edited by Vs. Azarov. Moscow: Gosudarstvennoe izdatel'stvo khudo-
  zhestvennoi literatury, 1956.
Stikhi i poemy. Edited by P. Viacheslavov. Moscow: Khudozhestvennaia literatura, 1964.
Stikhi i poemy. Edited by Vs. Azarov. Ufa: Bashkirskoe knizhnoe izdatel'stvo, 1972.
Stikhi i poemy. Moscow: Khudozhestvennaia literatura, 1976.
Stikhotvoreniia. Edited by I. Grinberg. Leningrad: Sovetskii pisatel', 1940.
Stikhotvoreniia. Edited by G.A. Morev. St. Petersburg: Akademicheskii proekt, 2000
  (forthcoming).
Stikhotvoreniia i poemy. Moscow: Gosudarstvennoe izdatel'stvo khudozhestvennoi liter-
  atury, 1958.
Stikhotvoreniia i poemy. Edited by E.P. Liubareva and S.A. Kovalenko. Moscow: Sovetskii
  pisatel', 1964.
Stikhotvoreniia i poemy. Minsk: Nauka i tekhnika, 1983.

Stikhotvoreniia i poemy. Edited by S.A. Kovalenko. Moscow: Moskovskii rabochii, 1984.
Stikhotvoreniia i poemy. Edited by I.L. Volgin. Moscow: Pravda, 1987.
Vom Schwarzbrot und von der Treue der Frau [Eduard Bagritzki]. Berlin: Verlag Volk und Welt, 1971.
Zvezda mordvina. Moscow: Molodaia gvardiia, 1931.
Zvèzda mordvina. Moscow: Detskaia literatura, 1972.

Other Works

Abramson, Henry. *A Prayer for the Government: Ukrainians and Jews in Revolutionary Times, 1917–1920.* Cambridge: Ukrainian Research Institute/Harvard University Press, 1999.
Afanas´ev, V. "Kommentarii k kommentariiam." *Literaturnaia gazeta,* 8 December 1956, 3.
Alexandrova, Vera. "Jews in Soviet Literature." In *Russian Jewry, 1917–1967,* edited by Gregor Aronson et al., 300–327. New York: Thomas Yoseloff, 1969.
"Almanakh pamiati Bagritskogo." *Literaturnaia gazeta,* 18 February 1934, 2.
Andreev, A. "Nash sovremennik. Zametki ob obraze Pushkina v sovetskoi poezii." *Zvezda* 6 (1959): 200–205.
Antokol´skii, Pavel. *Puti poetov.* Moscow: Sovetskii pisatel´, 1965.
Avins, Carol J. "Jewish Ritual and Soviet Context in Two Stories of Isaac Babel." In *American Contributions to the Twelfth International Congress of Slavists,* edited by Robert A. Maguire and Alan Timberlake, 11–20. Bloomington, Ind.: Slavica, 1998.
Azarov, Vsevolod. "Bagritskii i sovremennost´ (po neopublikovannym materialam)." *Novyi mir* 7 (1948): 201–14.
———. "Iz vospominanii o Bagritskom (lichnost´ i masterstvo)." *Russkaia literatura* 2 (1976): 151–58.
———. "Pevets molodosti." In Eduard Bagritskii, *Ptitselov. Stikhi i poemy,* 3–21. Moscow: Gosudarstvennoe izdatel´stvo detskoi literatury, 1960.
———. "Pushkinskaia tema v tvorchestve E. Bagritskogo." *Literaturnyi sovremennik* 1 (1937): 169–71.
———. "Put´ k 'Pobediteliam' (K chetyrekhletiiu so dnia smerti Eduarda Bagritskogo)." *Zvezda* 2 (1938): 175–84.
———. "U istokov pesni." *Znamia* 2 (1947): 159–65.
Babel, Isaac. *Collected Stories.* Translated by David McDuff. Harmondsworth, Eng.: Penguin, 1994.
Babel´, Isaak. *Sochineniia.* 2 vols. Edited by A.N. Pirozhkova. Moscow: Khudozhestvennaia literatura, 1991–92.
The Babylonian Talmud. Seder Zera´im. Translated and edited by Rabbi I. Epstein. London: Soncino, 1948.
Bagritskaia, L.G., comp. and ed. *Eduard Bagritskii: Vospominaniia sovremennikov.* Moscow: Sovetskii pisatel´, 1973.
"Bagritskii (Dziubin Eduard Georgievich)." In *Sovetskie pisateli. Avtobiografii.* Vol. 3: 34–42. Moscow: Khudozhestvennaia literatura, 1966.
Banchukov, Revol´d. "Odessa—Kuntsevo—vechnost´." *Vestnik,* 21 December 1999, 46–50.
Bank, Natal´ia. "'My poimany oba, my oba—v setiakh! . . .': Slovo v pamiat´ i zashchitu poeta Eduarda Bagritskogo." *Neva* 11 (1995): 202–6.

Bespalov, I.M. "Poeziia Eduarda Bagritskogo." In idem, *Stat'i o literature*, 151–88. Moscow: Gosudarstvennoe izdatel'stvo khudozhestvennoi literatury, 1959.

Bialik, Kh. N. "Mladenchestvo." Translated by Viacheslav Ivanov. In *Evreiskaia antologiia: Sbornik molodoi evreiskoi poezii*, edited by V.F. Khodasevich and L.B. Iaffe, 77–79. Berlin: Izdatel'stvo S.D. Zal'tsman, 1922.

Bibliia. Moscow: Izdanie Moskovskoi Patriarkhii, 1992.

Blium, A.V. *Evreiskii vopros pod sovetskoi tsenzuroi, 1917–1991*. St. Petersburg: Peterburgskii evreiskii universitet, 1996.

Blok, Aleksandr. *Sobranie sochinenii*. 10 vols. Moscow/Leningrad: Gosudarstvennoe izdatel'stvo khudozhestvennoi literatury, 1960–63.

Blum, Jakub. "Soviet Russian Literature." In *The Image of the Jew in Soviet Literature: The Post-Stalin Period*, 3–97. New York: Ktav, 1984.

Bobovich, Bor[is]. "Odnotomnik Eduarda Bagritskogo." *Komsomol'skaia pravda*, 21 October 1956, 3.

Bobyshev, Dmitrii. E-mail communication to Maxim D. Shrayer. 21 November 1999. Champaign, Ill., to Boston.

Boguslavskii, Viktor. "V zashchitu Kuniaeva." *Dvadtsat' dva* 16 (December 1980): 166–76.

Bokov, Viktor. Tape-recorded interview with Maxim D. Shrayer. 8 January 1998. Peredelkino, outside Moscow.

Bondarin, S[ergei]. "Eduard Bagritskii." *Novyi mir* 4 (1961): 130–43.

———. "Sud'by i stikhi." *Literaturnaia Rossiia*, 5 February 1965, 9.

———. "V gostiakh u vnukov." In idem, *Parus plavanii i vospominanii*, 194–210. Moscow: Sovetskaia Rossiia, 1971.

———. *Zlataia tsep'*. Moscow: Sovetskii pisatel', 1971.

Bonner, Elena. *Dochki-materi*. Moscow: Progress/Litera, 1994.

Bowra, Maurice, ed. *A Second Book of Russian Verse*. London: Macmillan, 1948.

Bozhatkin, M., ed. "Maloizvestnye stikhi Eduarda Bagritskogo." *Raduga* 6 (1970): 90–98.

Brod, Max. *Reübeni, Fürst der Juden: Ein Renaissanceroman*. Munich: K. Wolff, 1925.

——— [Maks Brod]. *Reubeni, kniaz' iudeiskii*. Translated [into Russian] by B. Zhukhovetskii. Moscow: Gosudarstvennoe izdatel'stvo, 1927. Reprint, Jerusalem: Biblioteka "Aliia," 1974.

———. *Reubeni, Prince of the Jews: A Tale of the Renaissance*. Translated by Hannah Waller. New York: Knopf, 1928.

———. *Reuveni sar ha-Yehudim: Roman*. Translated [into Hebrew] by Yitshak Lamdan. Tel Aviv: Shtibel, 1929.

Browder, Robert Paul, and Alexander F. Kerensky, eds. *The Russian Provisional Government, 1917*. Vol. 1. Stanford: Stanford University Press, 1961.

Brown, Edward J. *Mayakovsky: A Poet in the Revolution*. Princeton: Princeton University Press, 1973.

Bumiller, Kristin. "Rape as a Legal Symbol: An Essay on Sexual Violence and Racism." *University of Miami Law Review* 42 (September 1987): 75–91.

Cavaion, Danilo. "Ebracità come memoria oscura (Eduard Bagrickij)." In idem, *Memoria e poesia: Storia e letteratura degli ebrei russi nell'età moderna*. Rome: Carucci editore, 1988.

Cavanagh, Clare. *Osip Mandelstam and the Modernist Creation of Tradition*. Princeton: Princeton University Press, 1995.

Curtis, Lynn A. *Violence, Race, and Culture*. Lexington, Mass.: Heath, 1975.

Davies, Nick. *White Lies: Rape, Murder, and Justice Texas Style*. New York: Pantheon, 1991.

Dinershtein, E.A., ed. "Pis'ma [Eduarda Bagritskogo]." In *Literaturnoe nasledstvo* 74, 435–66. Moscow: Nauka, 1965.

Dinnerstein, Leonard. "The Fate of Leo Frank." *American Heritage* (October 1996): 99–109.

"Eduard Bagritskii." *Literaturnaia gazeta*, 18 February 1934, 1.

Epstein, Mikhail. "Judaic Spiritual Traditions in the Poetry of Pasternak and Mandelstam." Translated from the Russian by Ruth Rischin. *Symposium* 52.4 (Winter 1999): 205–31.

Erlich, Victor. *Modernism and Revolution: Russian Literature in Transition.* Cambridge: Harvard University Press, 1994.

Ermolaev, Herman. *Censorship in Soviet Literature, 1917–1991.* Lanham, Md.: Rowman & Littlefield, 1997.

Esenin, Sergei. *Sobranie sochinenii v piati tomakh.* Vol. 2. Moscow: Khudozhestvennaia literatura, 1966.

Ettinger, Shmuel. "The Position of Jews in Soviet Culture: A Historical Survey." In *Jews in Soviet Culture*, edited by Jack Miller, 1–21. New Brunswick, N.J.: Transaction, 1984.

Evgen´ev, A., and B. Runin. "Eduard Bagritskii (K piatiletiiu so dnia smerti)." *Novyi mir* 2 (1939): 253–67.

Fefer, Itsik. *Izbrannoe.* Moscow: Sovetskii pisatel´, 1957.

———. *Sbornik stikhov.* Moscow/Leningrad: Gosudarstvennoe izdatel´stvo khudozhestvennoi literatury, 1931.

Freidin, Gregory. *A Coat of Many Colors: Osip Mandelstam and His Mythologies of Self-Representation.* Berkeley: University of California Press, 1987.

Friedberg, Maurice. "Jewish Contributions to Soviet Literature." In *The Jews in Soviet Russia since 1917*, 3rd ed., edited by Lionel Kochan, 217–25. Oxford: Oxford University Press, 1978.

———. "Jewish Themes in Soviet Russian Literature." In *Jews in Soviet Russia*, ed. Kochan, 197–216.

———. "The Jewish Search in Russian Literature." *Prooftexts: A Journal of Jewish Literary History* 4.1 (January 1984): 93–105.

Friedman, Deb. "Rape, Racism and Reality." *Quest* 1.1 (Summer 1979): 40–52.

Gilman, Sander. *Jewish Self-Hatred: Anti-Semitism and the Hidden Language of the Jews.* Baltimore: Johns Hopkins University Press, 1986.

Ginzburg, Lidiia. "Vstrechi s Bagritskim." In *Den´ poezii. Leningrad*, 63–65. Leningrad: Sovetskii pisatel´, 1966.

Gitelman, Zvi. "The Evolution of Jewish Culture and Identity in the Soviet Union." In *Jewish Culture and Identity in the Soviet Union*, edited by Yaacov Ro´i and Avi Beker, 3–24. New York: New York University Press, 1991.

"Glubokii udar sovetskoi poezii." *Literaturnaia gazeta*, 18 February 1934, 2.

Gorev, M. *Protiv antisemitov.* Moscow/Leningrad: Gosudarstvennoe izdatel´stvo, 1928.

Grinberg, I. *Eduard Bagritskii.* Moscow/Leningrad: GIKhL, 1940.

Grübel, Rainer. "Russkii literaturnyi konstruktivizm." *Russian Literature* 17 (1985): 9–20.

Gunning, Sandra. *Race, Rape, and Lynching: The Red Record of American Literature, 1890–1912.* New York: Oxford University Press, 1996.

The Herder Dictionary of Symbols. Wilmette, Ill.: Chiron, 1994.

Herlihy, Patricia. *A History of Odessa.* Cambridge: Harvard University Press, 1986.

Hernton, Calvin C. *Sex and Racism in America.* New York: Grove Weidenfeld, 1965.

Horne, Gerald. "When Race and Gender Collide: The Martinsville Seven Case as a Case Study of the 'Rape-Lynch' Controversy." In *Challenging Racism and Sexism: Alternatives to Genetic Explanations*, edited by Ethel Tobach and Betty Rosoff, 211–18. New York: Feminist Press, 1994.

Jakobson, Roman. "On a Generation That Squandered Its Poets." In idem, *Language in Literature*, edited by Krystyna Pomorska and Stephen Rudy, 273–300. Cambridge: Belknap Press of Harvard University Press, 1987.

Kataev, Valentin. *Almaznyi moi venets*. Moscow: Sovetskii pisatel', 1979.

———. *Bezdel'nik Eduard*. Moscow: GIZ, 1925.

———. "Vstrecha." *Sobranie sochinenii v deviati tomakh*. Vol. 1, 419–27. Moscow: Khudozhestvennaia literatura, 1968.

Kaun, Alexander. *Soviet Poets and Poetry*. Berkeley: University of California Press, 1943. Reprint, Freeport, N.Y.: Books for Libraries, 1968.

Kerensky, Alexander. *The Crucifixion of Liberty*. Translated by G. Kerensky. New York: Krauss Reprint, 1972.

Kheifits, M. "Nashi obshchie uroki." *Dvadtsat' dva* 14 (September 1980): 156–66.

Khodasevich, V.F., and L.B. Iaffe, eds. *Evreiskaia antologiia: Sbornik molodoi evreiskoi poezii*. Berlin: Izdatel'stvo S.D. Zal'tsman, 1922.

Khodasevich, Vladislav, ed. and trans. *Iz evreiskikh poetov*. Berlin: Izdatel'stvo Z.I. Grzhebina, 1923.

Kisin, I. "Razmyshleniia o russkom evreistve i ego literature." *Evreiskii mir* 2 (1944): 164–72.

"Klassika i my." *Grani* 114 (1979): 126–55.

"Klassika i my." *Moskva* 1 (1990): 183–200; 2 (1990): 169–80; 3 (1990): 186–96.

"Klassika i my." *Poiski* 2 (1980): 65–88.

Kobrinskii, A. "K voprosu o kriteriiakh poniatiia 'russko-evreiskaia literatura.'" *Vestnik evreiskogo universiteta v Moskve* 5 (1994): 100–114.

Kolmogorov A.N., and A.V. Prokhorov. "O dol'nike sovremennoi russkoi poezii (Statisticheskaia kharakteristika dol'nika Maiakovskogo, Bagritskogo, Akhmatovoi)." *Voprosy iazykoznaniia* 1 (1964): 75–94.

Korey, William. *Russian Anti-Semitism, Pamyat, and the Demonology of Zionism*. Chur, Switz.: Harwood Academic Press, 1995.

———. *The Soviet Cage: Anti-Semitism in Russia*. New York: Viking, 1973.

Kornilov, Boris. *Stikhotvoreniia i poemy*. Leningrad: Sovetskii pisatel', 1960.

Kowalski, Luba Halat. "Eduard Bagritsky: A Selected Bibliography." *Russian Literature Triquarterly* 8 (1974): 540–42.

———. "Eduard Bagritsky: Life and Poetry." Ph.D. diss., Bryn Mawr College, 1966.

———. "Eduard Bagritsky: A Biographical Sketch with Three Unpublished Letters." *Russian Literature Triquarterly* 8 (1974): 472–81.

Kozhinov, Vadim. *Rossiia. Vek XX (1939–1964): Opyt bespristrastnogo issledovaniia*. Moscow: Algoritm, 1999.

———. *Zagadochnye stranitsy istorii XX veka*. Moscow: Prima B, 1995.

Krempien, Herbert. "Nachwort." In Eduard Bagritzki, *Vom Schwarzbrot und von der Treue der Frau*, 161–72. Berlin: Verlag Volk und Welt, 1971.

Krivulin, Viktor. *Okhota na mamonta*. St. Petersburg: Russko-Baltiiskii informatsionnyi tsentr, 1998.

———. Tape-recorded interview with Maxim D. Shrayer. 14 January 2000. St. Petersburg.

Kuniaev, Stanislav. "Legenda i vremia." *Dvadtsat' dva* 14 (September 1980): 136–55.

———. "Nash pervyi bunt." [Ch. 3 of his *Poeziia. Sud'ba. Rossiia*.] *Nash sovremennik* 3 (1999): 175–91.

———. "Russko-evreiskoe Borodino." [Ch. 5 of his *Poeziia. Sud'ba. Rossiia*.] *Nash sovremennik* 4 (1999): 169–97.

———. Tape-recorded interview with Maxim D. Shrayer. 26 May 1997. Moscow.

Kutik, Il´ia. E-mail communications to Maxim D. Shrayer. 6 December 1999 and 13 December 1999. Evanston, Ill., to Boston.

Kuzmin, M[ikhail]. "Eduard Bagritskii." *Literaturnaia gazeta*, 17 May 1933, 3.

LaFree, Gary D. "Male Power and Female Victimization: Toward a Theory of Interracial Rape." *American Journal of Sociology* 88:2 (1982): 311–28.

Larin, Iu. *Evrei i antisemitizm v SSSR.* Moscow: Gosudarstvennoe izdatel´stvo, 1929.

Laughlin, James, ed. *New Directions Anthology of Prose and Poetry.* Norfolk, Conn.: New Directions, 1941.

Lert, R[aisa]. *Na tom stoiu.* Moscow: Moskovskii rabochii, 1991.

———. "Vyskazannoe i nedoskazannoe. Kommentarii k diskussii." *Poiski* 2 (1980): 89–113.

Lessing, Theodor. *Der judische Selbsthass.* Berlin: Judischer Verlag, 1930.

Levin, Nora. *The Jews in the Soviet Union since 1917: Paradox of Survival.* 2 vols. New York: New York University Press, 1988.

Lezhnev, A[bram]. "E. Bagritskii." In *Literaturnye budni,* 127–61. Moscow: Federatsiia, 1929.

Lipkin, Semen. *Kvadriga.* Moscow: Knizhnyi sad/Agraf, 1997.

Lipkin, Semen, and Inna Lisnianskaia. Tape-recorded interview with Maxim D. Shrayer. 11 January 2000. Peredelkino, outside Moscow.

Liubareva, E.P. *Almaz gorit izdaleka . . .: Blokovskie traditsii v sovetskoi poezii.* Moscow: Sovetskii pisatel´, 1987.

———. "Eduard Bagritskii." In Eduard Bagritskii, *Stikhotvoreniia i poemy,* 5–46. Moscow: Sovetskii pisatel´, 1964.

———. *Eduard Bagritskii.* Moscow: Sovetskii pisatel´, 1964.

———. "Tak li nado tolkovat´ Bagritskogo?" *Voprosy literatury* 9 (1960): 67–70.

Losev, Lev. "Memuary E.L. Shvartsa." In Evgenii Shvarts, *Memuary,* edited by Lev Losev, 7–42. Paris: La presse libre, 1982.

Lumer, Hyman, ed. *Lenin on the Jewish Question.* New York: International Publishers, 1974.

Luplow, Carol A. "Isaak Babel´ and the Jewish Tradition: *The Childhood Stories.*" *Russian Literature* 15 (1984): 255–78.

L'vov, Arkadii. Telephone interview with Maxim D. Shrayer. 10 March 1998. Boston to Fort Lee, N.J.

———. "Vernost´ i otstupnichestvo Eduarda Bagritskogo." In idem, *Utolenie pechal´iu: Opyt issledovaniia evreiskoi mental´nosti,* 73–129. New York: Vremia i my, 1983.

Maiakovskii, Vladimir. *Polnoe sobranie sochinenii.* 13 vols. Moscow: Gosudarstvennoe izdatel´stvo khudozhestvennoi literatury, 1955–61.

Mandelstam, Osip. *Sobranie sochinenii,* edited by G.O. Struve and B.A. Filippov. 4 vols. Moscow: Terra, 1991.

———. *The Noise of Time,* translated by Clarence Brown. San Francisco: North Point, 1986.

Markish, Simon [Shimon]. "Eshche raz o nenavisti k samomu sebe." *Dvadtsat´ dva* 16 (December 1980): 177–91.

———. "The Example of Isaak Babel´." In *What Is Jewish Literature?,* edited by Hana Wirth-Nesher, 199–215. Philadelphia: Jewish Publication Society, 1994.

Markov, Vladimir, and Merrill Sparks, eds. *Modern Russian Poetry.* London: MacGibbon and Kee, 1966.

Mayer, Hans. *Outsiders: A Study in Life and Letters.* Cambridge: MIT Press, 1982.

Mezhirov, Aleksandr. Telephone interview with Maxim D. Shrayer. 12 May 1998. Boston to Portland, Oreg.

Miller, Jack, ed. *Jews in Soviet Culture.* New Brunswick, N.J.: Transaction, 1984.

Mirskii, D[mitrii]. "Evreiskie poety." *Literaturnaia gazeta,* 4 December 1935, 9.

————. "Tvorcheskii put' Eduarda Bagritskogo." In *Eduard Bagritskii. Al'manakh*, edited by Vladimir Narbut, 5–23. Moscow: Sovetskii pisatel', 1936.

Możejko, Edward. "Russian Literary Constructivism: Towards a Theory of Poetic Language." In *Canadian Contributions to the VIII International Congress of Slavists*, edited by Z. Folejewski et al., 61–70. Ottawa: Canadian Association of Slavists, 1978.

Myers, Martha A. "The New South's 'New' Black Criminal: Rape and Punishment in Georgia, 1870–1940." In *Ethnicity, Race, and Crime: Perspectives across Time and Place*, edited by Darnell F. Hawkins, 145–66. Albany: State University of New York Press, 1995.

Myrdal, Gunnar. *An American Dilemma.* New York: Harper, 1944.

Naiman, Anatolii. "Paladin poezii." *Russkaia mysl'* (April 30–May 6 1998): 14.

————. *Rasskazy o Anne Akhmatovoi.* Moscow: Khudozhestvennaia literatura, 1989.

Nakhimovsky, Alice Stone. "Bagritsky and Mandelshtam." In idem, *Russian-Jewish Literature and Identity*, 20–28. Baltimore: Johns Hopkins University Press, 1992.

Narbut, Vladimir, ed. *Eduard Bagritskii. Al'manakh.* Moscow: Sovetskii pisatel', 1936.

Obolensky, Dimitri, ed. *The Heritage of Russian Verse.* Bloomington: Indiana University Press, 1976.

Orbach, Alexander. *New Voices of Russian Jewry: A Study of the Russian-Jewish Press of Odessa in the Era of Great Reforms, 1880–1871.* Leiden: Brill, 1980.

Ozerov, Lev. "Mir otkrytyi nastezh'. . . ." In idem, *Masterstvo i volshebstvo: Kniga statei*, 207–17. Moscow: Sovetskii pisatel', 1972.

"Pafos i mechta revoliutsii." *Literaturnaia gazeta*, 18 February 1934, 1.

Pasternak, Boris. *Vozdushnye puti.* Moscow: Sovetskii pisatel', 1982.

Pinkus, Benjamin. *The Jews of the Soviet Union: The History of a National Minority.* Cambridge: Cambridge University Press, 1988.

Pipes, Richard. *The Formation of the Soviet Union: Communism and Nationalism, 1917–1923.* Rev. ed. Cambridge: Harvard University Press, 1997.

Poggioli, Renato. *The Poets of Russia, 1890–1930.* Cambridge: Harvard University Press, 1960.

Prokhorov, A.I. "E. Bagritskii v poslednii period tvorchestva (1928–1934 gg.)." *Uchenye zapiski Piatigorskogo pedagogicheskogo instituta* 11 (1956): 183–217.

"Redaktor." *Literaturnaia gazeta*, 18 February 1934, 2.

"Reubeni, David." In *Evreiskaia entsiklopediia*. Vol. 13, edited by A. Garkavi and L. Ketsenel'son, 447–50. St. Petersburg: Obshchestvo dlia Nauchnykh Evreiskikh Izdanii/Izdatel'stvo Brokgauz-Efron, n.d. (1906–1913); reprint, Moscow: Terra, 1991.

"Reubeni, David." In Mordecai Schreiber, ed. *The Shengold Jewish Encyclopedia.* Rockville, Md.: Shengold, 1998.

"Reuveni, David." In *Encyclopedia Judaica*. Vol. 14, 114–16. New York: Macmillan, 1971.

Rischin, Ruth. "The Most Historical of People: Yushkevich, Kuprin and the Dubnovian Era." In *The Short Story in Russia, 1900–1917.* Edited by Nicholas Luker, 23–52. Nottingham, Eng.: Astra, 1991.

Rosslyn, Wendy. "Bagritskii's *Duma pro Opanasa*: The Poem and Its Context." *Canadian-American Slavic Studies* 11.3 (Fall 1977): 388–405.

————. "Eduard Georg'evich Bagritskii." In *Reference Guide to Russian Literature*, edited by Neil Cornwell, 132–33. London: Fitzroy Dearborn, 1998.

————. "The Path to Paradise: Recurrent Images in the Poetry of Eduard Bagritsky." *Modern Language Review* 71.1 (January 1976): 97–105.

————. "The Unifying Principle of Bagritsky's 'Yugo-Zapad'." *Essays in Poetics* 4/1 (1979): 20–34.

Rozhdestvenskaia, I. *Poeziia Ed. Bagritskogo.* Leningrad: Khudozhestvennaia literatura, 1967.

Sandomersky [Dunham], Vera. "A Note on Soviet Poetry." In *New Directions Anthology of Prose and Poetry*, edited by James Laughlin, 517–21. Norfolk, Conn.: New Directions, 1941.

———. "Bagritsky, Edouard (1895–1934)." In *New Directions Anthology of Prose and Poetry*, edited by James Laughlin, 521–22. Norfolk, Conn.: New Directions, 1941.

Satunovkii, Ian. *Khochu li ia posmertnoi slavy*. Moscow: Biblioteka al´manakha "Vesy," 1992.

Selivanovskii, A. "Eduard Bagritskii." *Novyi mir* 6 (1933): 210–27.

Shafarevich, Igor´. "O rusofobii." *Vremia i my* 104 (1989): 161–62.

———. "Rusofobiia." *Nash sovremennik* 6 (1989): 167–91; 11 (1989): 162–72.

Schreiber, Mordecai, ed. *The Shengold Jewish Encyclopedia*. Rockville, Md.: Shengold Books, 1998.

Shklovskii, Viktor. "O serdtse." *Literaturnaia gazeta*, 18 February 1934, 2.

———. "Iugo-zapad." *Literaturnaia gazeta*, 5 January 1933, 3.

Shraer-Petrov, David [David Shrayer-Petrov]. "Serp i molot: Kuniaev i Shkliarevskii." In idem, *Moskva zlatoglavaia*, 262–91. Baltimore: Vestnik Information Agency, 1994.

Shrayer, Maxim D. "Anti-Semitism and the Decline of Russian Village Prose." *Partisan Review*, forthcoming.

———. "Jewish Questions in Nabokov's Art and Life." In *Nabokov and His Fiction: New Perspectives*, edited by Julian W. Connolly, 73–91. Cambridge: Cambridge University Press, 1999.

———. "Poeziia i evreistvo" [interview with Dmitrii Bobyshev]. *Nash Skopus* 18 (2000): 7–12.

———. *The World of Nabokov's Stories*. Austin: University of Texas Press, 1999.

Shteinberg, Arkadii. *K verkhov´iam*. Moscow: Sovpadenie, 1997.

Sicher, Ephraim. *Jews in Russian Literature after the October Revolution: Writers and Artists between Hope and Apostasy*. Cambridge: Cambridge University Press, 1995.

Sicher, Ephraim. "The Jewishness of Babel´." In Jack Miller, ed., *Jews in Soviet Culture*, 167–82. New Brunswick, N.J.: Transaction, 1984.

Sinel´nikov, Mikhail. "Ptitselov: K stoletiiu Eduarda Bagritskogo." *Moskovskie novosti* 29 October–5 November 1995: 25.

Siniavskii, Andrei. "Eduard Bagritskii." In *Istoriia russkoi sovetskoi literatury*, vol. 1, 397–420. Moscow: Izdatel´stvo AN SSSR, 1958.

Slavin, Lev. "Dobraia sila." In Eduard Bagritskii, *Izbrannoe*, 5–14. Moscow: Detskaia literatura, 1970.

Slonim, Marc [Mark Slonim]. *Soviet Russian Literature: Writers and Problems, 1917–77*. 2nd. ed. New York: Oxford University Press, 1977.

Slonim, Mark. "Pisateli-evrei v sovetskoi literature." *Evreiskii mir* 2 (1944): 146–64.

Smeliakov, Iaroslav. *Postoianstvo*. Moscow: Sovetskii pisatel´, 1991.

Sophocles. *Oedipus at Colonus*. Translated by Robert Fitzgerald. In *The Oedipus Cycle: An English Version*. New York: Harcourt, Brace & World, 1949.

Spivak, M.L. "Eduard Bagritskii: Memuary dlia sluzhebnogo pol´zovaniia, ili posmertnaia diagnostika genial´nosti." *Literaturnoe obozrenie* 5/6 (1996): 198–207; 1 (1997): 34–60.

"Stikhi E. Bagritskogo." *Volia Rossii* 1 (1929): 118.

Struve, Gleb. *Russian Literature under Lenin and Stalin*. Norman: University of Oklahoma Press, 1971.

Tannakh: The Holy Scriptures. Philadelphia: Jewish Publication Society, 1988.

Tarasenkov, Anatolii. "O natsional´nykh traditsiiakh i burzhuaznom kosmopolitizme." *Znamia* 1 (1950): 152–64.

———, gen. ed. *Russkie sovetskie pisateli. Poety. Bibliograficheskii ukazatel´*. Vol. 2. Moscow: Kniga, 1978.

————. "Pervyi tom sochinenii Eduarda Bagritskogo." In idem, Stat´i o literature, vol. 1, 227–35. Moscow: Gosudarstvennoe izdatel´stvo khudozhestvennoi literatury, 1958.

Tarlovskii, Mark. Sobranie stikhotvorenii. 2 vols. Edited by Evgenii Vitkovskii. Samizdat edition, Moscow: 1978.

Terras, Victor. A History of Russian Literature. New Haven: Yale University Press, 1991.

————. "Bagritsky." In idem, editor. Handbook of Russian Literature, 33–34. New Haven: Yale University Press, 1985.

————. Vladimir Mayakovsky. Boston: Twayne, 1983.

Thomson, Boris. Lot's Wife and the Venus of Milo: Conflicting Attitudes to the Cultural Heritage in Modern Russia. Cambridge: Cambridge University Press, 1978.

Tregub, S.[A.] Zhivoi s zhivymi. Sbornik statei. Moscow: Sovetskii pisatel´, 1949.

Troshchenko, E.[D.] "O polednikh proizvedeniiakh Bagritskogo." In Stat´i o poezii, 33–47. Moscow: Sovetskii pisatel´, 1962.

Tsybenko, V.A. Eduard Bagritskii (Ocherk tvorchestva). Edited by A.A. Volkov. Novosibirsk: Novosibirskii gosudarstvennyi pedagogicheskii institut, 1970.

Vainshtein, Mikhail. "'Otnyne ia drugoi . . .' (Illiuzii i prozrenie Eduarda Bagritskogo)." In A list´ia snova zeleneiut . . . (Stranitsy evreiskoi russkoiazychnoi literatury), 133–56. Jerusalem: Kakhol´-Lavan, 1988.

Vavilov, S.I., et al., eds. Bol´shaia sovetskaia entsiklopediia. Soiuz sovetskikh sotsialisticheskikh respublik. Moscow: OGIZ SSSR, 1947.

Venclova, Tomas. "Chuvstvo perspektivy. Razgovor Tomasa Ventslovy s Iosifom Brodskim." Strana i mir 3.45 (1988): 143–54.

Veshnev, V., ed. Neodolennyi vrag: Sbornik khudozhestvennoi literatury protiv antisemitizma. Moscow: Federatsiia, 1930.

Vitkovskii, Evgenii. "Koshelek na mostovoi." Manuscript, 3 pp.

"Vnimanie bor´be s antisemitizmom." Pravda, 19 February 1929, 1.

Volgin, I.L. "Eduard Bagritskii." In Eduard Bagritskii, Stikhotvoreniia i poemy, 5–20. Moscow: Pravda, 1987.

Vykhodtsev, P.S., ed. Istoriia russkoi sovetskoi literatury. 2nd ed. Moscow: Vysshaia shkola, 1974.

Woll, Josephine. "Russians and 'Russophobes': Antisemitism on the Russian Literary Scene." Soviet Jewish Affairs 19.3 (1989): 3–21.

Yarmolinsky, Avram, ed. A Treasury of Russian Verse. New York: Macmillan, 1949.

Yudkin, Leon I. "In the Eye of the Revolution: Russia." In idem, Jewish Writing and Identity in the Twentieth Century, 59–77. New York: St. Martin's, 1982.

"Za ideinuiu chistotu sovetskoi poezii." Literaturnaia gazeta, 30 July 1949, 2.

Zaslavskii, D. Evrei v SSSR. Moscow: Izdatel´stvo "Emes", 1932.

Zelinskii, Kornelii. "O druge." Literaturnaia gazeta, 18 February 1934, 2.

————. "Odna vstrecha u M. Gor´kogo (Zapis´ iz dnevnika)." Voprosy literatury 5 (1991): 144–70.

————. "Vsevolod Bagritskii." Znamia 3 (1948): 131–33.

Zhabotinskii, Vladimir. "O 'evreiakh i russkoi literature.'" In idem, Izbrannoe. Jerusalem: Biblioteka-Aliia, 1978.

Zholkovskii, A.K., and M.B. Iampol´skii. Babel´/Babel. Moscow: Carte Blanche, 1994.

Zipperstein, Steven J. The Jews of Odessa: A Cultural History, 1794–1881. Stanford: Stanford University Press, 1985.

Znakomy, Leonid, and Dan Levin. "A Decade of Soviet Poetry." In New Directions Anthology of Prose and Poetry. Edited by James Laughlin, 621–27. Norfolk, Conn.: New Directions, 1941.

APPENDIX

~

Russian Text of the Poems

I. Эдуард Багрицкий, «Происхождение»

ПРОИСХОЖДЕНИЕ

Я не запомнил—на каком ночлеге
Пробрал меня грядущей жизни зуд.
Качнулся мир.
4 Звезда споткнулась в беге
И заплескалась в голубом тазу.
Я к ней тянулся . . . Но, сквозь пальцы рея,
Она рванулась—краснобокий язь.
8 Над колыбелью ржавые евреи
Косых бород скрестили лезвия.
И все навыворот.
Все как не надо.
12 Стучал сазан в оконное стекло;
Конь щебетал; в ладони ястреб падал;
Плясало дерево.
И детство шло.
16 Его опресноками иссушали.
Его свечой пытались обмануть.
К нему в упор придвинули скрижали,
Врата, которые не распахнуть.
20 Еврейские павлины на обивке,
Еврейские скисающие сливки,
Костыль отца и матери чепец—
Все бормотало мне:
24 «Подлец! Подлец!»
И только ночью, только на подушке
Мой мир не рассекала борода;
И медленно, как медные полушки,
28 Из крана в кухне падала вода.

133

Сворачивалась. Набегала тучей.
Струистое точила лезвие . . .
—Ну как, скажи, поверит в мир текучий
32　Еврейское неверие мое?
Меня учили: крыша—это крыша.
Груб табурет. Убит подошвой пол,
Ты должен видеть, понимать и слышать,
36　На мир облокотиться, как на стол,
А древоточца часовая точность
Уже долбит подпорок бытие.
. . . Ну как, скажи, поверит в эту прочность
40　Еврейское неверие мое?
Любовь?
Но съеденные вшами косы;
Ключица, выпирающая косо;
44　Прыщи; обмазанный селедкой рот
Да шеи лошадиный поворот.
Родители?
Но в сумраке старея,
48　Горбаты, узловаты и дики,
В меня кидают ржавые евреи
Обросшие щетиной кулаки.
Дверь! Настежь дверь!
52　Качается снаружи
Обглоданная звездами листва,
Дымится месяц посредине лужи,
Грач вопиет, не помнящий родства.
56　И вся любовь,
Бегущая навстречу,
И все кликушество
Моих отцов,
60　И все светила,
Строящие вечер,
И все деревья,
Рвущие лицо,—
64　Все это встало поперек дороги,
Больными бронхами свистя в груди:
—Отверженный! Возьми свой скарб убогий,
Проклятье и презренье!
68　Уходи!—
Я покидаю старую кровать:
—Уйти?
Уйду!
72　Тем лучше!
Наплевать!

1930

II. Эдуард Багрицкий, «Февраль»

ФЕВРАЛЬ

Вот я снова на этой земле.
                Я снова
Прохожу под платанами молодыми,
Снова дети бегают у скамеек,
4   Снова море лежит в пароходном дыме . . .

Вольноопределяющийся, в погонах,
Обтянутых разноцветным шнуром,—
Это я—вояка, герой Стохода,
8   Богатырь Мазурских болот, понуро
Ковыляющий в сапогах корявых,
В налезающей на затылок шапке . . .

Я приехал в отпуск, чтоб каждой мышцей,
12   Каждой клеточкой принимать движенье
Ветра, спутанного листвою,
Голубиную теплоту дыханья
Загорелых ребят, перебежку пятен
16   На песке и соленую нежность моря . . .

Я привык уже ко всему: оттуда,
Откуда я вырвался, мне обычным
Казался мир, прожженный снарядом,
20   Пробитый штыком, окрученный туго
Колючей проволокой, постыло
Воняющий потом и кислым хлебом . . .

Я должен найти в этом мире угол,
24   Где на гвоздике чистое полотенце
Пахнет матерью, подле крана—мыло,
И солнце, бегущее сквозь окошко,
Не обжигает лицо, как уголь . . .

28   Вот снова я на бульваре.
                Снова
Иван-да-марья цветет на клумбах,
Человек в морской фуражке читает
Книгу в малиновом переплете;
32   Девочка в юбке выше колена
Играет в дьяболо; на балконе

Кричит попугай в серебряной клетке.

И я теперь среди них как равный,
36 Захочу—сижу, захочу—гуляю,
Захочу (если нет вблизи офицера)—
Закурю, наблюдая, как вьется плавный
Лист над скамейками, как летают
40 Ласточки мимо часов управы . . .

Самое главное совершится
Ровно в четыре.
                    Из-за киоска
Появится девушка в пелеринке,—
44 Раскачивая полосатый ранец,
Вся будто распахнутая дыханью
Прохладного моря, лучам и птицам,
В зеленом платье из невесомой
48 Шерсти, она вплывает, как в танец,
В круженье листьев и в колыханье
Цветов и бабочек над газоном.

Домой из гимназии . . .
                    Вместе с нею—
52 Откуда-то, из позабытого мира,
Кружась, летят звонки перемены,
Шепот подруг, ангелок с тетради
И топот учителя в коридоре.
56 Пред ней платаны поют, а сзади
Ее, хрипя, провожает море . . .

Я никогда не любил как надо . . .
Маленький иудейский мальчик—
60 Я, вероятно, один в округе
Трепетал по ночам от степного ветра.

Я, как сомнамбула, брел по рельсам
На тихие дачи, где в колючках
64 Крыжовника или дикой ожины
Шелестят ужи и шипят гадюки,
А в самой чаще, куда не влезешь,
Шныряет красноголовая птичка
68 С песенкой тоненькой, как булавка,
Прозванная «Воловьим глазом» . . .

Как я, рожденный от иудея,
Обрезанный на седьмые сутки,

72   Стал птицеловом—я сам не знаю!

      Крепче Майн-Рида любил я Брэма!
      Руки мои дрожали от страсти,
      Когда наугад раскрывал я книгу . . .
76   И на меня со страниц летели
      Птицы, подобные странным буквам,
      Саблям и трубам, шарам и ромбам.

      Видно, созвездье Стрельца застряло
80   Над чернотой моего жилища,
      Над пресловутым еврейским чадом
      Гусиного жира, над зубрежкой
      Скучных молитв, над бородачами
84   На фотографиях семейных . . .

      Я не подглядывал, как другие,
      В щели купален.
                      Я не старался
      Сверстницу ущипнуть случайно . . .
88   Застенчивость и головокруженье
      Томили меня.
                   Я старался боком
      Перебежать через сад, где пели
      Девочки в гимназических платьях . . .

92   Только забывшись, не замечая
      Этого сам, я мог безраздумно
      Тупо смотреть на голые ноги
      Девушки.
               Стоя на табурете,
96   Тряпкой она вытирала стекла . . .

      Вдруг засвистело стекло по-птичьи—
      И предо мной разлетелись кругом
      Золотые овсянки, сухие листья,
100   Болотные лужицы в незабудках,
      Женские плечи и птичьи крылья,
      Посвист полета, журчанье юбок,
      Щелканье соловья и песня
104   Юной соседки через дорогу,—
      И наконец, все ясней, все чище,
      В мире обычаев и привычек,
      Под фонарем моего жилища
108   Глаз соловья на лице девичьем . . .

Вот и сейчас, заглянув под шляпу,
В слабой тени я глаза увидел.
Полные соловьиной дрожи,
112　Они, покачиваясь, проплывали
В лад каблукам, и на них свисала
Прядка волос, золотясь на коже . . .

Вдоль по аллее, мимо газона,
116　Шло гимназическое платье,
А в сотне шагов за ним, как убийца,
Спотыкаясь о скамьи и натыкаясь
На людей и деревья, шепча проклятья,
120　Шел я в больших сапогах, в зеленой
Засаленной гимнастерке, низко
Остриженный на военной службе,
Еще не отвыкший сутулить плечи—
124　Ротный ловчило, еврейский мальчик . . .

Она заглядывала в витрины,
И средь прозрачных шелков и склянок
Таинственно, не по-человечьи,
128　Отражалось лицо ее водяное . . .

Она останавливалась у цветочниц,
И пальцы ее выбирали розу,
Плававшую в эмалированной миске,
132　Как маленькая махровая рыбка.

Из колониального магазина
Потягивало жженым кофе, корицей,
И в этом запахе, с мокрой розой,
136　Над ворохами листвы в корзинах,
Она мне казалась чудесной птицей,
Выпорхнувшей из книги Брэма . . .

　　.　.　.　.　.　.　.　.　.　.　.　.　.　.

А я уклонялся как мог от фронта . . .
140　Сколько рублевок перелетало
Из рук моих в писарские руки!
Я унтеров напаивал водкой,
Тащил им папиросы и сало . . .
144　В околодок из околодка,
Кашляющий в припадке плеврита,
Я кочевал.
　　　　　Я пыхтел и фыркал,

Плевал в бутылки, пил лекарство,
148   Я стоял нагишом, худой и небритый,
Под стетоскопами всех комиссий . . .

Когда же мне удавалось правдой
Или неправдой—кто может вспомнить?—
152   Добыть увольнительную записку,
Я начищал сапоги до блеска,
Обдергивал гимнастерку—и бойко
Шагал на бульвар, где в платанах пела
156   Голосом обожженной глины
Иволга, и над песком аллеи
Платье знакомое зеленело,
Покачиваясь, как дымок недлинный . . .

160   Снова я сзади тащился, млея,
Ругаясь, натыкаясь на скамьи . . .
Она входила в кинематограф,
В стрекочущую темноту, в дрожанье
164   Зеленого света в квадратной раме,
Где женщина над погасшим камином
Ломала руки из алебастра
И человек в гранитном пластроне
168   Стрелял из безмолвного револьвера . . .

Я знал в лицо всех ее знакомых,
Я знал их повадки, улыбки, жесты.
Замедленный шаг их, когда нарочно
172   Стараешься грудью, бедром, ладонью
Почувствовать через покров непрочный
Тревожную нежность девичьей кожи . . .
Я все это знал . . .
                  Улетали птицы . . .
176   Высыхала трава . . .
                  Погибали звезды . . .
Девушка проходила по свету,
Собирая цветы, опустив ресницы . . .
Осень . . .
              Дождями пропитан воздух,
180   Осень . . .
              Грусти, погибай и сетуй!
Я сегодня к ней подойду.
                  Я встану
Перед ней.
          Я не дам ей свернуть с дороги.
Достаточно беготни.

                    Мужайся!

184   Возьми себя в руки.
                    Кончай волынку!
Заколочен киоск . . .
                 У часов управы
Суетятся голуби.
               Скоро—четыре.
Она появилась за час до срока,—
188   Шляпа в руках . . .
               Рыжеватый волос,
Просвеченный негреющим солнцем,
Реет у щек . . .
              Тишина.
           И голос
Синицы, затерянной в этом мире . . .
192   Я должен к ней подойти.
              Я должен
Обязательно к ней подойти.
            Я должен
Непременно к ней подойти.
           Не думай,
Встряхнись—и в догонку.
           Довольно бреда! . . .
196   А ноги мои не сдвигались с места,
Как будто каменные.
           А тело
Как будто приковалось к скамейке.
И встать невозможно . . .
           Бездельник! Шляпа!

200   А девушка уже вышла на площадь,
И в темно-сером кругу музеев
Платье ее, летящее с ветром,
Казалось тоньше и зеленее . . .

204   Я оторвался с таким усильем,
Как будто накрепко был привинчен
К скамье.
           Оторвался—и без оглядки
Выбежал за нею на площадь.
208   Все, о чем я читал ночами,
Больной, голодный, полуодетый,—
О птицах с нерусскими именами,
О людях неизвестной планеты,
212   О мире, в котором играют в теннис,

Пьют оранжад и целуют женщин,—
Все это двигалось предо мною,
Одетое в шерстяное платье,
216   Горящее рыжими завитками,
Покачивающее полосатым ранцем,
Перебирающее каблучками . . .

Я положу на плечо ей руку:
220   «Взгляни на меня!
                  Я—твое несчастье!
Я обрекаю тебя на муку
Неслыханной соловьиной страсти!
Остановись!»
            Но за поворотом—
224   В двадцати шагах зеленеет платье.
Я ее догоняю.
            Еще немного
Напрягусь—мы зашагаем рядом . . .

Я козыряю ей, как начальству,
228   Что ей сказать? Мой язык бормочет
Какую-то дребедень:
                —Позвольте . . .
Не убегайте . . .
            Скажите, можно
Вас проводить? Я сидел в окопах! . .

232   Она молчит.
         Она даже глазом
Не поведет.
        Она убыстряет
Шаги.
      А я рядом бегу, как нищий
Почтительно нагибаясь.
              Где уж
236   Мне быть ей равным! . .
               Я как безумный
Бормочу какие-то фразы сдуру . . .

И вдруг остановка . . .
              Она безмолвно
Поворачивает голову—я вижу
240   Рыжие волосы, сине-зеленый
Глаз и лиловатую жилку
На виске, дрожащую в напряженьи . . .
«Уходите немедленно»,—и рукою

244   Показывает на перекресток . . .
                                        Вот он—
        Поставленный для охраны покоя—
        Он встал на перепутье, как царство
        Шнуров, начищенных блях, медалей,
248   Задвинутый в сапоги, а сверху—
        Прикрытый полицейской фуражкой,
        Вокруг которой кружат в сияньи,
        Желтом и нестерпимом до пытки,
252   Голуби из святого писанья
        И тучи, закрученные как улитки . . .
        Брюхатый, сияющий жирным потом
        Городовой.
                         С утра до отвала
256   Накачанный водкой, набитый салом . . .

        .   .   .   .

        Студенческие голубые фуражки;
        Солдатские шапки, треухи, кепи;
        Пар, летящий из мерзлых глоток;
260   Махорка, гуляющая столбами . . .

        Круговорот полушубков, чуек,
        Шинелей, воняющих кислым хлебом,
        И на кафедре, у большого графина—
264   Совсем неожиданного в этом дыме—
        Взволнованный человек в нагольном
        Полушубке, в рваной косоворотке
        Кричит сорвавшимся от напряженья
268   Голосом и свободным жестом
        Открывает объятья . . .
                              Большие двери
        Распахиваются.
                         Из февральской ночи
        Входят люди, гримасничая от света,
272   Топчутся, отряхают иней
        С полушубков—и вот они уже с нами,
        Говорят, кричат, подымают руки,
        Проклинают, плачут.
                         Сопенье, кашель,
276   Толкотня.
                    На хорах трещат перила
        Под напором плеч.
                         И, взлетая кверху,

Пятерни в грязи и присохшей крови
Встают, как запачканные светила . . .

280 В эту ночь мы пошли забирать участок . . .
Я, мой товарищ студент и третий—
Рыжий приват-доцент из эсеров.

Кровью мужества наливается тело,
284 Ветер мужества обдувает рубашку.
Юность кончилась . . .
                              Начинается зрелость . . .
Грянь о камень прикладом! Сорви фуражку!

Облик мира меняется.
                              Нынче утром
288 Добродушно шумели платаны.
                                        Море
Поселилось в заливе.
                              На тихих дачах
Пели девушки в хороводах.
                                   В книге
Доктор Брэм отдыхал, прислонив централку
292 К валуну.
              Мой родительский дом светился
Язычками свечей и библейской кухней . . .

Облик мира меняется . . .
                              Этой ночью
Гололедица покрывает деревья,
296 Сучья лезут в глаза, как живые.
                                        Море
Опрокинулось над пустынным бульваром.
Пароходы хрипят, утопая.
                                        Дачи
Заколочены.
                     На пустынных террасах
300 Пляшут крысы.
                         И Брэм, покидая книгу,
Подымает ружье на меня с угрозой . . .
Мой родительский дом разворован.
                                        Кошка
На холодной плите поднимает лапки . . .

304 Юность кончилась нынче . . . Покой далече . . .
Ноги шлепают по воде.

　　　　　　　　　　　　Проклятье!
　　　Подыми воротник и закутай плечи!
　　　Что же! Надо идти!
　　　　　　　　　　　　Не горюй, приятель!
308　Дождь!
　　　　　　　Суетливая перебранка
　　　Воронья на акациях.
　　　　　　　　　　　Дождь.
　　　　　　　　　　　　　　Из прорвы
　　　Катящие в ацетиленовом свете
　　　Мотоциклисты.
　　　　　　　　　　И снова черный
312　Туннель—без конца и начала.
　　　　　　　　　　　　　　　Ветер,
　　　Бегущий неизвестно куда.
　　　　　　　　　　　　По лужам
　　　Шагающие патрули.
　　　　　　　　　　И снова—
　　　Дождь.
　　　　　　　Мы одни—в этом мокром мире.

316　Натыкаясь на тумбы у подворотен,
　　　Налезая один на другого, камнем
　　　Падая на мостовую, в полночь
　　　Мы добрели до участка . . .
　　　　　　　　　　　　　　Вот он,
320　Каменный ящик, закрытый сотней
　　　Ржавых цепей и пудовых крючьев,—
　　　Ящик, в который понабивались
　　　Лихорадка, тифозный озноб, запойный
324　Бред, бормотанье молитв и песни . . .

　　　Херувимы, одетые в шаровары,
　　　Стояли подле ворот на страже,
　　　Словно усатые самовары,
328　Один другого тучней и ражей . . .

　　　Откуда-то изнутри, из прорвы,
　　　Шипящей дождем, вырывался круглый
　　　Лошадиный хрип и необычайный
332　Заклинательный клич петуха . . .
　　　　　　　　　　　　　　　Привратник
　　　Нам открыл какую-то щель.
　　　　　　　　　　　　　И снова
　　　Загремели замки, закрывая выход . . .

Мы прошли по коридорам, похожим
336 На сновиденья.
                    Кривые лампы
Качались над нами.
                         По стенам кверху,
К продавленному потолку, взбегали,
Сбиваясь в комки, раскрутясь в спирали,
340 Косые тени . . .
                         На длинных скамьях,
Опершись подбородками на эфесы
Сабель, похрапывали городовые . . .
И весь этот лабиринт сходился
344 К дубовым воротам, на которых
Висела квадратная карточка: «Пристав»!! .

Розовый, в лазоревых бакенбардах,
Разлетающихся от легчайшего дуновенья,
348 Подобно ангелу с гимназической тетради,
Он витал над письменным прибором,
Сработанным из шрапнельных стаканов,
Улыбаясь, тая, изнемогая
352 От радушия, от нежности, от счастья
Встречи с делегатами комитета . . .

А мы . . . стояли, переминаясь
С ноги на ногу, пачкая каблуками
356 Невероятных лошадей и попугаев,
Вышитых на ковре . . .
                         Нам, конечно,
Было не до улыбок.
                         Довольно . . .
Сдавай ключи—и катись отсюда к черту!
360 Нам не о чем толковать.
                         До свиданья . . .

Мы принимали дела.
                    Мы шлялись
По всем закоулкам.
                         В одной из комнат
В угол навалены были грудой,
364 Как картофель, браунинги и наганы.
Мы приняли их по счету.
                         Утром,
Полусонные, разомлев от ночной работы,
Запачканные участковой пылью,

368   Мы добыли арестантский чайник,
        Жестяной, заржавленный, и пили,
        Обжигаясь и шлепая губами,
        Первый чай победителей, чай свободы . . .

372   Голубые дожди омывали землю,
        По ночам уже начиналось тайно
        Мужественное цветенье каштанов.
        Просыхала земля . . .
                          Разогретой солью
376   Дуло с берега . . .
                    В раковине оркестра,
        Потерявшейся в гуще платанов,
        Марсельеза, приподнятая смычками,
        Исчезала среди фонарей и листьев.

380   Наша улица, вымытая до блеска
        Летним ливнем, улетала к заливу,
        Подымавшемуся, как забор зеленый,—
        Строй платанов, вытянутый на диво.
384   И на самом верху, в завитушках пены,
        Чуть заметно покачивался картонный
        Броненосец «Синоп».
                       И на сизой туче
        Червяком огня извивался вымпел . . .
388   Опадали акации.
                 Невидимкой
        Дух гниющих цветов пробирался в море,
        И матросы отплясывали в обнимку
        С полногрудыми девками из слободки.

392   За рыбачьими куренями, на склонах
        Перевалов, поросших клочкастой мятой,
        Под разбитыми шлюпками, у снесенных
        Купален, отчаянные ребята—
396   Дезертиры в болтающихся погонах—
        Дулись в двадцать одно, в карася, в солдата,
        А в пещере посапывал, как теленок,
        Змеевик самогонного аппарата.

400   Я остался в районе . . .
                     Я стал работать
        Помощником комиссара . . .
                      Вначале
        Я просиживал ночи в сырых дежурках,

Глядя на мир, на проходивший мимо,
404 Чуждый мне, как явленья иной природы.
Из косых фонарей, из густого дыма
Проступали невиданные уроды . . .

Я старался быть вездесущим . . .
                                В бричке
408 Я толокся по деревенским дорогам
За конокрадами.
                        Поздней ночью
Я вылетал на моторной гичке
В залив, изогнувшийся черным рогом
412 Среди камней и песчаных кочек.
Я вламывался в воровские квартиры,
Воняющие пережаренной рыбой.
Я появлялся, как ангел смерти,
416 С фонарем и револьвером, окруженный
Четырьмя матросами с броненосца . . .
(Еще юными. Еще розовыми от счастья.
Часок не доспавшими после ночи.
420 Набекрень—бескозырки. Бушлаты—настежь.
Карабины под мышкой. И ветер—в очи.)

Моя иудейская гордость пела,
Как струна, натянутая до отказа…
424 Я много дал бы, чтобы мой пращур
В длиннополом халате и лисьей шапке,
Из-под которой седой спиралью
Спадают пейсы и перхоть тучей
428 Взлетает над бородой квадратной . . .
Чтоб этот пращур признал потомка
В детине, стоящем подобно башне
Над летящими фарами и штыками
432 Грузовика, потрясшего полночь . . .

         . . . .

Я вздрогнул.
                   Звонок телефона
Скрежетнул у самого уха . . .
«Комиссара? Я. Что вам?»
436 И голос, запрятанный в трубке,
Рассказал мне, что на Ришельевской,
В чайном домике генеральши Клеменц,
Соберутся Семка Рабинович,

440   Петька Камбала и Моня Бриллиантщик,—
       Железнодорожные громилы,
       Кинематографические герои,—
       Бандиты с чемоданчиками, в которых
444   Алмазные сверла и пилы,
       Сигарета с дурманом для соседа . . .
       Они летали по вагонным крышам
       В крылатках, раздуваемых бурей,
448   С револьвером в рукаве фрака,
       Обнимали сторублевых гурий,
       И нынче у генеральши Клеменц—
       Им будет крышка.
                              Баста!

452   В караулке ребята с броненосца
       Пили чай и резались в шашки.
       Их полосатые фуфайки
       Морщились на мускулатуре . . .
456   Розовые розоватостью детства,
       Большерукие, с голубыми глазами,
       Они передвигали пешки
       Восторженно с места на место,
460   Моргали, шевелили губами,
       Задумчиво, без малейшей усмешки
       Подпевали, притопывая каблуками . . .

       Мы взгромоздились на дрожки,
464   Обнимая за талии друг друга,
       И остроугольная кляча
       Потащила нас в теплую темень . . .

       Нужно было сунуть револьвер
468   В щелку ворот, чтобы дворник,
       Зевая и подтягивая брюки,
       Открыл нам калитку.
                              Молча.
       Мы взошли по красной дорожке,
472   Устилавшей лестницу.
                              К двери
       Подошел я один.
                              Ребята,
       Зажав меж колен карабины,
       Вплотную прижались к стенке.

476   Все—как в тихом приличном доме . . .
       Лампа с темно-синим абажуром

Над столом семейным.
                    Гардины,
Стулья с мягкой спинкой.
                         Пианино,
480 Книжный шкаф, на шкафе—бюст Толстого.
Доброта домашнего уюта
В теплом воздухе.
                    Над самоваром
Легкий пар.
                На чайнике накидка
484 Из плетеной шерсти—все в порядке . . .

Мы вошли, как буря, как дыханье
Черных улиц, ног не вытирая
И не сняв бушлатов.
                         Нам навстречу,
488 Кланяясь и потирая нервно
Руки в кольцах, выкатилась дама
В парике, засыпанная пудрой.
Жирная, с отвислыми щеками . . .
492 «Антонина Яковлевна Клеменц!
Это вы?—Мы к вам пришли по делу»,—
Я сказал, распахивая двери.

За столом велась беседа.
                         Трое
496 Молодых людей в земгусарской форме,
Барышни, смеющиеся скромно.
На столе—пирожные, конфеты.

Я вошел и стал в изумленьи . . .
500 Черт возьми! Какая ошибка!
Какой это чайный домик!
Друзья собрались за чаем.
Почему же я им мешаю? . .
504 Мне бы тоже сидеть в уюте,
Разговаривать о Гумилеве,
А не шляться по ночам, как сыщик,
Не врываться в тихие семейства
508 В поисках неведомых бандитов . . .

Но какой-то из моих матросов
Подошел к столу и мрачным басом
Проворчал:
                    «Вот этих трех я знаю.
512 Руки вверх!

Берите их, ребята! . .
Где четвертый? . . Барышни в сторонку! . . »
И пошло.
И началось.
На совесть.
У роскошных земгусар мы сняли
516 Кобуры с наганами.
Конечно,
Это были те, за кем мы гнались . . .
Мы загнали их в чулан.
Закрыли—
И приставили к ним караул.

520 Мы толкали двери.
Мы входили
В комнаты, наполненные дрянью . . .
Воздух был пропитан душной пудрой,
Человечьим семенем и сладкой
524 <Одурью> ликера.
Сквозь томленье
Синего тумана пробивался
Разомлевший, еле-еле видный
Отсвет фонаря . . . (как через воду).
528 На кровати, узкие, как рыбы,
Двигались тела под одеялом . . .
Голова мужчины подымалась
Из подушек, как из круглой пены . . .
532 Мы просматривали документы,
Прикрывали двери, извиняясь,
И шагали дальше.
Снова сладким
Воздухом нас обдавало.
Снова
536 Подымались головы с подушек
И ныряли в шелковую пену . . .

В третьей комнате нас встретил парень
В голубых кальсонах и фуфайке.
540 Он стоял, расставив ноги прочно,
Медленно покачиваясь торсом
И помахивая, как перчаткой,
Браунингом . . . Он мигнул нам глазом:
544 «Ой! Здесь целый флот! Из этой пушки
Всех не перекокаешь. Я сдался . . . »

А за ним, откинув одеяло,
Голоногая, в ночной рубашке,
548 Сползшей с плеч, кусая папиросу,
Полусонная, сидела молча
Та, которая меня томила
Соловьиным взглядом и полетом
552 Туфелек по скользкому асфальту . . .

. . . .

«Уходите!—я сказал матросам . . . —
Кончен обыск! Заберите парня!
Я останусь с девушкой!»
                              Громоздко
556 Постучав прикладами, ребята
Вытеснились в двери.
                              Я остался.
В душной полутьме, в горячей дреме
С девушкой, сидящей на кровати . . .
560 «Узнаете?»—но она молчала,
Прикрывая легкими руками
Бледное лицо.
                    «Ну что, узнали?»
Тишина.
              Тогда со зла я брякнул:
564 «Сколько дать вам за сеанс?»
                                        И тихо,
Не раздвинув губ, она сказала:
«Пожалей меня! Не надо денег . . . »

Я швырнул ей деньги.
                              Я ввалился,
568 Не стянув сапог, не сняв кобуры,
Не расстегивая гимнастерки,
Прямо в омут пуха, в одеяло,
Под которым бились и вздыхали
572 Все мои предшественники,—в темный,
Неразборчивый поток видений,
Выкриков, развязанных движений,
Мрака и неистового света . . .

576 Я беру тебя за то, что робок
Был мой век, за то, что я застенчив,
За позор моих бездомных предков,

За случайной птицы щебетанье!

580 Я беру тебя, как мщенье миру,
Из которого не мог я выйти!

Принимай меня в пустые недра,
Где трава не может завязаться,—
584 Может быть, мое ночное семя
Оплодотворит твою пустыню.

Будут ливни, будет ветер с юга,
Лебедей влюбленное ячанье.

1933–1934

III.   Other Russian Poems Quoted in the Text

1. Эдуард Багрицкий, «От чёрного хлеба и верной жены . . .» (p. 4)

От черного хлеба и верной жены
Мы бледною немочью заражены . . .

Копытом и камнем испытаны годы,
Бессмертной полынью пропитаны воды,—
И горечь полыни на наших губах . . .
Нам нож—не по кисти,
Перо—не по нраву,
Кирка—не по чести
И слава—не в славу:
Мы—ржавые листья
На ржавых дубах . . .
Чуть ветер,
Чуть север—
И мы облетаем.
Чей путь мы собою теперь устилаем?
Чьи ноги по ржавчине нашей пройдут?
Потопчут ли нас трубачи молодые?
Взойдут ли над нами созвездья чужие?
Мы—ржавых дубов облетевший уют . . .

2. Эдуард Багрицкий, «Контрабандисты» (p. 8)

Так бей же по жилам,
Кидайся в края,

Бездомная молодость,
     Ярость моя!
Чтоб звездами сыпалась
     Кровь человечья,
Чтоб выстрелом рваться
     Вселенной навстречу,
Чтоб волн запевал
     Оголтелый народ,
Чтоб злобная песня
     Коверкала рот,—
И петь, задыхаясь,
     На страшном просторе:
«Ай, Черное море,
     Хорошее море! . . . »

3. Эдуард Багрицкий, «Стихи о поэте и романтике» (p. 10)

Депеша из Питера: страшная весть
Очерном предательстве Гумилева . . .

4. Эдуард Багрицкий, «ТВС» (p. 11)

А век поджидает на мостовой,
Сосредоточен, как часовой.
Иди—и не бойся с ним рядом встать.
Твое одиночество веку под стать.
Оглянешься—а вокруг враги;
Руки протянешь—и нет друзей;
Но если он скажет: «Солги»,—солги.
Но если он скажет: «Убей»,—убей.

5. Эдуард Багрицкий, «Весна» (p. 13)

И поезд, крутящийся
     В мокрой траве,—
Чудовищный вьюн
     С фонарем в голове.

6. Александр Блок, «Соловьиный сад» (p. 59)

Я, бедняк обездоленный, жду,
Повторяя напев неизвестный,
В соловьином звенящий саду.

7. Владимир Маяковский, «Февраль» (p. 65)

Толпа плывёт
        и вновь
            садится на́ мель,
И вновь плывет,
          русло
             меж камня вырыв.
[. . .]
Знамена несут,
        несут
           и несут.
В руках,
      в сердцах,
           и в петлицах—а́ло.
[. . .]
Но мы
      ответили
          гневом дыша:
—Обратно
      земной
         не завертится шар.
слова
     переделаем в дело!—
И мы
     дошли,
        в Октябре заверша
То, что февраль не доделал.

8. Эдуард Багрицкий, «Февраль»
(draft of the long poem of the same title) (p. 66)

Вся любовь моя, весь мой голос и зренье,
Кровь, еще не испорченная . . .
Кости, еще не источенные ревматизмом,
Сладкое юношеское вдохновенье,
[. . .]
Слово <. . .> неиспорченное: свобода!
Все это отдано было без счета
Марту 17-го.

9. Эдуард Багрицкий, «Февраль» (1923)
   («Темною волей судьбы...») (р. 66)

Новые дали открылись,
Новые дали—заре.
Так в феврале мы трудились,
Чтоб победить в Октябре!

10. Эдуард Багрицкий, «На битву с богом» (рр. 76–77)

Трубит труба в убогой синагоге,
И дряхлые молельщики идут:
Через кусты, по выжженной дороге,
Едва-едва, согбенные, ползут.
[. . .]
И древний бог легенд и песнопений
Теперь ничто. Он ветер, дым и прах,
Он истомленною проходит тенью,
Он тает облаком в пустых песках.
Настало время силы и свободы,
Расправил плечи изнуренный раб.
И, позабыв томительные годы,
Встает, кто был покинут, нищ и слаб.

11. Эдуард Багрицкий, «Происхождение» (draft) (р. 79)

Где ты, мой мир! [. . .]
Я шел к своим. Но в сумерке чернея,
Горбаты, угловаты и дики,
В меня кидали ржавые евреи
Обросшие щетиной кулаки . . .
Отверженный! Как я запрет нарушу,
Как сочетаю после в бытие
Вот эту неприкаянную сушу
И злое одиночество мое.

12. Эдуард Багрицкий, «Папиросный коробок» (p. 81)

> Вставай же, Всево́лод, и всем володай,
> Вставай под осеннее солнце!
> Я знаю: ты с чистою кровью рожден,
> Ты встал на пороге веселых времен!

13. Эдуард Багрицкий, «Разговор с сыном» (p. 82)

> Я прохожу по бульварам. Свист
> В легких деревьях. Гудит аллея

14. Эдуард Багрицкий, «Разговор с сыном» (p. 82)

> В красных рубашках, в чуйках суконных,
> Рыжие лабазники, утаптывая грязь,
> На чистом полотенце несут икону . . .
> И матерый купчина с размаху—хлоп
> И в грязь и жадно протягивает руки,
> Обезьяна из чиновников крестит лоб,
> Лезут приложиться свирепые старухи.
> Пух из перин, как стая голубей . . .
> Улица настежь распахнута . . . И дикий
> Вой над вселенной качается: «Бей!»

15. Эдуард Багрицкий, «Разговор с сыном» (p. 82)

> Мир в этих толпах — он наш навек . . .
> [. . .]
> Сын мой! Одним вдохновением мы
> Нынче палимы.

16. Эдуард Багрицкий, «Разговор с сыном» (p. 83)

> Там, где погром проходил, рыча [. . .]
> Мы на широких несем плечах
> Жажду победы и груз громадный.
> Пусть подымаются звери на гербах
> В черных рубахах выходят роты [. . .]
> Пусть истребитель на бешеной заре
> Отпечатан черным фашистским знаком [. . .].

17. Эдуард Багрицкий, «Разговор с сыном» (p. 83)

Время настанет—и мы пойдем,
Сын мой, с тобой по дорогам света . . .
Братья с Востока к плечу с плечом
С братьями освобожденной планеты.

18. Эдуард Багрицкий, «Последняя ночь» (p. 83)

Еврейские домики я прошел.
Я слышал свирепый храп
Биндюжников, спавших на биндюгах,
И в окнах была видна
Суббота в пурпуровом парике,
Идущая со свечой.

Index

About the Author

Maxim D. Shrayer was born in Moscow, Russia, in 1967. Having immigrated to the United States in 1987, Shrayer studied comparative literature and literary translation at Brown University. In 1995, he received a Ph.D. in Russian literature from Yale University. Shrayer has published three collections of Russian verse, *Herd above the Meadow* (1990), *American Romance* (1994), and *New Haven Sonnets* (1998). His English-language fiction, poetry, and translations have been featured in a number of publications, including *AGNI*, *The Massachusetts Review*, *Midstream*, *Salmagundi*, and *Southwest Review*. An assistant professor of Russian literature at Boston College, Shrayer is the author of *The World of Nabokov's Stories* (1999) and the editor of the forthcoming *Anthology of Russian-Jewish Literature: Two Centuries of a Dual Identity*.